D1457311

INTO THE RED

ALYA GUSEVA

Into the Red

*The Birth of the Credit Card Market
in Postcommunist Russia*

STANFORD UNIVERSITY PRESS

STANFORD, CALIFORNIA

Stanford University Press
Stanford, California

©2008 by the Board of Trustees of the
Leland Stanford Junior University.
All rights reserved.

No part of this book may be reproduced or transmitted in any form or
by any means, electronic or mechanical, including photocopying and
recording, or in any information storage or retrieval system without the
prior written permission of Stanford University Press.

Printed in the United States of America
on acid-free, archival-quality paper

Library of Congress Cataloging-in-Publication Data

Guseva, Alya, 1974–
    Into the red : the birth of the credit card market in postcommunist
Russia / Alya Guseva.
        p. cm.
    Includes bibliographical references and index.
    ISBN 978-0-8047-5838-3 (cloth : alk. paper)
    1. Credit cards—Russia (Federation) 2. Consumer credit—Russia
(Federation) I. Title.

HG3756.R8G87 2008
332.7'650947—dc22   2007051839

Typeset by Classic Typography in 10/14 Janson

To my children, Dasha and Artyom

Contents

Tables and Figures

Acknowledgments

If publishing a book is similar to bearing a child, then mine was a long and protracted pregnancy with many unexpected turns and distractions, but a swift and easy delivery. This book started as my dissertation project more than eight years ago, but it has changed in ways I could not have foreseen.

Numerous colleagues in the social sciences read and commented on separate chapters, engaged me intellectually in discussions of the ideas I presented at conferences, and gave me advice along the way, among them Patrik Aspers, Bruce Carruthers, Barry Cohen, Stephen Kalberg, Mark Mizruchi, Dan Monti, Marc Schneiberg, Andrew Spicer, as well as other junior professors at Boston University: Emily Barman, Julian Go, and Laurel Smith-Doerr (who have already published their first books, thus strongly motivating me to finish mine). BU Sociology Chair John Stone should be credited for suggesting the title and Juliet Johnson for the advice to shorten it. Juliet and Gerry McDermott read the entire manuscript, and their comments and advice helped me strengthen my arguments. Valery Yakubovich was the sounding board for many of my ideas, reading and commenting on several of the chapters' drafts and generously sharing his expertise and passion for research in the economic sociology field. Russian economic sociologist Olga Kuzina, whom I met during my first field trip to Moscow, has become my collaborator and a close friend. From her I learned a great deal about the Russian transitional economy and Russian economic sociology. She conducted several of the interviews for this project. Finally, I am indebted to Ákos Róna-Tas, who has been my teacher and mentor, and then coauthor and friend for more than ten years. He witnessed this project germinate from a tiny seed of an idea into a large-scale, multicountry collaborative effort, on which we now work together.

Earlier versions of the chapters were presented at meetings of the American Sociological Association, Society for the Advancement of Socio-Economics and International Institute of Sociology, MIT–Harvard Economic Sociology Colloquium, Russian Studies Workshop at the University of Chicago, and to audiences at Boston University, University of California, Irvine, University of California, San Diego, University of Wisconsin–Madison, International University Bremen (Germany), and Oxford University.

I am thankful to all my Russian interviewees, many of whom are pioneers and die-hard enthusiasts of the Russian credit card market, in particular, Pavel Stromsky, Vladimir Shavanichev, and Pavel Ivanov, as well as Valery Torkhov and Valery Shipilov, who generously shared their time and insights with me, invited me to give talks, and put their networks at my disposal.

This project would have not been possible had I not had an opportunity to come to the United States to study at the University of California, San Diego. I owe it to Dr. Gerald Kent and his wife, Barbara, who sponsored me and made it happen. Jerry should also be credited with the topic of this book, which emerged from our regular lunch conversations while I was a student at UC San Diego.

I would also like to thank my editor at Stanford University Press, Margo Beth Crouppen. I have always found it peculiar when writers rave about their editors in acknowledgment sections using words like "incredible," "encouraging," and "caring." Margo has been all this and more. It is to her and a team of professionals at Stanford University Press, most notably my production editor Mariana Raykov, that I owe that swift and easy delivery. They have given me the support that every writer ought to have, making the potentially scary and difficult process easy and enjoyable.

My family deserves special words of thanks. My mother did not live to see this day, but she was always my biggest fan, encouraging me to do great things. I inherited the love of books and learning from my father, an avid book collector whose home library numbers over five thousand volumes. I hope he will find a place for my book on one of his shelves. My husband's daily question, "Have you submitted your manuscript yet?" kept me on track when I wanted to slack off. He read it from cover to cover, helped me with the figures, and did not scoff at my last-minute requests to change them in the wee hours of the morning. In retrospect, I am amazed he was able to put up with my obsessive writing for so long. My daughter, Dasha, was patiently crafting her own books (with illustrations!) while I was writing mine. I think it was her way of showing me that it was indeed possible. My son Artyom's impending birth put me on a tight deadline, pushing me to complete the manuscript only a few weeks before he came into the world.

I dedicate this book to my children, with gratitude for the inspiration they have given me and with the hope that one day they will publish theirs.

This project is based, in part, on work supported by the National Science Foundation (NSF) under Grant No0242076. Any opinions, findings, and conclusions or recommendations expressed in this material are those of the author and do not necessarily reflect the views of the NSF. Parts of Chapters 1 and 5 were previously published as "Building New Markets: A Comparison between Russian and American Credit Card Markets" in the *Socio-Economic Review* 2005, 3:437–66. Parts of Chapter 1 were also published with Ákos Róna-Tas as "Uncertainty, Risk and Trust: Russian and American Credit Card Markets Compared" in *American Sociological Review* 2001, 66(5):623–46. American Sociological Association and Oxford University Press kindly allowed me to use these materials. Parts of Chapter 3 were previously published as "Friends and Foes: Informal Networks in the Soviet Union" in *East European Quarterly* 2007, 41(3):323–47.

INTO THE RED

Introduction

I received my first three credit cards shortly after setting foot on American soil. I was a foreign undergraduate who had come to spend one year at an American university. Credit card applications only asked for my dorm address and a copy of my student ID. A week later, three "no-annual-fee" credit cards, each with a limit of $300 to $500, were rushed to me. I was more surprised than flattered: these companies were willing to trust me with more than $1,000! How did they know I would not spend it all and go home without paying off my debt? It was 1993, the year when several nonbank companies (GM and AT&T among them) aggressively entered the U.S. credit card market. One of their marketing tools was heavy recruitment on university campuses: get students hooked on cards early, and you will bring up an entire generation of card users. At least in my case, they got it right: fourteen years later, I am still here, diligently paying my bills.

What I did not know back then was that a mature credit card market such as the one found in the United States rests on a solid foundation of stable working institutions (credit bureaus, statistical scoring of credit, and debt collections), which render trust between the card issuer and cardholder irrelevant (Guseva and Róna-Tas 2001). Institutions do so not only by estimating the risk of default for each applicant, but also by assessing the profitability of prospective customers for the bank. As I see it now, GM and AT&T did not trust me, of course. In fact, they could not trust me because they knew close to nothing about me. But trust was beyond the point. What they did know was that I was a student at a prominent four-year college. So they counted on four years of interest and finance charges with a low probability of default thanks to the "Bank of Mom and Dad."

About a year later, while traveling in Moscow, I came across advertisements by Russian banks offering Visas and MasterCards. This puzzled me even more. Russia at that time was struggling to stabilize its nascent banking industry and revamp its legal system, which was ill prepared to handle market-related disputes, let alone card defaults or sophisticated card fraud. There were no ready-made institutional solutions such as credit reporting and debt collection. The Russian state was pursuing macroeconomic stabilization, handling periodic market crashes, and trying to avert social and political tensions as a result of plummeting living standards for the majority of the population. In other words, it was preoccupied with more pressing problems than helping a fledgling credit card market on its feet. Issuing cards in such an environment seemed to me a perfect recipe for failure. How did banks know which cardholders would use the cards honestly and responsibly?

This was my initial question when I started my research. Later, I discovered additional problems that emerging credit card markets faced. For instance, despite what the reader may expect, when credit cards first appeared in Russia, they were not swept up eagerly by enthusiastic users. On the contrary, banks faced a serious problem of building consumer demand. Moreover, not only did they have to make the cards appealing to prospective cardholders, but they also had to convince merchants to sign up to accept cards in their shops. As a result, my research question expanded, and it now included a more general focus on the emergence of a completely new market in the transitional context. How was a market for credit cards built entirely from scratch? What sorts of solutions did banks rely on? How were cash-loving, credit-averse Russians, distrustful of private banks, transformed into card-carrying consumers? What was the effect of the ongoing restructuring of Russian financial institutions on the process of market building?

My analysis covers the period from 1988, when the first commercial banks were founded in Russia, to the present. During this period of almost two decades, Russia went from just a handful of banks to having more than two thousand at their peak in 1996; from rare glimpses of Visas in the hands of foreign tourists in the 1970s and 1980s, to the first reluctant card programs in the beginning of the 1990s, and to more than seventy-five million cards issued by Russian banks to Russian customers by January 2007; and from consumers' exclusive reliance on cash to their borrowing more than a trillion rubles at a growth rate of close to 100 percent a year in a recent buying frenzy. How these breathtaking changes occurred in the midst of Russia's postcommunist transition and what obstacles had to be overcome is the subject of this book.

While the book focuses on Russia, the Russian experience is not unique. In the 1990s, credit card markets were springing up in all of the former Soviet-bloc countries of Eastern and Central Europe, with the number of issued cards steadily rising throughout the region (Figure I.1). These countries

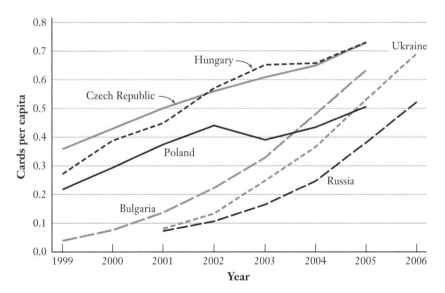

Figure I.1 Number of Cards per Capita in Russia and Select Countries of Eastern and Central Europe from 1999 to 2006

Source: Data from the European Central Bank (www.ecb.int), the Bank of Russia (www.cbr.ru), and the National Bank of Ukraine (www.bank.gov.ua). No data for 1999 and 2000 for Russia and Ukraine. Data for 2006 only for Russia and Ukraine.

share a common past, and their emerging markets face similar problems. Moreover, market actors in these countries frequently draw on similar solutions because they look for them among their shared socialist legacies. Therefore, where applicable I have drawn parallels between what I found in Russia and other Eastern and Central European countries' experiences.

The emergence of credit card markets from the ruins of communism is symbolic of the transition from an economy based on the principle of redistribution to one based on exchange, and from chronic shortages to abundance. Instead of patiently waiting for state-rationed apartments, cars, and electric appliances and saving for years, individuals and households can now go into debt and buy these goods on the open market. Referring specifically to the emergence of revolving credit cards in Russia, a 2002 issue of the Moscow-based magazine *Afisha* gleefully wrote: "This year, full-blown capitalism appeared. We got the opportunity to participate fully in the consumerist orgy like citizens of Western countries" ("Russians Get Taste for Credit as Consumerism Takes Hold" 2003).

Developing markets for credit cards are also part of a larger trend of the global expansion of multinational credit card brands. The very concept of the credit card is global: the name *Visa* illustrates this point perfectly. Credit card companies act as agents of globalization when they seek to expand their card empires from the core Western countries, some of which (such as the United States) are already near saturation, to Eastern Europe, the Middle East, and parts of Asia and Africa (in line with Wallerstein's [1998] world systems theory). The spread of Western popular culture and foreign travel exposes Russian consumers to the idea of credit cards as a necessary attribute of the middle-class lifestyle, challenging the cash-centered view of market transactions and establishing the social acceptability and desirability of bank-procured financing. What this book will demonstrate, however, is that the effect of globalization is not unidirectional. While international credit cards are transforming Russian society and culture, the reverse tendency is also taking place. Principles of card distribution, circulation, and acceptance developed and perfected in the West are undergoing modifications in the process of adapting better to Russia's local realities.

Approach, Data, and Analysis

This is a case study of one emergent credit card market. The Russian postcommunist transition and its implications made Russia a particularly challenging environment in which to build a credit card market. According to Flyvbjerg's classification of strategies for case selection, Russia is an *extreme/deviant* case, which is usually chosen "[t]o obtain information on unusual cases, which can be especially problematic . . . in a more closely defined sense" (Flyvbjerg 2001, 79). Learning about market building in such inhospitable conditions draws attention to the obstacles that developing credit card markets can encounter (from very specific obstacles, such as the problem of simultaneously recruiting both cardholders and merchants, to the most basic ones, such as missing credit bureaus and inefficient courts) without taking anything for granted, and simultaneously enables one to appreciate the resourcefulness of market actors in their quest to establish a working market order.

The data for this book come from several field visits to Moscow, Russia, in 1998, 1999, and 2003–2005, where I conducted semistructured interviews with representatives of banks, bank associations, credit card networks, card-processing companies, and experts of the plastic card market. I also gathered bank application materials and relevant publications in specialized journals and periodicals. In addition to this qualitative data, I collected publicly available quantitative data from Visa, the Central Bank of Russia, and several card industry publications. These data reflect trends at the level of individual banks, credit card brands, and the overall Russian market.

The main goal of this project was to discover what credit card markets are like, and what it takes to build one *de novo*, especially in the challenging conditions of a transitional economy. For this reason, my nonrandom sample that is also almost entirely limited to the city of Moscow should not be viewed as a drawback; the data it yields well serve the goal of uncovering the mechanisms of market building in a postcommunist context.[1]

The selection of Moscow as a site is well justified: although the city of Moscow makes up only 6 percent of the total population of Russia, it attracts two-thirds of foreign investment and provides almost a quarter of the country's tax revenues ("Russia's Capital: Beacon or Bogey?" 1997). In addition to being a political capital of Russia, Moscow is undeniably its financial capital. According to the Central Bank of Russia, more than half of Russia's banks are registered in Moscow, and among the thirty leading banks, only six are not based in Moscow ("1000 bankov Rossii" 2007). In 2004, Moscow and the Moscow region accounted for 28 percent of all bank cards issued in Russia, while St. Petersburg, Russia's second largest city, only contributed 8 percent (Adrianova 2004).

Additionally, the two time periods during which the interviews were collected (1998–99 and 2003–2005) provided for a longitudinal look at the process of market maturation. I have combined my primary data analysis with secondary accounts of the Russian market from market actors, analysts, and policymakers from across the country. Finally, where applicable, I have compared and contrasted my case with some other countries' credit card markets to give the reader a sense of how common the social mechanisms that I discovered are.

Anatomy of the Market

Postsocialist transitional countries are unique for studying markets as dynamic systems that emerge, grow, and change, helping to challenge the traditional equilibrium models prevalent in much of economic theory. What makes these emerging market economies particularly fascinating is that they enable us to look at markets at their points of conception and follow them along their developmental trajectories, including failed solutions and abandoned paths that usually are cleansed from organizational and institutional memories. This sociological voyeurism pays off: not only does it provide an opportunity to examine the "hows" of market development, but also the "whys," as much of market development is path dependent, and examining the early formative stages is essential for understanding what markets eventually become.

Moreover, this examination of the emerging market economies has an important implication for better understanding the domestic market. Few American consumers appreciate the complexity of the American credit card market. Like many other markets in developed economies, this one has become fully institutionalized, with many of its practices and inner logic routinized and taken for granted. It operates like a "black box": most of the cardholders and even middle-level bank management are only familiar with "input" and "output" functions, having a vague understanding of what happens on the inside. Consumers are familiar with card applications (or preapproved offers), receiving cards in the mail, using them to pay for retail purchases, including Internet transactions, and paying their monthly bills. But they know little about the instruments card issuers have at their disposal to conduct screening, monitoring, and sanctioning. Various consumer advocate groups are trying to learn more about the process of lending decision making to help those who have been rejected by mainstream card issuers. U.S. national credit bureaus, for instance, have been pressured by these groups and by market regulators to educate consumers about what goes into calculating credit scores and how they can improve their numerical values.

Even issuers themselves often have a vague understanding of what goes into the score. At an early stage of this project, I conducted an informal interview with a card specialist in one of the local San Diego banks, and asked her the main question I was preparing to ask during my subsequent field trip to Moscow: how do banks decide who can be issued a card and who should be denied? Her answer was surprisingly short, but also emblematic of the point I am making. She explained that everything is automated, and the bank uses scoring models to make these decisions. She did not know which factors mattered more than others and could not elaborate on how the model was developed. In contrast, during my interviews in Russia, I was impressed by how much bank employees were aware of the nuts and bolts of card issuance, including the details of screening, verification, and monitoring of transactions. I was lucky that many were willing to share their knowledge with me.

Thus, the Russian credit card market in its formative stages lends itself particularly well to this theoretically grounded and methodologically informed investigation of the principles and logic involved in its creation. At the same time, it promises to shed light on several topics of interest to economic sociologists: the challenges of two-sided markets; the role of networks in market making; the problems of institution building and constituting consumer demand; and the globalization of practices, institutional configurations, and (consumer) culture, to name a few.

Outline of the Book

In the next chapter, "The Architecture of Credit Card Markets," I build a theoretical framework for the empirical Chapters Four, Five, Six, and Seven. I focus on the structure of credit card markets and the four key problems that their makers face: uncertainty, complementarity, the need to build consumer demand, and the imperative to foster interbank cooperation. I detail how American card issuers handled these problems.

Chapter Two, "Market Building in the Transitional Context," continues building on the theoretical foundation for the analysis of the credit card market. I recreate key debates on the course of postcommunist reforms in Russia and detail the challenges of building markets and creating institutions. Here I introduce the two main contributions that I am hoping to make in this book: first, to demonstrate that Russian card issuers rely on networks to constitute *mass* markets, and second, to expand the idea of networks to include those sets of ties that connect nodes of different levels, both individuals and organizations.

Chapter Three, "Setting the Stage: Consumer Credit and Banking Before and During the Transition," places the Russian credit card market in historical perspective, offering a brief overview of the Soviet economic system and surveying Soviet-era (pre-1990) and transitional (post-1990) consumer credit and banking, early card programs, and the particularities of the first plastic cards issued in Russia. The chapter argues that while the Russian economy and society overall were not well prepared for the advent of credit cards, the socialist period produced several legacies that subsequently played key roles in shaping the credit card market.

The next three chapters draw directly on empirical fieldwork: each concentrates on one of the three successive but overlapping card-marketing strategies (elite issuing, mass issuing of salary cards, and mass issuing of cards through retail establishments) and analyzes them within the framework set up in Chapter One.

Chapter Four, "Inner Circles: Card Issuing at the Dawn of the Market," addresses elite-issuing strategies: distributing cards through personal networks of bankers or by anchoring prospective applicants in their own networks, unrelated to the bank. The three main goals that Russian banks pursued during this early period were ruling out fraud, verifying applicants' overall honesty, and most important, establishing reliable channels of communication through which cardholders could be contacted to inquire about or negotiate a late payment. At that time, cards were mostly issued as a status symbol, and banks did not invest in developing card acceptance among merchants.

Chapter Five, "The Stick But No Carrot: Disseminating Cards Through Employers," analyzes the banks' first attempt to develop the mass card market in Russia via salary projects, which became the main channel of card distribution in Russia in the 1990s (and until as recently as 2003 for some banks). Salary projects involved agreements between banks and enterprises to issue cards to all of the enterprises' employees while depositing their salaries directly to card-issuing banks. Employing the lens of uncertainty and complementarity, I discuss the role of employers in helping banks both access and control potential cardholders. I demonstrate how banks rely on networks to mass-issue cards and focus specifically on the networks' *relational* benefits, those that enable banks to use the relations employers have with their employees to reduce uncertainty in lending.

In Chapter Six, "The Carrot, at Last: Will Consumer Lending Lead the Way for Russia's Credit Card Market?," I address the recent boom of consumer lending in Russia and detail why this is the most successful attempt at market building so far. I contrast this method of card issuance with salary projects, which, while managing to increase the number of cards in circulation, did not lead to greater use of cards for retail purchases. Here I further extend the argument developed in the previous chapter on the role of networks in promoting mass markets, but focus on their *locational* benefits, because retail organizations attract consumers but do not help banks screen them. Card issuing at retail locations has been instrumental in increasing the number of revolving credit cards and stimulating card purchases, but it also has underscored the lack of effective prescreening methods.

Chapter Seven, "The Missing Piece of the Puzzle: The Struggle to Institutionalize Interbank Information Sharing and Create Credit Bureaus," addresses the process of debating and passing the law on credit bureaus to help banks screen, monitor, and sanction borrowers and sustain mass lending. I detail the challenges of this process in the context of Russia's highly concentrated and fiercely competitive market and argue that state involvement is necessary, but that it is also limited in its capacity to promote cooperation between banks. This chapter draws attention to the role that global actors played in articulating the principles of credit reporting in Russia.

In the concluding chapter, Chapter Eight, "The Russian Credit Card Market Through the Lens of Continuity and Change," I reflect on the major changes experienced by the credit card market since its inception, focusing on the current trends. I then suggest that the Russian credit card market is both a site of continuity with the past and a force bringing major changes to society, leading the Russians out of the communist past and into the consumerist future, out of the red and into the red.

CHAPTER ONE

The Architecture of Credit Card Markets

> America began to change on a mid-September day in 1958, when the
> Bank of America dropped its first 60,000 credit cards on an unassuming
> city of Fresno, California. That's a word they liked to use in the credit
> card business to characterize a mass mailing of cards: a "drop," and it
> is an unwittingly apt description. There had been no outward yearning
> among the residents of Fresno for such a device, not even the dimmest
> awareness that such a thing was in the works. It simply arrived one day,
> with no advance warning, as if it had dropped from the sky.
>
> —JOSEPH NOCERA[1]

These cards were the precursors of today's Visa cards. By the end of the following year, Bank of America had mailed two million more cards to the unsuspecting residents of several larger California towns and cities, including
"untrustworthy" Los Angeles, home to "the fast Hollywood crowd, the blue
suede shoe boys" (from the words of a BofA executive, quoted in Nocera 1994,
29; see also Wolters 2000). Eight years later, during the pre-Christmas sale of
1966, several Chicago banks mailed another five million unsolicited cards.

What is so remarkable about these mailings? After all, millions of Americans today routinely receive "preapproved" offers for credit cards in the mail.
What was different then was that individuals received *actual cards*, ready to be
used in merchants' establishments, without applying for them, without being screened, and apparently, even without their names being verified. In
some cases, cards were mailed to prison inmates, individuals long deceased,
infants, and even dogs. For example, Shepherdson (1991, 128) reports that
"[a] dachshund named Alice Griffin was sent not one but four cards, one of

which arrived with the promise that Alice would be welcomed as a 'preferred customer' at many of Chicago's finest restaurants."

As a result of issuing cards indiscriminately and entirely foregoing preliminary screening, after the first fifteen months of Bank of America's credit card program, its official losses amounted to $8.8 million—a huge sum of money for a bank at that time. Instead of the expected 4 percent of delinquent accounts (the average for loans), default accounts comprised 22 percent. Fraud was rampant and collections—another risk-management mechanism—were problematic, because the bank had never established a special collections department, so confident had it been in its clients. The situation was especially difficult in Los Angeles. There, Bank of America faced a major moral hazard, as credit cards seemed to corrupt even once-honest clients. New cardholders perceived credit lines as free money and ran up bills without any intention of paying them back (Nocera 1994).

The Chicago experiment with unsolicited mailings was even more disastrous, with credit cards corrupting merchants and postal workers. Merchants worked together with criminals to supply fraudulent slips to banks, while postal workers were discovered "carting off bags of unmailed credit cards to sell on the black market" (Nocera 1994, 58). Some cardholders disputed purchases they had actually made, and banks often preferred to pay rather than argue, given the already negative reputation that credit cards had earned. The situation in Chicago spiraled completely out of control when the press reported the story of a bank clerk who slipped and fell while carrying several boxes of unprocessed merchant credit card slips that were blown away by the wind. Another time, a truck loaded with new credit cards flipped over, and newspapers published photographs of people grabbing handfuls of cards for future use. The total losses of the Chicago banks were estimated at $6 million, although some analysts believed them to have been no less than $25 million (Nocera 1994, 59–61).

The story detailed by Joseph Nocera in his award-winning book, *A Piece of the Action*, is striking. Bank of America mailed credit cards to strangers without prescreening and name verification at the same time that an applicant for a regular small personal loan was required to provide a detailed family history during a face-to-face interview with the bank's credit officer. What is even more stunning is that Chicago banks repeated the unsolicited credit card mailings almost a decade later, having known by then about the losses that Bank of America had experienced earlier. What can explain the seemingly irrational and self-destructive approach of these banks?

This chapter will provide the answer to this question by discussing ways in which the credit card market is different from other markets and identifying the main challenges that emerging credit card markets face. It will draw on historical material to reveal how these challenges were tackled by American credit card issuers, and will offer insights into the strategies of Russian banks that will be addressed in full in the subsequent chapters.

Demand-Side Increasing Returns and Complementarity

Credit card markets are a classic example of demand-side increasing returns (DSIR) markets, where the value to the consumer of each additional product increases with the number of items already in use by others (Katz and Shapiro 1985; Saloner, Shepard, and Podolny 2001). Other examples of such markets include markets for telephones, faxes, and other means of communication that presuppose connectedness and compatibility. For example, owning a telephone if none of your friends or acquaintances owns one is useless, but acquiring one when there are others you can call is beneficial because you are joining an already existing user group. Also, each additional device increases the value of owning the existing ones. Once the number of users reaches a critical mass (Granovetter 1978), new membership starts to snowball. The network starts growing on its own, attracting new members by virtue of its sheer size.

This logic of increasing returns is exemplified in path-dependent processes that are brought about by small random events but receive positive feedback and get locked in (David 1986). One of the key implications is that such processes are hard to initiate, but once they are under way and are set on a particular path, they are difficult to reroute. Once a demand for a particular product is locked in, it becomes self-reinforcing: consumers want more of this particular product over others like it.

But how do companies get the first consumers interested? This is the fundamental marketing question that often is not easily answered. But in the case of credit cards, it is even more complicated. The problem is that the value of owning a card does not increase directly in proportion to the number of those who already have cards. The value increases indirectly: more card-holders means that more merchants will accept the cards, and this, in turn, will attract more individuals to sign up to become cardholders. This is an example of a two-sided market (Rysman 2006; Armstrong 2006; Rochet and Tirole 2005), a market that connects the two segments, merchants and consumers, through an intermediary (in this case, a bank that issues cards); each of the segments is sensitive to how well the intermediary performs in the other segment. Another classic example of a two-sided market, discussed by Rysman (2003), is the market for Yellow Pages directories, whose success also depends on the extent to which the directory publishers are capable of convincing sellers to advertise and consumers to buy them. In practice, Yellow Pages are usually distributed to consumers for free. In this case, directory promoters need to find a credible way to signal to sellers that they have direct access to consumers who would favor their directory over the competition. Telephone companies have traditionally been more successful than independent publishers in promoting Yellow Pages directories precisely because of their consumer coverage. Two-sided markets can also be conceptualized in terms of the "hardware-software" paradigm (Rysman 2003; Katz and Shapiro 1985), where "hardware" (for instance, VCRs) becomes more available if more "software" (compatible VCR tapes) is provided, which in turn depends on the availability of "hardware." The more there are people who own VCRs of a particular format, the more valuable it is to own one of the same format, as tapes of this format will be more available from video rental stores.

Thus, just like the promoters of VCRs who had to target two segments of the market simultaneously: consumers and video-store owners, credit card issuers also had to recruit merchants and cardholders at the same time. Reaching critical mass in one group sends positive feedback to the other group and encourages more of the members of the other group to join as well. Cardholders and merchants are said to be mutually *complementary*, as one group cannot function without the other and the growth in each group makes joining the other more attractive (Milgrom, Qian, and Roberts 1991). Therefore, no cardholders, no merchants, and vice versa. Unless the vicious circle is broken, the market simply will not take off. Once positive feedback is received, the numbers of cardholders and merchants start growing in a complementary fashion: "As more consumers have a particular card brand and more merchants take that card brand, it becomes harder and harder for other merchants *not* to take that card brand" (Evans and Schmalensee 1999, 151, emphasis mine).

But where should credit card promoters start? Bank of America executives believed that they had found the solution to this chicken-and-egg problem: instead of recruiting cardholders via traditional means, they decided to *create* them (Nocera 1994, 26, emphasis mine) by "dropping" cards onto a large number of consumers at once. According to Kenneth Larkin, Bank of America vice president who oversaw their first "drop," "it was the only way to initially assure merchants that there would be enough cardholders to make accepting the cards worthwhile" (Shepherdson 1991, 130). History proved that they were right. In addition to three hundred merchants who signed up in advance, the mass mailing in Fresno drew another eight hundred merchants in the next five months. By the end of 1959, about the same time that Bank of America posted multimillion-dollar losses, the BankAmericard program attracted more than twenty thousand merchants to accept its credit cards. Eight years later, more than eight hundred banks were involved in the card business, and thirty-two million cards were issued in that year alone, the majority through unsolicited mailings (Nocera 1994, 57). President Nixon outlawed unsolicited mailings in 1970, but by that time, twelve years after the Fresno "drop," BankAmericard cards were present in forty-four American states and Master Charge (precursor of MasterCard) cards in forty-nine, and around twenty-nine million people had used the cards at least once, which was more than 20 percent of the adult population at that time.

Thus, unsolicited mailings of cards helped American banks solve the initial problem of complementarity: as a result of signing up a large number of cardholders, banks managed to attract merchants, which prompted even more cardholders to join. The cost that banks had to pay for this campaign in the short run was steep: in the haste of getting cards to as many people as possible in the shortest time possible, the applicants were not screened, and banks incurred serious financial losses.[2] Were the banks that undertook card programs not as big and stable, and had they not had as much organizational slack—resources that could be shed without a devastating impact on organizational performance—they would not have been likely to recover financially. Yet, the market was successfully born, and the staggering losses accompanying its early development were soon forgotten by all but business historians.[3]

How did the Russian banks approach the complementarity problem? Despite the entirely different context, they were in the same predicament because they, too, were starting the market from scratch.[4] By the time the first cards were issued in Russia, there were already some Russian merchants who accepted cards in their establishments, along with twenty-five million merchants who accepted the Visa and MasterCard brands worldwide. But neither of the two groups could generate a demand for credit cards among the Russian consumers. A handful of domestic merchants who accepted cards were high-end hotels and hard-currency stores that served the needs of foreign travelers and holders of foreign-issued cards, which were completely out of reach for the majority of Russians. The foreign-card acceptance network attracted the Russian elite, who with the fall of communism received an opportunity to travel abroad and quickly accepted cards as unalienable signs of one's elite status. But the limited number of elite cards could not trigger the interest of many Russian merchants to join. So neither the elite cards nor the merchants' acceptance network mainly serving visitors with foreign cards could lead the way for a domestic credit card market.

Parts of Nocera's book were translated into Russian and published in the mid-1990s by one of Russia's leading magazines covering the plastic card industry. It is conceivable that many of the Russian bankers engaged in promoting cards knew of the story, but they undoubtedly took it as an example of how *not* to market cards. They would not dare "drop" cards the "American way" because in the context of transitional Russia it would be a suicidal tactic. As much as they did not trust their prospective customers, they were also suspicious of mail being intercepted or stolen. In the 1990s, Russian banks did not even mail monthly statements, citing considerations of confidentiality and security and requiring cardholders to pick them up in person. Most of the banks were small, undercapitalized, and lacked the resources that helped Bank of America to withstand the blow of losses and persist with its credit card program. These banks were also extremely unstable, growing fast but failing frequently.

The Russian card issuers' initial strategy was to issue cards, after an exhaustive analysis of each case, to applicants who had a direct or indirect social tie to the bank, who were visible politically or socially, or who were anchored in some other way that made the bank reasonably confident that they would not default. But very soon, the Russian banks realized, just as Bank of

America had thirty-five years earlier, that slow and careful recruitment of cardholders was like swimming against a strong current. It was not bringing them closer to their destination: a market where the numbers of cardholders and merchants are increasing in a complementary manner, and growth is generated by the externalities of demand. They needed the equivalent of a steamship. And they did build the ship. They turned toward employing organizations, peddling cards *en masse* to entire work collectives, creating cardholders instead of recruiting them. The employing organizations provided access, and in some cases served as guarantors; the banks sold and serviced the cards. Employing organizations also enabled the banks to avoid the large initial losses that plagued the American credit card market. To the extent that companies exercised control over their employees, they ensured the Russian banks' ability to monitor cardholders and helped them to control uncertainty, to which we turn next.

The Problem of Uncertainty

Issuing a credit card is the beginning of a potentially long-term relationship between the bank and the client (and between the merchant and the bank), which imposes certain responsibilities on each of the parties. American-style unsolicited card mailings, while successful in solving the problem of *complementarity*, underscored the dangers of ignoring the *uncertainty* involved in credit lending and foregoing the preliminary screening of prospective cardholders.

According to Beckert (1996), the ubiquitous nature of uncertainty in economic life creates a particular problem for neoclassical economic equilibrium models, and at the same time opens up rich possibilities for sociological contributions to the understanding of economic processes (see also Podolny 1994). In his insightful analysis, Beckert demonstrates that uncertainty prevents actors from knowing in advance which of the alternative courses of action is the most rational to pursue because their relative benefits would often only become clear afterward. Beckert argues that actors are "intentionally rational," that is, they aspire to be rational but frequently fail, and questions how they nevertheless make choices when they do not know what the best course of action is. His answer points toward social devices, such as traditions and routines, norms and institutions, social structure and power. These devices limit the actors' flexibility by cutting down on the number of alternatives in the decision-making process. As a result, social devices reduce ambiguity and speed up decision making.

Banks use several methods to protect themselves from irresponsible or malicious borrowers and to reduce the uncertainty inherent in lending (Table 1.1). First, they can lower the amount of uncertainty they experience by reducing their *exposure*. For instance, they can limit the size or the term of the loan. Second, they can ask for various *guarantees* that protect the bank from possible losses either by deterring the client from defaulting or by compensating the bank if the default has occurred. This is the strategy used by pawnshops, which take collateral that is worth more (sometimes much more) than the loan they are extending. This gives the borrower a strong incentive to pay the loan back. Banks also take collateral: mortgages and auto loans are collateralized by real estate and cars—goods that the loans finance. Third, some Russian banks in my sample argued that they charged borrowers high interest or high fees on various loan-related services hoping that this would *compensate* them for possible losses. Unlike guarantees, which are individual and nontransferable (borrower A provides collateral that would be sold to compensate the lender if borrower A defaults), the logic of charging high interest rates to compensate for possible losses works on the aggregate level: diligent borrowers will end up paying for those who default. A similar logic applies in the health insurance industry, in which the young and healthy subsidize the healthcare expenses of those who are not so healthy and no longer young.

None of these approaches is effective (at least, none on their own) (Guseva and Kuzina 2004). Limiting credit lines and shortening the term of the credit card or loan reduces the bank's potential profits. Taking collateral when lending on credit cards is cumbersome (and some Russian banks were

TABLE 1.1

Methods of Reducing Uncertainty in Lending
(Excluding Screening and Sanctioning)

	Limiting exposure	Asking for guarantees	Compensating for possible losses
Examples	Smaller, shorter-term loans	Security deposits, collateral	High interest rates, user and other fees; making "good" clients pay for the "bad"
Problems	Reduces bank's profit	Freezes borrowers' assets, turns banks into pawnshops	Can aggravate the problem of adverse selection

not only willing to take liquid assets, such as savings accounts, but also real estate or stocks and bonds). Besides, it requires borrowers to freeze their liquid assets (usually for a larger amount than the size of the credit line), and essentially reduces the bank to a version of a pawnshop. As for increasing the interest rate, this strategy may backfire: according to Stiglitz (2000), raising interest rates will only attract high-risk borrowers and can consequently aggravate the problem of adverse selection.[5]

A much more effective and commonly used method of reducing uncertainty in lending is prescreening, an attempt to separate good risks from bad ones. In our analysis of a specific case of uncertainty in lending, Ákos Róna-Tas and I (Guseva and Róna-Tas 2001) focus on the two ways to prescreen cardholders: (1) in a case-by-case fashion by carefully establishing the trustworthiness of each applicant (expert judgment), or (2) *en masse* through the calculation of risk based on statistical models.

In a classic work, *Risk, Uncertainty and Profit* (1957 [1921]), Knight distinguishes risk, the situation in which actors are able to assign probabilities to future events, from uncertainty, when such probabilities cannot be assigned in any meaningful way. Future probabilities are assigned based on the analysis of past observations. For example, the correlation between past cardholders' demographics, financial status, and credit history on the one hand, and their success in repayment of credit on the other, serves as an indicator of current applicants' future chances of paying off their balances.

The calculation of risk is preferable to case-by-case decision making, because it predicts better (Dawes, Faust, and Meehl 1989), allows for processing a greater volume of applications, reduces the need to have highly trained credit officers, and enables bundling and selling accounts on secondary markets (Rosenthal and Ocampo 1988). But the ability to classify, compare, and calculate is not innate to human beings, who have limited cognitive capacities (Simon 1986). In support of Beckert's (1996) argument about "social devices," we point toward social institutions such as credit bureaus that help economic actors to turn uncertainty into risk (Guseva and Róna-Tas 2001). Credit bureaus accumulate, verify, and classify data and often preprocess it (with the help of credit-scoring models) to assist credit card issuers in calculating the risk of default or, even, the profitability of prospective customers.

A typical scoring model uses observed empirical data from past and current accounts (both "good" and "bad") classified into homogeneous groups based on meaningful criteria: occupation, type of residence, age, length of time at present address, extent of financial indebtedness, and so forth. The goal is to estimate the probability of applicants defaulting, given their jobs and residential and financial histories.[6] The process renders decisions specific to groups and is completely routinized.[7] Despite the biases that might be built into the system, this formalization speeds up and systematizes application processing.

Although credit-scoring models can differ significantly from one bank to another, most of them combine three kinds of predictions: (1) willingness to pay, (2) ability to pay, and (3) accountability. *Willingness to pay* is gauged through previous payment history, including late payments, bankruptcies, or accounts turned over to collections. Is the cardholder reliable enough to abide by the rules specified in the contract? *Ability to pay* is assessed as a combination of the amount of current indebtedness and income. Will the cardholder have enough funds to pay off the loan? The cardholder's *accountability* is the perceived ability of the bank to reach him or her in order to verify suspicious card activity, remind about a missed payment, negotiate on the terms of the repayment or apply sanctions (Sztompka 1999). Accountability is assessed based on the applicant's occupation and the length of time spent with the current employer and at the current residence. Homeownership, for instance, signals higher accountability, and not just greater ability to pay, because homeowners can be traced more easily than renters.

In addition to predicting the likelihood of default, advanced models can also try to evaluate whether the cardholder is someone who would be profitable for the bank. Curiously, these assessments do not necessarily coincide. An American credit card holder who is deemed both reliable (a good past record of kept commitments, operationalized as good credit history) and capable of repayment (regular and sufficient income) can be less profitable for the bank than someone who is not as disciplined or periodically falls on hard times. The former may be paying the monthly balance on time and in full, avoiding interest and late fees, and using credit cards mainly for convenience, whereas the latter may revolve the balance from month to month, paying interest and, perhaps, an occasional late fee. According to Manning (2000, 13), 57 percent of American households were revolvers (44.5 million) in 2000, while 43 percent (33.5 million) were convenience credit card users (zero credit card debt). Although banks may hail discipline and responsibility when it comes to repayment of credit (qualities possessed in abundance by convenience users), it is revolvers that procure the livelihood of the credit card industry.

Each characteristic of the applicant is assigned a score. All scores are summed up automatically, and a final score is compared to a preset cutoff point. An applicant whose score is below the cutoff is rejected. This ensures that uncertainty is reduced to the maximum extent possible, and that the decision rendered is perfectly rational. Thus, rationality is achieved at the cost of choice. Loan officers and bank managers lose discretion over the process.[8]

Of course, perfect rationality does not always prevail. Sometimes loan officers are allowed to override scoring decisions that fall in close proximity to the cutoff point. The overrides are usually justified on the grounds of possessing information about the applicant that was not included in the scoring (for example, very recently acquired information), or information that seriously challenges the data provided by the credit bureau. Thus, despite the standardization, impersonality, and calculation of the prescreening and card-issuing processes in the United States, expert judgments also play an occasional role in these decisions.

In the absence of credit bureaus and ways to score applicants' risk, lenders rely on case-by-case expert judgments or two other methods of prescreening: rules and point systems.[9] If expert judgments and risk calculation are positioned at opposite ends of the informal-formal continuum, rules and point systems fall in between (Table 1.2); both are more formalized than judgments but less formalized than calculation of risk. Rules can include a variety of principles, from simple eligibility rules and commonsense observations to

TABLE 1.2

*Formalization of Decision Making with
the Use of Different Screening Methods*

Expert judgments	Least formalized
Rules	
Point systems	
Risk calculation	Most formalized

Source: Ákos Róna-Tas, "Credit Card Markets in East European Emerging Economies," talk given at Harvard Business School, November 16, 2006. Used by permission.

more specific formalizations from particular experiences. More often, these rules have a limiting or prohibitive nature exemplifying the bank's having learned from its (bad) experiences. Rather than evaluating each case individually, banks apply rules to groups of cases.

Point systems superficially look like credit scoring (risk calculation): applicants are assigned numerical values for each of their characteristics, which are then summed up. However, in a point system, as opposed to a credit-scoring system, both characteristics (variables) and their weights (numerical scores assigned to different values) are not arrived at as a result of the statistical analysis of previous borrowers' behavior, but are based on common sense and the idiosyncratic experiences of those who develop a particular point system. For instance, it is reasonable to suppose that married people are less likely to default on their loans, so a point system would assign a higher score to someone who is married. But how much higher? And what about those who have never been married or who are divorced or widowed? Do they pose the same risk for the bank and should therefore be lumped into one category of "nonmarrieds"? Or should they be treated separately? Without the solid statistical analysis of the previous borrowers' behavior, experts can disagree on these matters depending on their background or personal experiences, and the resulting point systems can be completely inaccurate. So while providing more standardization and significantly speeding up decision making, point systems are not necessarily more effective than rules or expert judgments.

As a method of last resort, banks can rely on sanctioning those who have failed to repay their debt or were involved in fraud; sanctions involve legal action and/or collections. But without effective prescreening, sanctioning can fail. It is difficult to sanction those who obtained a loan or a credit card under false pretenses or based on incorrect personal information because the bank would have to locate that person first. Therefore, in addition to distinguishing between those who would probably repay and those who would most likely not, prescreening also helps insure that the borrower would be available for future sanctioning if necessary, in other words, that he or she could be tracked down and held accountable (Sztompka 1999, 47, 87). In addition, prescreening carries out an important mission of sanctioning: to spoil the chances of obtaining future loans. In other words, despite the multitude of methods to reduce uncertainty, prescreening is irreplaceable; it is probably more important than all other methods combined.

Quite paradoxically, the two problems, complementarity and uncertainty, require contradictory solutions (Table 1.3). The problem of uncertainty requires careful prescreening, and it can be time-consuming (if prescreening uses experts to decide on prospective borrowers); thus, it only allows for a slower market expansion. In addition, prescreening narrows down the pool of potential applicants by weeding out "poor risks" and yielding a smaller number of "suitable" cardholders. Slower market expansion and smaller pool size jeopardize the problem of complementarity. Thus, careful screening prevents card issuers from quickly reaching a critical mass of cardholders necessary for getting merchants interested, receiving positive feedback, and acheiving ultimate market success. Moreover, in emerging markets, which usually lack necessary formal institutions such as credit bureaus, lenders have to resort to social networks to prescreen and monitor prospective borrowers. This sets natural limitations on the size of the issuers' clientele and further prevents lenders from solving the problem of complementarity. In other words, if one *is* too careful in screening, the market may never develop. But if one *is not* too careful and issues cards quickly but indiscriminately, chasing complementarity, market expansion can bring ruin: card issuers may be faced with mounting defaults and fraud.

Card issuers in emerging markets must carefully balance these two competing pressures: to jumpstart the market and to control uncertainty. Of the two problems, complementarity is temporary. It is only important initially and becomes irrelevant once the card-acceptance network is established and the demand for cards becomes self-generated. Nevertheless, card issuers never lose the desire to issue more cards; only in established markets this becomes part of the usual market competition. Unlike complementarity, the challenge

TABLE 1.3

Contradictory Solutions to Uncertainty and Complementarity Problems in Emerging Credit Card Markets

	Uncertainty	Complementarity
Solutions	Careful prescreening	Quickly issuing cards *en masse* in order to attract merchants
Consequences	Slower market expansion, smaller pool of potential customers	Card issuing in the absence of prescreening can aggravate the problem of adverse selection and jeopardize the future economic soundness of the market

of uncertainty is permanent. As much as it has to be solved by each new debu-
tante on the card-issuing scene, existing card issuers are also regularly revis-
ing their screening and monitoring approaches to react to market changes, to
accommodate new products, or to appeal to new consumer groups.

In mature credit card markets, there is also a tension between two competing pressures: issuing more cards on the one hand, and containing uncertainty on the other. For these markets, mass issuance of cards is no longer
about jump-starting the market, but rather about expanding one's card program and increasing profits. The lure of moneymaking is restrained by the
concern of money loss, exemplified in the tensions between two bank divi-
sions, risk management and sales.[10]

So while the first U.S. credit card issuers solved the *complementarity* problem, they aggravated the problem of *uncertainty*. It was clear that for subsequent market growth banks needed to find a permanent solution to uncertainty: they had to design ways to effectively prescreen, monitor, and sanction
their customers. In the next section, I discuss how this task was eventually ac-
complished in the American consumer-lending market.

How the Problem of Uncertainty Was Managed in the United States

By the time the first credit cards were issued in the United States, the country had already boasted a long-standing tradition of collecting individual
credit histories and a fairly large number of small local credit bureaus (Calder
1999; Mandel 1990). Early forms of credit reporting in the United States
were developed in response to the needs of commercial credit. As wholesalers' businesses outgrew the circles of retailers that they knew personally,
information about prospective buyers became crucial. Colonial merchants
routinely provided credit recommendations of potential customers to one
another through their correspondence or by word of mouth. Sometimes,
prospective buyers would themselves provide references regarding their reliability to wholesalers. At other times, when it was merchants who initiated
the request, information about prospective buyers could be solicited from
their customers, friends, and relatives (Madison 1974).

Lewis Tappan founded the first commercial credit bureau in the United
States in 1841. His Mercantilist Agency later became what is now known as

Dun & Bradstreet Company (Foulke 1941). Small-scale credit agencies were also organized by individual merchants or by groups of merchants. The nineteenth-century credit rating relied heavily on the collection of clinical (in-depth) information about borrowers from the members of their communities: attorneys, bank clerks, and other merchants, but also their friends, neighbors, hairdressers, and butchers (Olegario 1999; Cohen 1999). This work was performed by traveling or resident reporters and by local correspondents and community members themselves, among them cashiers, postmasters, sheriffs, storekeepers, and most important, young lawyers (Lovett 1975; Madison 1974). Attorneys were seen as an invaluable source of information and often aggressively recruited. However, because at least initially credit reporting was a stigmatized pursuit, primarily young or unsuccessful lawyers became correspondents, and then usually for a limited period of time. For many of them, credit reporting was attractive, as it supplied them with a constant flow of debt-collection cases.

The main problem at that time was that credit reporting relied on information obtained from local social ties. Although this guaranteed rich information and provided ways of constantly monitoring the borrower's spending, it also inevitably meant a limited scope of lending.

The mass migration and urbanization of the late-nineteenth to early-twentieth century necessitated an information exchange between local credit bureaus about borrowers moving to other localities. In 1906, six local bureaus organized the National Association of Mercantile Agencies, whose membership in 1927 numbered eight hundred, and in the mid-1950s, 1,700 bureaus (Pagano and Jappelli 1993).[11] This was a gradual process toward disembedding credit reporting from social relations.

The content of reported information was also changing. Initially, it supplied rich information in the form of detailed freestyle narratives. But by the turn of the twentieth century, narratives were gradually replaced by formal ratings, and richness of information was supplanted by quantification and prediction, both signs of the continuing rationalization of credit reporting. Consequently, credit reporting grew dramatically in scope (Carruthers and Cohen 2001).

In 1965, the Credit Data Corporation (CDC) organized the first nationwide, computer-based credit bureau. The CDC managed to convince several California banks to subscribe to their services (at fifty cents an inquiry) "on the condition that they open their credit files to Credit Data's microfilming teams" (Jordan 1967, 67). Bank of America alone supplied eight million items of information (Miller 1971, 75). Within the next two years, the CDC also signed the other major banks in California and New York, large financial and credit card companies, large chain retailers, and major oil companies. The CDC was eventually acquired by TRW (now Experian), which became the largest repository of personal credit information in the United States and likely in the world. Today, each of the three national credit-reporting systems (Experian, Equifax, and TransUnion) maintains about 190 million credit files.[12] Two billion pieces of data are entered monthly into their credit records, and about one billion credit reports are used annually in the United States (Associated Credit Bureaus 2001; see also Miller 2003).

By the early 1960s, a few American companies, most notably, Fair Isaac Corporation, started to develop statistical solutions to the problems of screening and monitoring by offering banks powerful automated tools for managing their prospective and current customers. National repositories of credit histories and formalized decision making made credit accessible to a wider group of people and allowed banks to quickly process a much larger volume of applications (Leyshon and Thrift 1999). Moreover, they rendered any social interaction between lenders and borrowers completely irrelevant. According to Evans and Schmalensee (1999, 50), 84 percent of the credit cards held by individuals in the United States in 1995 were issued by banks with which the cardholders had no other banking relationship.

Today cards in the United States are offered to millions of strangers via mailed-in "preapproved" offers, but unlike the unsolicited card mailings of the 1950s and 1960s, this strategy does not result in uncontrollable losses for the banks. The problem of uncertainty is managed in the U.S. credit card market by drawing on institutional resources, nationwide computerized credit bureaus, and credit-scoring methods. U.S. banks can quantify risk and prescreen while maintaining a high volume of operations. Institutions obviated the need for close social ties between banks and their customers, and provided the U.S. market with virtually unlimited potential for growth. But this required banks to cooperate and open the files of their existing clients to third parties. Interbank cooperation is a solution to the problem of uncertainty, and resistance to cooperation is the third problem that credit card market promoters face, in addition to uncertainty and complementarity.

Interbank Cooperation

Cooperation is indispensable for credit card markets because, unlike most other credit markets, they are based on an interchange system—a system of mutual transactions between the members of the network. The network consists of several types of players (Figure 1.1). Most commonly, there are banks that issue cards to individuals (called *issuers*), and there are those that provide equipment for card acceptance, authorize purchases, and reimburse merchants after receiving payments from issuing banks (called *acquirers*). There could also be a separate processing company if neither of the two banks is large enough to process payments in-house, and another bank that settles accounts. The same bank can perform all of those roles: issue cards, acquire merchants, and process and settle payments, but in competitive systems and especially in the global environment when cardholders travel internationally, issuing and acquiring are performed by different banks.

It is essential for a seamless working of the system that a Visa card issued in Beijing is accepted by a store in Boston and vice versa. Acquiring banks need to be assured that issuing banks will not delay payments (acquirers usually compensate merchants before the issuing banks compensate them). Merchants need to know that their acquiring bank will reimburse them for the purchase promptly. Issuing banks and their customers need to know that

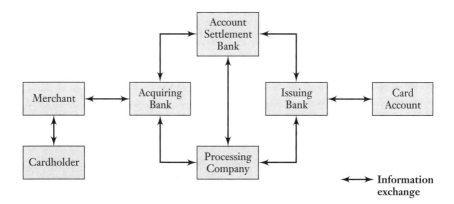

Figure 1.1 Interchange Network in a Credit Card Market

merchants will readily accept cards in lieu of cash. Both issuers and acquirers need to know that the processing company and the bank that settles payment will perform their duties quickly and honestly. What this means, however, is that while any two banks can compete in the issuing or acquiring market, nevertheless, they must cooperate and abide by the rules that benefit the whole network. Moreover, all network participants need to have faith in the fairness of the rules and their enforceability.

These rules are developed by Visa, MasterCard, and other card associations and sent regularly to all member banks, which are required to follow them and are severely fined if they break the rules. The rules are quite detailed: they describe issuers' and acquirers' rights and duties and indicate specific steps for resolving conflicts among cardholders, merchants, and their banks (for instance, they clearly define which bank has to pay for fraudulent charges).

But there was a time, in the 1960s, before these rules were institutionalized, when U.S. banks opportunistically cheated on each other trying to obtain a competitive edge. This is how Nocera (1994, 68) describes interchange relations within the BankAmericard system, the first multibank credit card network and a precursor of Visa:

> Card-issuing banks would receive sales drafts from a merchant bank and then sit on them for weeks at a time, earning interest on money that did not really belong to them. Or they would unilaterally refuse to accept certain sales drafts from a merchant bank, claiming they were invalid for some preposterous reason. Or the merchant bank would lie about the size of the merchant discount, in order to lower the fee it had to pay to the credit card bank.[13] These measures would then bring retaliation. "I thought a bank was shafting us on the merchant fee they sent us," recalls one banker, "so I decided we would just start sending them zero. Two weeks later, the head of their card program called the head of ours and started screaming, 'You are sending us zero, you bastard! I *know* your merchant discount isn't zero.'"

The main reason for this chaos was that the original interchange system developed by Bank of America was largely an informal one, and it essentially stopped working when the number of card-issuing banks in the network grew. Bank of America was also losing other banks' trust in its impartiality, and as a result, its power to "discipline and punish" (Nocera 1994, 67–69). Allowing banks to benefit in the short run, these opportunistic strategies served to undermine the entire market, eroding that very faith on which markets rest (Spicer and Pyle [2003] call this effect "reputational externalities," alluding to how the negative reputations of individual banks are extrapolated to all of the banks in the market). The solution came from a third party, a new organization named National BankAmericard Inc. (later Visa), a for-profit, member-owned company. As a result, power was shifted away from Bank of America, giving all member banks equal rights and responsibilities. National BankAmericard standardized the interchange fees and made advertising campaigns a prerogative of the network, not of individual banks as it had been before. In addition, it introduced severe penalties for banks accused of breaking the rules of the system in order to use the power of example to dissuade other banks from noncompliance. This was a political solution to the problem of cooperation, demonstrating that markets are as much political formations as they are networks (Fligstein 2001). This illustrates the second paradox of credit card markets: there is an intrinsic contradiction between the propensity of banks to engage in direct competition and the need to cooperate to sustain exchange.[14]

The U.S. banks were the pioneers in building the credit card acceptance network and working out the principles of the interchange system, first in the United States, and later internationally as Visa and MasterCard expanded overseas. Therefore, Russian issuers of Visas no longer faced the same problem: they became part of a member-bank network with already articulated rules. But the Russian credit card market illustrates another element of this tension between competition and cooperation: the problem of interbank information sharing.

Pooling account information, usually with the help of credit bureaus, is a crucial means to prescreen, monitor, and sanction cardholders and is a key solution to the problem of uncertainty on a mass scale. Yet Russian banks are paralyzed by a collective action problem. They fear other banks would free ride: access information about their customers without reciprocating. By restricting access to their account information, Russian banks charge "information rents" and limit competition, locking customers in (Pyle 2002). Thus, the Russian version of the second paradox, the contradiction between the urge to compete and the goal of curbing uncertainty, arises because fiercely competitive banks refuse to share their customers' account information and to contribute to the formation of credit bureaus.

Creating Consumers, Building Demand

Disseminating credit cards to thousands of individuals does not automatically mean they will use them to pay for purchases. Turning people into cardholders is not the same as turning them into card-using consumers. Even with the cards in their wallets, they may still prefer cash to cards, or saving over borrowing. Consumer culture indispensable for the success of credit card markets includes the willingness to go into debt and to borrow from banks (rather than friends and family), and the readiness to pay interest. Americans had already developed these traits by the time the first bank credit cards appeared in the United States, and today they constitute the cultural foundations of contemporary American consumer society. In the Russian case, traditional preferences for cash and for saving over borrowing prevailed, and despite consistent growth of the number of cards in the 1990s, it was not accompanied by the growth of card-purchase volume. Arming individuals with cards was not enough to make them spend.

A recent surge of interest in the study of concrete markets among economic sociologists ranges from industrial production markets (White 1981; Burt 1992; Uzzi 1996; Fligstein 2001; Podolny 2005), to biotechnology (Powell, Koput, and Smith-Doerr 1996; Podolny 2005), to labor markets (Granovetter 1995 [1974]; Fernandez, Castilla, and Moore 2000; Yakubovich 2005), to financial exchange markets such as securities and stock markets (Baker 1984; Zukerman 1999; Abolafia 2001; Knorr-Cetina and Brugger 2002; MacKenzie and Millo 2003; Podolny 2005), and even markets for art, photography, wine, and book publishing (Powell 1985; Aspers 2001; Podolny 2005; Velthuis 2005).[15] But little attention has been paid to the problem of constructing consumer demand. In this sense, most economic sociologists are not much different from neoclassical economists who assume that firms and markets emerge when entrepreneurs fill existing niches. For example, in the recent edition of *The Handbook of Economic Sociology*, Swedberg discusses Harrison White's position on the social construction of markets: "If businessmen are correct in their calculations, they will be able to locate a niche in the market for their products, which their customers acknowledge by buying a certain volume at a certain price" (2005, 245; see also Zuckerman 1999 for a critique of a position that ignores consumer side). The irony of such a position is that the argument about the social constitution of markets is made with an assumption of consumer demand existing objectively and independently, waiting to be tapped by an entrepreneur with a vision. White's own words establish the focus of his work even more squarely away from demand and consumption: "Markets are tangible cliques of producers watching each other. Pressure from the buyer side creates a mirror in which producers see themselves, not consumers" (1981, 543).

Competition is undoubtedly the essence of the market that distinguishes it from other ways of organizing economic activity. Nevertheless, it is a mistake to think of markets exclusively through the prism of producers struggling for a bigger market share. While this book focuses mainly on the banks' vision of the market, its problems, and ways to solve them, what I hope to demonstrate is that consumers' collective behavior decides the shape and the ultimate fate of the market, and that consumers should not be downplayed as mere objects of banks' competition.

The traditional emphasis on production "with no more than occasional gestures towards consumption" (Zelizer 2005, 332) reflects a deep-seated problem in contemporary sociology. Frenzen, Hirsch, and Zerrillo attribute it to the historic context in which both economics and sociology developed, a period "when the industrial production was still young and manufactured goods were still commodities for which consumer demand greatly exceeded the available supply," resulting in scarcity and allowing market actors and scholars of the market to take consumer demand for granted (Frenzen, Hirsch, and Zerrillo 1994, 403). Modern production capacities outstrip consumers' ability to consume, isolating the problem of demand and bringing it to the forefront.

Nevertheless, there are some welcome exceptions to this general trend. Zuckerman (1999) raises the issue of consumer demand in his work on securities markets—mediated markets, where demand depends on financial analysts' perceptions of different products. Analysts are the main shapers of demand even though it is mass consumers who eventually buy securities. It is to these market critics that producers pay the most attention. Zuckerman's main question is how consumers evaluate alternative products on the market, and his answer is that they rely on critics, who legitimize new products and put them in the appropriate categories of already existing products.

While Zuckerman examines the problem of consumer demand, which is rare in economic sociology, his work reflects another prevalent trend in the literature, namely, the focus on the functioning of existing markets, rather than on the emergence of entirely new markets. Even a few sociological studies with promising titles, such as White's "Where Do Markets Come From?" (1981) or Abolafia's *Making Markets* (2001), concentrate exclusively on what existing markets are rather than on how new markets are built. As a result, there is little opportunity to ask a question that I am asking here: how do producers generate demand for entirely new products—those that cannot easily fit into an existing category?

In established markets, the problem of consumer demand shifts to product differentiation. For instance, it is no longer necessary to build consumer demand for credit cards in the U.S. market. Strong consumer demand exists for this category of products because they have been long established as the instrument of everyday use, enabling such long-distance transactions as car rentals, hotel bookings, and Internet purchases. Yet, different card issuers (banks or multinationals) are competing within the same accepted category of cards, offering various perks in order to entice consumers to switch to their particular card brand or a specific card product.

One notable exception to the trend of studying already existing markets is the work of Zelizer (1978) on the rise of life insurance in nineteenth-century America. She explicitly addresses the problem of initial consumer resistance to an emergent market for life-insurance services. Potential consumers of life insurance considered it culturally unacceptable to put a price tag on human life. Life-insurance policies challenged the prevailing distinction between sacred (life) and profane (monetary value), and exemplified the difficulty of building demand for a new product. What eventually made life insurance sell was the process of "sacralization"—"the transformation of the monetary evaluation of death into a [secular] ritual" (1978, 605). The notion of a "good death" started to involve financial arrangements for family members left behind. Life-insurance money was portrayed as a source of remembrance and a way to achieve immortality in the eyes of living relatives. This was a cultural solution to the problem of creating demand. New cultural frameworks helped change the initial negative perceptions of life insurance.

Like Zelizer's, this book is about the development of a new market, and about the problem of creating demand for an entirely new product. But because credit card markets are two-sided markets, the resistance to credit cards is of a more complex nature than the resistance to life insurance. In addition to several *cultural* elements, such as distrust of banks, traditional reliance on savings and cash to pay for purchases, and informal no-interest borrowing from friends and family, the resistance to the spread of credit cards has an important *strategic* element: the barrier of complementarity. Not only were prospective Russian consumers wary of or uncomfortable with noncash payments or bank-procured credit, but they were also resistant because they were waiting for merchants to join first (who, in turn, were waiting for consumers to sign up). When it comes to solutions to the problem of building demand, my story also parts with Zelizer's. Instead of constituting new *cultural* frames for card use, cashless transactions, bank-procured credit, and interest payments, Russian banks found a *structural* solution to the problem of resistance to using cards in merchants' locations. Instead of trying to bring the two parties—merchants and consumers—together, they jumped on the bandwagon of a rapidly growing retail sector. By offering cards in large chain stores and newly built shopping malls, banks positioned themselves squarely as facilitators of merchant-customer transactions. Postcommunist consumers could not resist the glitter and exuberance of retail, and did not have to be persuaded for much longer.

Marketing literature identifies *place* as one of the four P's of distribution (the others being Product, Price, and Promotion; for a review, *see* Frenzen, Hirsch, and Zerrillo 1994, 414–17). Decisions on how to attract prospective consumers are essential to the successful distribution of any product, but they become critical for the subsequent survival of two-sided markets when the issue of complementarity is looming on the horizon.

Conclusion

To sum up, credit card issuers in emerging credit card markets are faced with four problems. They have to solve the problem of uncertainty, recruit a large number of cardholders in order to inspire complementary growth of card-accepting merchants' outlets, promote interbank cooperation, and build demand for cards among consumers, especially if there are strong cultural preferences for cash and against borrowing.

The additional challenge is that solutions to some of these problems are contradictory: while the principle of complementarity requires quick mass dissemination of cards, managing uncertainty relies on careful prescreening. The need to establish mechanisms of interbank information sharing puts to the test the ability of bank competitors to cooperate.

In the next chapter, I continue building the theoretical scaffolding to support the empirical discussion of credit card market creation. I review market transitions and institutionalist and social network literature to formulate solutions to the problems outlined in this chapter and to set up the agenda for the rest of the book.

CHAPTER TWO

Market Building in the Transitional Context

The course of the Russian postcommunist transition was modeled on the Western neoliberal idea that markets arise spontaneously once private owners are created and the restraints on entrepreneurial activity are lifted. In order to achieve this, the economy has to be liberated from the socialist state, its "grabbing hand" amputated to prevent it from meddling in the free workings of emerging markets. This approach viewed the market as an inevitable force that, once unleashed, engulfed societies and argued that institutions would "follow private property," as Shleifer and Vishny confidently predicted in their book *The Grabbing Hand: Government Pathologies and Their Cures* (1998, 11).[1] Moreover, Western economic advisors (known as "the Washington consensus") argued that to prevent popular upheaval and overcome the inertia of the bureaucrats, these profound changes had to be implemented in one big sweep of shock therapy. They also advocated a radical break from the past, believing that transitioning societies are like *tabula rasa*, on which policymakers could chart the outlines of a new economic order (for a critique of this argument, see Stark 1996; Clarke 2002b; McDermott 2002). Joseph Stiglitz, Nobel laureate, former chief economist of the World Bank and a subsequent vocal critic of the neoliberal reform model, summarized it as "a blitzkrieg approach[, which] during the 'window of opportunity' provided by the 'fog of transition' would get the changes made before the population had a chance to organize to protect its previous vested interests" (Stiglitz 2001, 154).

The Washington consensus got it all wrong, however. The collapse of communism in Eastern Europe did not destroy the entire social structure of the "old regime," leaving the actors free to build markets on its ruins; on the contrary, numerous socialist legacies persisted and influenced transitional outcomes, suggesting that postcommunist development is path-dependent (Róna-Tas 1998). Moreover, advocates of this approach misunderstood the role of the state, mistakenly considering it a hindrance rather than a key actor in regulating markets and enforcing contracts. They also overestimated the power of the markets to give rise to "right" institutions. The Russian banks' long-standing resistance to interbank information sharing, despite their general agreement that credit bureaus were urgently needed, illustrates the latter point perfectly. While the banks had been sharing negative information about defaults and fraud informally, on the level of personal networks, no bank was ready to make their full account information open to all of the other banks.

The extreme optimism of the neoliberal approach was significantly toned down following the Asian financial crisis and the subsequent aftershocks in Eastern Europe in the late 1990s. The revised recommendations of the International Monetary Fund (IMF) and the World Bank to emerging economies included comprehensive institutional reform. The version of institutionalism that dominates policymaking views institutions as "rules of the game." According to this perspective, institutions establish a system of incentives and sanctions that govern individual behavior in markets and are chosen by market actors as efficient solutions to lower the costs of transacting, including searches, screening, and enforcement of contracts (Williamson 1975).

This approach suffers from three shortcomings. First, it focuses exclusively on the intentionality of institutional design (Williamson 1975; Langlois 1986). However, sociologists and other institutional economists have argued that new institutional and organizational forms can emerge in an unintended fashion as a result of a legitimacy contagion, evolutionary logic, or path-dependency (Schotter 1986; DiMaggio and Powell 1991; Arthur 1994; Nelson 1994).

Second, traditional neoinstitutional accounts only consider formal institutions (laws, regulations, and codes) and overlook informal ones (stable organizational practices and patterns of behavior, norms, customs, and traditions). Sociologists agree that it is necessary to establish formal rules and that this task must be carried out by states because states, as opposed to individuals or organizations, are rarely subject to the problem of free riding. Moreover, if political power is key in institution building, then market building is first and foremost state building. This argument has been made specifically in the context of postcommunism, and more generally, in the historical context of Western capitalist development (Polanyi [1944] 1957; Carruthers 1996; Fligstein and Mara-Drita 1996; Dobbin and Dowd 2000). In his discussion of the Russian transition, Burawoy echoes Polanyi's idea that "there is no market road to market economy"; this road has to be paved by a strong state (Burawoy 1996, 1115; see also Frye 2000; Johnson 2000; Bruszt 2002). But unlike neoinstitutional economists, sociologists recognize that formal top-down institutional reform will not lead to the desired results if formal laws clash with deep-rooted informal practices and traditions (Sztompka 1996; Nee 2005). Such informal elements play a prominent role in the process of institutional change because they help to frame some institutional arrangements as more legitimate and acceptable than others (Ingram and Clay 2000).

Finally, sociologists have rejected the claim that institutions are created as efficient solutions to market problems and that they persist as long as they remain efficient. They demonstrate that inefficient institutions can nevertheless persist due to legitimacy and inertia. Besides, organizations can adopt practices for reasons other than efficiency: to mimic other successful organizations or as a result of normative pressures from professional communities (DiMaggio and Powell 1983).

Bi-Level Networks as Building Blocks of Mass Markets

What happens when an emerging market experiences problems that actors cannot solve on their own, yet the state is not able to step in? The "neoliberals versus statists" debate is the reconfiguration of the old "markets versus hierarchies" debate. In his 1975 volume *Markets and Hierarchies*, Williamson argues that when markets are not able to solve the transaction-cost problem in an adequate manner (whether because of high uncertainty or prevailing opportunism among market actors), hierarchies are built instead, their organizational structure ensuring against poor performance, opportunism, and malfeasance. Granovetter (1985) famously rejects this dichotomy of uncertain and opportunistic markets on the one hand, and trustworthy and transparent "everyone-pursuing-common-goals" hierarchies on the other, as false. There are as much uncertainty, vertical bargaining, and opportunism in organizations as there are opportunities to curb them in markets. These opportunities, argues Granovetter, mainly come from networks; professional and personal ties as well as interlocking directorates allow for solving ubiquitous market uncertainty and opportunism.

Therefore, social structure is a solution to the situation when both markets and hierarchies fail. It also explains why, in real life, they nevertheless function despite obvious shortcomings: according to Granovetter, they are regulated through social ties. In this book I show that the Russian credit card market did not miraculously emerge on its own, nor was it built top down through a sustained state effort to pursue an institutional reform; rather, it was created through the actions of the market participants themselves, who made use of existing and emerging elements of social networks.

Economic sociology boasts a substantial bibliography documenting the presence and important role of social networks in enabling and facilitating exchange in contemporary markets (for example, Baker 1984; Granovetter 1985; Uzzi 1996; White 2002).[2] Only a few of these accounts, however, address the ties connecting sellers and their customers, and those are usually limited to small-business and venture-capital banking (see, for instance, Uzzi 1999; Mizruchi and Stearns 2001). None of these sources claim that networks are essential in creating *mass* markets. Moreover, historically, while social networks were the skeleton of local exchange, as mass national markets emerged, networks started to break down under the pressure of greater geographic, social, and cultural distances between transaction parties. The networks were replaced by other forms of governance, such as formal institutions and professions that enabled transactions between strangers sharing little or nothing in terms of social circles or culture (Zucker 1986).

This book draws attention to the role of networks in the construction of *mass* markets, specifically, their ability to help sellers both access and assess their prospective consumers. The reason that traditional approaches are unable to account for the presence of networks in mass markets is that the analysis is always restricted to relations between nodes of the same level: either individuals or organizations, or either informal interpersonal relations between producers/entrepreneurs or power/property relations between firms, never combining the two. Moreover, interorganizational ties are often reduced to interpersonal ones (through interlocking directorates, for instance). When some scholars allow for the variability in the *type* of the tie (Granovetter 1985; Powell, Koput and Smith-Doerr 1996; Uzzi 1996), relations are still between nodes of the same *level*.

Yet, such uni-level networks can only capture a partial snapshot of a mass market, which is by definition a market in which large firms (organizations) produce goods or services for mass consumption (therefore, for consumption of a large number of individual actors). For instance, an analysis of interorganizational ties between card-issuing banks and employers does not capture the crucial role that employers play in helping banks disseminate cards to individual workers.

I argue that networks can contribute to the creation of a mass-consumer market, but only when networks combine the nodes of two different levels: both organizations and persons. Organizations usually have relationships with large groups of individuals, whether employer-employee relationships or merchant-customer ones. If card issuers can persuade organizations to provide them with access to these individuals, they would instantly reach scores of potential cardholders. For example, the banks' strategy of capitalizing on retailers' ability to attract customers to their shops and to malls utilizes what I call a *locational* benefit of bi-level networks: in order to reach mass consumers, a company needs to identify a way that they can be targeted as a group.

Retailers only assist banks in providing access to prospective cardholders without helping to prescreen them. But in the case of card issuing through employers, they not only provide banks with access to their employees but also help in managing the problem of uncertainty. In this arrangement, employers amplify the usual ability of social networks to reduce uncertainty by channeling information and producing greater transparency and trust (Granovetter 1985). Organizational structure anchors individuals firmly in intraorganizational relations, both vertical and horizontal, making it easier for issuing banks to monitor them. I call this a *relational* benefit of bi-level networks. Such networks produce informal controls substituting for the lack of formal institutional arrangements (credit bureaus) to screen and sanction cardholders.

But how do banks get organizations interested in providing them with access to individual consumers? Arrangements with retailers can range from zero (banks open their booths in large malls without a specific agreement with any of the stores) to bilateral agreements to issue co-branded cards (usually with large stores, such as IKEA), which also offer various loyalty perks (discounts, promotions, and so forth). Salary projects—card issuing to workers through their employers—presuppose well-specified formal agreements signed by both the bank and the employer. While in both cases banks start by using organizations as middlemen who provide access or "introduce" them to their potential cardholders, they end up successfully reformulating their own role as a middleman between companies and individuals (Figure 2.1).

In the case of salary projects, banks promise to simplify the process of wage payment for employers. Traditionally, wages in Russia were paid in cash and employers were subject to high transaction costs because the cash had to be transported, secured, and dispensed. Banks offer to directly deposit employees' wages in the newly opened personal accounts and to issue cards linked to these accounts. In the case of cards distributed in retail locations,

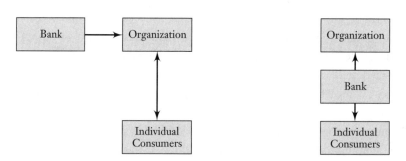

Phase 1: Bank approaches employer

Phase 2: Bank positions itself as a middleman

Figure 2.1 How Banks Use Bi-Level Networks to Access Prospective Consumers

banks enable purchases that otherwise would not happen if consumers lack cash, freeing merchants from the need to finance purchases themselves. Thus, in both cases of consumer credit and salary projects, the arrangements between banks and organizations are framed as mutually beneficial: banks obtain access to prospective customers, and companies no longer have to provide services for which they are professionally not suited.

These strategies are not limited to emerging markets in a transitional context. There are plenty of examples of sellers turning to organizations both to reduce uncertainty and to facilitate access to mass consumers in modern capitalist societies such as the United States. This includes marketing cards on university campuses or next to airline terminals (specifically, those with mileage programs), relying on lists provided by credit bureaus to send out preapproved applications, and selling group insurance policies through employers.[3] In the latter example, employers not only help insurance companies to access prospective consumers, but also reduce the problem of adverse selection and help them turn uncertainty into quantifiable risk. This suggests that new markets can emerge by capitalizing on already existing markets. Specifically, the Russian credit card market has been relying on labor and retail markets.

The idea of analytically tying organizations and individuals as nodes in the same network is borrowed from organizational literature, which treats both of them as actors (Scott et al. 2000), however, downplaying relationships between them. I focus on the ties between them because they are sought after by banks and other companies struggling to create new markets. These ties are not necessarily meaningful social relationships like the ones linking friends or colleagues. Organizations, even if they are our employers, usually do not know us closely, but they nevertheless possess some information about us and have a certain degree of control over us. At the very least, we need them to provide services or goods. We come to organizations to fulfill these needs, and this is why our ties to organizations become such valuable assets for market makers striving to reach their prospective customers. Access that organizations provide can involve different degrees of coercion. For example, applying for a credit card in a store where one just saw an item that is too expensive to be paid for in cash is entirely voluntary. Employees, on the other hand, have no choice if their administration has signed an agreement with a particular bank to carry out a salary project at the company. They cannot opt out and continue receiving their wages in cash. Moreover, unlike American workers who can request that their payroll department directly deposit their wages to any bank, Russian employees must work with the bank chosen by their employer.

My aim is to explain the logic and process of constructing a mass credit card market in Russia, and this cannot be done adequately without references to bi-level networks that combine both individuals and organizations. Moreover, only when both organizations and persons are included can we start appreciating how existing roles and relations are recalibrated to assist current needs. For example, a relationship between "a corporate bank" and "a firm, which is this bank's corporate client" is transformed into a relationship between "a retail bank" and "an employer that makes its employees available to the bank as potential customers." Likewise, a relationship between "employer" and "employee" can be transformed into a relationship between "retailer" and "consumer" in situations when salary cardholders could use them in factory-owned stores and eateries. What the Russian credit card market exemplifies is that individual actors do not conjure markets out of thin air, in an orderly response to perceived opportunities. In the absence of formal institutions, they create markets from the fragments of social structure, such as networks and organizations (Stark 1996; Sedaitis 1998; McDermott 2002), which are fitted to new uses. This is not the "inescapable socialist legacies" argument, however (see McDermott 2002 for a critique), because the shape of the future is not predetermined. These fragments are like Lego blocks: they preserve some irreducible traces of the old structure, but they can be reattached in more than one way. Relations between pieces can be recalibrated over time and become multiplex, with the nodes playing several different roles at the same time. Old fragments such as Soviet-period organizations and networks have been joined by new ones, particularly large chain stores and shopping malls, which have emerged in the last decade.

Institution Building and Globalization

While social networks and informal practices clearly play a key role in the process of creating the Russian credit card market, they cannot fully replace a wide range of formal institutions such as a legal system, banking regulations, accounting standards, credit bureaus, collection agencies, bankruptcy laws, debtors and privacy protection, and so forth. While bi-level networks allow Russian banks to monitor and control salary cardholders, in the case of consumer lending they put banks on shaky ground because disseminating cards in retail locations is essentially giving them to strangers. These people are instant consumers willing to use their newly obtained cards on the spot, but the banks' ability to weed out those who won't pay is limited. Thus, the future success of the credit card market in Russia hinges on the development of the institutions of credit reporting and collections.

Social networks not only serve as mechanisms of informal governance (as is the case with salary projects), but they also are a source of formal institutional emergence and change. Referring to social networks as the link between individual actions and macro outcomes, Granovetter contends that "networks are where cooperation and trust and domination and compliance are actually produced" (Krippner et al. 2004, 116). Institutional development is therefore intertwined with social network dynamics, or, in McDermott's terminology, politics becomes embedded in local networks (McDermott 2002).

Globalization expands the reach of networks across national borders and adds transnational actors such as international financial and policy organizations, transnational corporations, foreign governments, and international professional associations to the list of sources that influence nation-states' steps in adopting or creating formal institutional solutions. Johnson (2007) discusses the role of a transnational community of central bankers in the transformation of postcommunist central banks. Bockman and Eyal (2002) provide ample evidence that professional ties between Western and Eastern European economists helped transmit Western neoliberal market principles to Eastern Europe. Especially when there is a struggle between rival conceptions or frameworks, networks help mobilize alliances, exert influence, and produce outcomes that benefit network members at the expense of outsiders. Therefore, globalization diffuses the power of nation-states, subjecting them to direct institutional and indirect normative pressures and reconfiguring their relations with national markets (Ó Riain 2000; Robinson 2001; Halliday and Carruthers 2007).[4]

Viewed in such a light, the creation of markets and market institutions is no longer a domestic issue in which informal norms and social networks interact with the legislative power of the nation-state, but is the result of the combined efforts of a much bigger and more complex network of global actors. As I will discuss in Chapter Seven when analyzing the development of credit reporting, international credit bureaus such as Experian and TransUnion influenced the process of crafting the historic legislation establishing the creation and operation of credit bureaus in Russia, and the final decision on the bureaus' organizational form was the one that suited these foreign players the best.

However, local actors are unlikely to completely give in to global pressures. While traditional globalization studies have warned of global cultural and institutional convergence, they are now being complemented by more cautious studies of "glocalization," demonstrating the power of local actors to resist one-directional globalizing processes and use the pressures of globalization selectively by fusing them with their local practices (Guillén 2001). Even though Russian-issued Visas and MasterCards look almost identical to those issued by U.S. banks, what this book demonstrates is that there is a great difference in what kinds of bank-cardholder relations they represent, and in how the cards are issued by banks and used by consumers. And since the abilities of local actors to resist global pressures differ, advances of globalization are uneven and often unpredictable.

Conclusion

In this chapter I introduced bi-level networks and argued that only when we conceive of networks involving nodes of two different levels can we then appreciate the role that networks play in creating mass-consumer markets. Bi-level networks help banks reach individual consumers. Those networks that tie banks to employers and employees also give rise to stable and predictable patterns of behavior shaping informal institutional mechanisms of controlling uncertainty. While networks compensate for the lack of formal institutional arrangements like credit bureaus, they are also instrumental in helping bring them about as they channel ideas, resources, and influence, both on a local scale and globally.

Building a credit card market from scratch is a formidable task in itself. But constructing one out of the ruins of communism is even more challenging because of the pervasiveness of the socialist legacies and the added burden of the transition. The next chapter focuses on these additional challenges and also discusses the early card programs and the technical peculiarities of the first Russian cards.

CHAPTER THREE

Setting the Stage

Consumer Credit and Banking Before and During the Transition

The Russia of the early 1990s did not provide hospitable soil for a new credit card market to take root. It had just emerged from a heavily distorted mono-bank economy where shortages prevailed and personal favors ruled, and where individuals relied exclusively on cash and had little regard for formal borrowing. What Russia was looking at was an almost decade-long period of economic and political instability punctuated by periodic market crashes, culminating in the spectacular collapse of the government-promoted State Treasury bond pyramid in August 1998. This chapter details Russia's skill in navigating this obstacle course, and ties its nascent card market to its Soviet and transitional history and the developing commercial banking industry.

The Soviet Economic System and Consumer Credit

The key features of Soviet-type economies were central planning, bureau-
cratic coordination of production, and public ownership of the means of production. Central planning was sought as a refuge from the seemingly chaotic
nature of the market, an argument that was especially compelling after the
Great Depression of the 1930s. Plans for industries and individual enterprises
were generated centrally, usually based on their previous performance, potential, and the needs of the economy. Matching plans were generated for factories that produced spare parts, whereas delivery and sales were guaranteed to
ensure rationality and efficiency of production and consumption. "Everything
is planned and the plan is everywhere. There is—as seems perfectly natural—
a five-year plan, an annual plan and a monthly plan, and this includes educa-
tional establishments (achievement plans for the class, the school, the district,
the region, and republic . . .), hospitals, restaurants, snack-bars, canteens, fire
brigades, research institutes and the police" (Heller 1988, 73).

Central planning was instrumental in spurring rapid industrialization in
the 1920s and 1930s, and during the post–World War II rebuilding of the
devastated country, but the resulting economy was deficient on several
counts. First, despite the existence of the plan, industries and enterprises
were subject to soft rather than hard budget constraints (Kornai 1980). It
meant that, irrespective of their economic performance, publicly owned enterprises were never bankrupted or coerced to shed surplus labor in the way
that private businesses are when pressured by market forces. Fulfillment of
the plan at whatever the cost was the only performance criterion, while output was judged entirely on quantity rather than quality. So no matter how
inefficient or wasteful enterprises were, they could count on the state's continual capital investments. As a result, there was little incentive to innovate,
improve the quality, diversify, or in any other way produce with the end consumer in mind. Second, since the mechanism of central planning was built
for the main purpose of rapid industrialization, Soviet-type economic development was skewed in the direction of heavy industry, especially toward the
sectors working for national defense, while light and other consumer industries catering to individual needs were downplayed and could not keep up
with increasing consumer demand (Goldman 1983). Third, the mastermind
of central planning overlooked one crucial factor: the complexity of the

economy and the virtual impossibility of effectively orchestrating production and distribution from the Kremlin. As a result, in addition to inadequate production of consumer goods, their distribution across the country was uneven, which resulted in chronic shortages.

The problem of shortages persisted well into the transitional period of the 1990s. But it was during Brezhnev's rule (1964–1982) that these problems became ubiquitous, as a result of both underproduction and inadequate distribution. One observer of that time described with a great deal of humor that "supplies of consumer goods are about as unpredictable as the weather." One city, for example, "can be overstocked with cross-country skis and yet go several months without soap for washing dishes . . . [Elsewhere he] found an ample supply of accordions but local people complained they had gone for weeks without ordinary kitchen spoons or tea samovars." Getting the things one needed was further complicated by the highly unpredictable hours of store operation, including frequent "cleaning days," "inventory days," "repair," and so on. It is no surprise then that people spent "an enormous amount of time . . . shopping, selling, trading, scouting, and queuing for deficit commodities," hoping to be in the right place at the right time. For this purpose many women always brought *avos'ki* (string bags) with them, the word itself deriving from the Russian word for *maybe* or *perhaps*, while men very often carried briefcases. The observer was struck by how businesslike those Russian men looked, only to discover that "briefcases were more likely to be loaded with oranges, hoards of toothpaste or pairs of shoes than with books or papers" (Smith 1976, 62).

The scarcity of consumer goods in official distribution channels led to rationing and made consumer credit unnecessary. To purchase a car, for instance, one would often have to be on a waiting list for as long as ten years, plenty of time to accumulate enough cash. Contrary to states that stimulate economic growth by encouraging consumption as part of their macroeconomic policy, the Soviet state was promoting long-term savings, including, in addition to regular savings accounts, various insurance annuity schemes. By the time of late socialism, this practice led to so-called "monetary overhang," the situation in which the population had more money overall than they could spend.[1]

While Party elites had access to a network of special stores, which exchanged affordable deficit consumer goods and foodstuffs for continuous loyalty to the regime, common folk had to fend for themselves. The way to do it was to apply one's wits to beating the system. Friends were instrumental in helping to achieve this. According to numerous accounts of everyday life in the Soviet Union, friends compensated for inadequate formal distribution of goods with informal provisions of food, clothing, housing, access to health care, children's education, concerts, and soccer games. If they could not provide for their friends, they were willing to place their networks at their friends' disposal. "The friends of friends, as well as the acquaintances of friends, turn the whole of Soviet society into closely interwoven networks where there are only one or at most two individuals between you and an official or salesperson whose favor you need" (Shlapentokh 1989, 176). Thus, a close look at the Soviet shortage economy (Kornai 1980) reveals that it was simultaneously an economy of favors (Ledeneva 1998), where goods and services unavailable in the public distribution system traveled via exclusive personal ties. These ties, which came to dominate virtually every aspect of Soviet life—both in the private and public domains—are one of the socialist legacies that defined the essence and the structure of the early credit card market in Russia.[2] The trust, loyalty, and enhanced information flow and control that such ties engender helped banks issue the first cards in the absence of institutional mechanisms that regulate uncertainty in mature markets.

In addition to helping overcome shortages, friends helped friends in situations of financial need. Seventy-five percent of the Soviet people regularly borrowed money from one another (Pavlov 1975), and 20 percent of large-city dwellers borrowed specifically from neighbors (Iankova 1979). But it is in situations when beating the system would unexpectedly open up opportunities for a big-ticket purchase before one had a chance to save up that borrowing from one's friends and family became crucial. "Do not have a hundred rubles, but have a hundred friends," quotes Ledeneva (1998) from a well-known Russian folk saying. There is abundant anecdotal evidence of friends lending money to friends to buy their first car or to make the first payment on their new co-op apartment. Such informal loans were usually interest-free, made solely on personal trust, with the terms of repayment rarely set in stone. Often they were renegotiated repeatedly. Many loans were paid later than originally promised, and some (usually smaller and more routine ones) were never repaid.

At the same time, formal bank consumer credit was severely limited (Neuhauser 1993). Some stores offered installment plans for large-ticket items, but working collectives and enterprises had to request such credit on their employee's behalf.[3] These loans were provided for the short term, and usually one at a time. The employer automatically deducted monthly installments from the person's paycheck. Since there were practically no layoffs and wages were paid regularly, the state-owned enterprise could essentially guarantee the bank and the store (both state-owned) that the loan would be repaid on time.[4] Moreover, a rigid mechanism of administrative control limited mobility across companies and geographic areas by requiring all individuals to have *propiska*, registration at their place of residence through the local police (Popov 1995).

Such a form of credit provision was essentially an extension of the welfare state, helping people to optimize consumption and compensating for universally low wages. The ability of employers to procure consumer loans for their workers during the Soviet period exemplifies their generally paternalistic role in the lives of their employees. In addition to being employed, workers could count on their workplaces for deficit goods, healthcare, subsidized recreation, and daycare for their children. In return, workers developed a sense of devotion to their employers and working collectives, many working at the same place for their entire lives. This socialist legacy of employment stability and employers' control over workers' lives, epitomized in the well-known Chinese "iron rice bowl" phenomenon, came to define the essence of "salary projects," the distribution of cards via employers.

Despite the willingness of enterprises to apply on their workers' behalf, installment credit was not very popular, the result of both lack of quality goods in official distribution channels and the strong aversion to borrowing and living in debt held by many Russians who had grown up under the Soviet regime. Thus, the two most common ways to pay for expensive goods in the former Soviet Union were to save and pay up front or to borrow informally from friends and family. Notably, informal borrowing was not viewed in the same negative terms as formal borrowing because it was interest-free and was routinely misrecognized as "friends helping friends" (Ledeneva 1998).

Nascent Commercial Banking

If consumer credit has a short history in Russia, private commercial banking is an even younger institution. For most of its history (from the 1930s to

1987), the Soviet banking system consisted of one single state-owned bank: Gosbank, which acted simultaneously as the Central Bank, capital investment bank, and retail bank. It controlled the printing of currency, managed gold reserves, allocated capital to enterprises in accordance with the overall production plan, and attracted an excess of household cash to low-interest savings and demand accounts through a nationwide network of local retail branches called *sberkassa* (Spicer and Pyle 2003). These funds were available to the state as a source of additional revenue.

In 1987, the Soviet monobank system was reorganized, and four specialized banks were founded, all state-owned: Vneshekonombank (Foreign Economic Relations Bank), Promstroybank (Industrial and Construction Bank), Zhilsotsbank (Housing and Social Investment Bank), and Sberbank (Retail Savings Bank) ("Gosudarstvenny Bank SSSR" 2006). In 1988, a series of new laws, notably, the Law on Cooperation, opened possibilities for private entrepreneurial activity, including private commercial banking.[5] That year, only twenty-five banks were founded. But from the early 1990s, Russian commercial banks began to mushroom: if at the beginning of 1990 there were about three hundred banks, by the end of the next year, their number reached 1,360, and there were more than 2,500 at their peak in 1995.

Many of the first commercial banks were built as branches of the recently formed specialized state banks. The Central Bank at that time encouraged such commercialization as part of the continual reform of the Soviet monobank system. In addition, many banks were founded on very pragmatic grounds of helping the nascent cooperative movement, various entrepreneurial efforts legitimized by the new Law on Cooperation. Vyacheslav Zakharov was at that time deputy head of the board of Soviet Gosbank, overseeing the process of registering new commercial banks. He remembers that the first registered commercial bank, Soyuzbank (located in the Kazakh city of Chimkent), was founded by Chimkent co-op members who became wary of dealing with the local branch of the state-owned Zhilsotsbank, which constantly demanded kickbacks:

> If one wants to open an account, one needs to pay. This service has to be paid for, and that one has to be paid for as well. The co-op members got together and asked themselves, why should they pay Zhilsotsbank for all these services if the law allowed them to organize their own bank. So they

decided to organize their own bank. Of course, they would have to pay the bank they would organize, but it would be their own bank. When they went ahead and Zhilsotsbank found out about their initiative, it immediately waived all the service fees, promising free-of-charge service (from *Rozhdenie kommercheskih bankov* by Krotov and Lapshov [1998], quoted in Buylov and Shushunova 2003, 27).

But it was too late, as the co-op members had already gone into the banking business themselves. Similarly, Alexandr Smolenskiy, a well-known oligarch and founder of Stolichny bank (subsequently, one of the largest Russian card issuers), admitted that his decision to organize a bank was mainly to circumvent the bureaucracy of state banking, which was inefficient or openly hostile to newly formed cooperatives (Buylov and Shushunova 2003).

The level of professionalism in those first private banks was very low. Even specialists with experience working in a Soviet bank were not prepared for running new commercial banks because banking in the Soviet economic system was so different from what it has to be in a market-driven system. Moreover, commercial banking attracted a lot of enthusiasts who lacked any training in finances or even economics. For instance, banks were founded by scientists, engineers, and even, in at least two known cases, by an emergency doctor and a dentist (Buylov and Shushunova 2003). Indeed, very few of my interviewees in 1998–1999 had any economic or financial background at all, most coming from research institutes and security forces.

Newly organized banks jumped at every opportunity to earn money. For the first ten years, many of their activities hardly resembled those considered usual for commercial banks. For instance, according to Lyudmila Trubnikova, head of the department on Registration of Commercial Banks, part of the Planning and Economic Division of Gosbank, "In 1989, many banks received the major portion of their profit not from banking proper, but from trade. At that time, there was an inflated demand for personal computers, and many banks managed to import large quantities of computers, sold them, and then reported the profit they received as banking profit in their annual reports" (Buylov and Shushunova 2003, 26). Moreover, many went so far as to include import and trade into their charters. This was a result of the eclectic background of their founders; the overall lack of understanding, even among Gosbank specialists, of what commercial banking should be doing;

and the particular structure of opportunities that existed in Russia at that time: on one hand, formidable institutional and cultural barriers to conducting the usual banking activities (such as lending), and on the other, the existence of a plethora of lucrative opportunities elsewhere.

Many of the Russian commercial banks made their initial capital on financial speculations. In the early-to-mid-1990s inflation was very high, which allowed banks to take advantage of the differences in exchange rates and receive quick and easy profits. For instance, short-term bank-to-bank lending became an extremely popular way of making money. However, to pursue it, banks needed financial resources that few of them had, as the first commercial banks were small and had few assets. In their quest for financial resources, they turned to the state, the only actor in postcommunist countries that had accumulated significant amounts of capital, since the majority of the enterprises were still not privatized, and the population's savings were either consumed by hyperinflation or stashed away under mattresses. At that time the Russian government was reorganizing the state banking system and was looking for ways to hold and disburse state budget funds intended for capital investment and salaries of employees in state-owned enterprises and municipal organizations. As a temporary solution, the government decided to appoint several private commercial banks to administer and allocate these budgetary resources until a state treasury could be established. These banks were given the status of "authorized agents" of the state, this honor proudly displayed on the first page of their annual reports. Not just any bank could get its snout into this "feeder," but only those who had good political connections. In the absence of any government oversight on how these budget resources were managed, "authorized" banks were able to use this arrangement to their advantage: they routinely held this money for several days or weeks, using it to finance their speculative deals and short-term lending, and pocketed the accrued surplus. Therefore, working with state budget resources became the most treasured and vied-for privilege, as well as a mark of prestige and success. There was no need to worry about improving banking technologies, developing new services or infrastructure, so easy was it to make a profit.

This was the system that paved the way for some banks toward rapid growth and high concentration of bank capital. Intimate proximity to the power apparatus, which was considered one of the most serious assets banks could possess, allowed chosen banks to engage in the redistribution of GNP to their advantage. Thus, to a large extent, banks simply lived off the state property accumulated over the decades preceding the reforms (Shadalin 1997).

Starting in 1995 state budget resources became scarcer, and banks had to find new sources of capital. Privatization of state-owned enterprises and in particular the loans-for-shares program (Johnson 1997) became such a source, engaging banks in a wild race for large state companies with high market value. The loans-for-shares program was first proposed by a group of powerful oligarchs, the owners of the largest Russian banks, who had already built up their financial power and were interested in increasing their holdings of industrial enterprises. They offered to furnish the Russian government with low-interest loans in order to breach the gaping holes in its budget, but in exchange they asked for the opportunity to control state shares in forty-three major industrial enterprises, many of them the true gems of the Russian national economy: highly profitable resource-based companies in the oil and metallurgical industries. The irony was that often the money banks ended up paying for shares was the state's own money transferred to them as a result of their "authorized" status. The program was intended to run for five years; during this period the government could buy its shares back. If the government failed to do the buyback, the banks were supposed to sell the shares through auctions in 2000. They did, but curiously enough, the banks organizing the auctions were the ones that ended up placing the winning bids. This was a defining moment of the Russian reform and the one indicative of its course: as the result of a series of incestuous transfers of money and influence, a bankrupted state handed the best of its industrial holdings over to a group of powerful financial tycoons. In 1995, 70 percent of state budget revenues were provided through twelve loans-for-shares swaps, including the one involving Yukos, recently stripped of its assets, with its owners Khodorkovskiy and Lebedev found guilty of tax fraud and imprisoned.

All throughout this period, banks engaged in fierce competition, but instead of consumers, they were mainly vying for the benevolence of state officials. At times, this competition reached the point of open, public hostility. Banks traded attacks through mass media outlets, which the largest of them owned as part of their empires, and published compromising information about one another's financial conditions (Dinello 1998). A bank that was the target of a smear campaign could be denied participation in a privatization tender or auction or might become the subject of a long, exhaustive inspection by the Central Bank. Even if such a review found nothing wrong, which was rare, it took time. In addition, an outside inspection damaged the bank's reputation and inevitably affected the already limited collective trust of the general population in financial institutions.[6]

One more source of bank revenues in the mid-1990s were the State Treasury bonds, initiated by the state as another way to finance its chronic budget deficits. This was a government-supported several-years-long financial pyramid, which yielded over 80 percent annual interest even with correction for inflation. To be able to pay existing bond holders, the state had to continue issuing new bonds until the pyramid finally collapsed in August of 1998, bringing down with it many banks, including several of the largest ones, and sending the ruble exchange value into a deep plunge. There was no deposit insurance in Russia at that time, and the government was faced with a banking crisis of catastrophic proportions that could have potentially devastating social and political consequences. In a desperate attempt to get the situation under control, the government offered the depositors of the largest banks (Mostbank, MENATEP, SBS-Agro, Inkombank, Promstroybank, Mosbiznesbank, Rossiyskiy Kredit, and Avtobank) an opportunity to voluntarily transfer their deposits to state-owned Sberbank to benefit from an ad-hoc guarantee extended by the Central Bank of Russia, the main owner of Sberbank. The major drawback was that ruble-denominated deposit accounts would be transferred into demand accounts, which had significantly lower interest rates, while dollar-denominated accounts would have to be converted into rubles based on the September 1, 1998 exchange rate. Although Sberbank guaranteed the return of all money in full, it would only start dispensing it on November 15, more than two months after this offer, while accounts would continue losing their value in the meantime (Panfilova and Kiseleva 1998). Many depositors nevertheless chose this option instead of playing an uncertain game of waiting to have their banks liquidated and their deposits returned (in retrospect, in a few cases it took two years just to start bankruptcy proceedings). For instance, Jack and Gall (1998, 2) quote one such depositor: "I had 10,000 rubles: that was worth $1,500 back in August. And now the rate has changed so much it is [already] worth just a third of that." Sberbank turned out to be the big winner of this crisis. As a result of this transfer, it gained about five hundred thousand new accounts, and significantly increased its share of household deposits to 85 percent (its share has since been gradually declining and was at 60 percent in 2004) (EIU 2005).

The August 1998 crisis was not Russia's first large scale banking crisis. In 1995, with a combined number of cards issued by all card networks close to a million, the Russian market for interbank lending collapsed, sending several local card networks and a number of large banks, including card pioneer Kredobank, tumbling. These banks' card programs were abandoned or, as was the case of Kredobank, transferred to other, more stable banks. This was the first major test for Russia's card market.

While the easy profits in the early-to-mid-1990s undoubtedly helped jump-start commercial banking in Russia, they came at a high price. They compensated for frequent bad management decisions made by ill-trained and inexperienced bankers, and they obviated the need for improving banking technologies and providing better training. In addition, some of these earning practices directly led to the destabilization of banking in Russia. For instance, short-term interbank lending tied the entire banking community into a web of mutual dependence. In the absence of adequate reserves, one bank's trouble in returning a loan was likely to create a domino effect, which was precisely the problem behind the 1995 "Black Thursday."

Indeed, as a result of periodic market crises, the number of bank failures during the 1990s has been as impressive as the number of banks founded. The total number of registered banks has been declining from over 2,500 in 1995 to about 1,600 by the middle of 1998. Between 1994 and 1997, 922 banks had their licenses revoked (Smirnov 1998, 10). As part of Central Bank-imposed regulations in the wake of the August 1998 crisis, 720 more banks were put on "death row," reducing the country's total number of banks to just over 1300.

Bank closings contributed to overall banking instability and added to a pervasive mistrust in financial institutions. In the absence of deposit insurance, consumers grew extremely distrustful of Russia's banking sphere, preferring cash (better yet, foreign cash) to any forms of savings or payments that involved banks (Spicer and Pyle 2003).

Early Card Programs

Foreign credit cards had been accepted in select Soviet retail locations for several decades before the local Russian banks issued the first cards. Granted, these cards were owned by foreign visitors, and used exclusively in hard-currency stores and hotels of the Intourist chain catering to foreigners. The first foreign card company to enter Russia was American Express, which opened its representative office in Moscow in 1958, while the first AmEx cards were accepted starting in 1961. Diners Club cards turned up in the late 1960s, and Visa (at that time BankAmericard), EuroCard (a European partner of MasterCard), and Japanese JCB made their appearance in the 1970s.[7]

The first Soviet cards were issued only in 1988, the year that Vneshekonombank issued Visa cards to the Soviet Olympic team departing for the Summer Olympic Games in Seoul. The next year, Vneshekonombank followed with a limited issue of MasterCard Gold cards intended for high-level Party officials and their wives, reasoning that carrying suitcases full of cash to pay for expensive goods while abroad was both inconvenient and embarrassing.

The year 1989 saw two other banks, state-owned Sberbank and a newly-established privately-owned Kredobank, engage in disseminating cards (Andreev et al. 1998, 15–16). Sberbank carried out a limited issue of Visa cards as part of an experiment to test a system of noncash transactions. According to Vyacheslav Drapash, who was at that time Sberbank's deputy head of the Division of Automation, in 1988 Sberbank was involved in developing a state-sponsored program of creating a national noncash payment system for individuals and organizations. The program intended to issue both debit and credit cards. In February 1989, Sberbank set up three ATM machines, two in the main office for Sberbank's own employees and one more in its Dzerzhinskiy branch, all three in Moscow. About five thousand Visa cards were issued in the following several months. They combined both credit and debit features and two kinds of currency, depending on the geography of their use. For instance, in the USSR, cards worked as ruble cards and could offer up to 500-ruble credit lines (balances had to be settled in one month and during this time did not accrue any interest). If taken abroad, the cards only worked as debit cards, but accepted charges in hard currency (this last feature was only available to those who had bank accounts abroad). Cards were issued free of charge to Sberbank's own employees and Soviet political elites (this would be a second card for Mikhail Gorbachev and other Polit-buro members, making them much better endowed than an average Russian even sixteen years later).[8] Common folk residing on the territory of Sber-bank's Dzerzhinskiy branch were offered cards with a symbolically low an-nual fee. Although subsequent pilot projects in Sberbank's branches in Kiev (Ukraine) and Chelyabinsk-40 (a small satellite town of Chelyabinsk, an in-dustrial city in the Ural mountains) tried to persuade stores and gas stations to accept these cards, the architects of the program were admittedly more concerned with testing the mechanisms of noncash transactions than with building an economically viable card network. Their ambitious plans to move the program to an even larger scale could not be realized, however. With the collapse of the Soviet Union and ensuing economic reforms, the goal of creating a national system of noncash payments lost its priority for Sberbank. But the story of Visa cards in Russia was just beginning.

It is to a young enterprising interpreter by the name of Igor Lipanov, who was in the midst of negotiations between Sberbank and Visa, that Kre-dobank owes the distinction of being the first Russian bank to carry out mass card distribution. Igor Lipanov headed this program in Kredobank and be-came one of the legendary figures in the history of the Russian credit card market. As opposed to tiny programs by Vneshekonombank intended as publicity campaigns, and unlike Sberbank, whose program was more im-pressive but was reportedly only focused on technology testing, Kredobank viewed its program first and foremost as a commercial undertaking. Still, the program was targeting elite rather than mass clients, specifically those who often traveled abroad or worked for Western or joint-venture companies in Moscow. During the four years of its card program (from 1991 to 1995), Kredobank issued ten thousand cards, the majority of them debit cards. Some of the cardholders, however, were allowed to draw overdrafts on their accounts, but those were usually the customers who were well-known to the bank: "respectable, well-to-do people affiliated with respectable companies" (*solidnye lyudi, solidnoe materialnoe polozhenie, solidnye organizatsii*).[9] In addi-tion to being the first to mass-market cards in Russia, Kredobank is also re-membered as the smithy of card specialists, many of whom subsequently founded card programs in other large banks, following the spectacular col-lapse of Kredobank in the midst of the 1995 crisis of Russia's interbank lend-ing market.

None of these three banks (Vneshekonombank, Sberbank, and Kredobank) was troubled by any of the issues with which American banks had to deal at the onset of their credit card programs. Sberbank's program was a pilot experiment, mostly concerned with the technical side of noncash payments. The goal of the other two card programs was not so much to develop a domestic market for credit cards but to provide an opportunity for some of their elite clients to make credit card purchases abroad. Thus, they could, at least for a while, ignore the problem of complementarity, because attracting domestic merchants was not their priority. Uncertainty was also of little concern since the first cardholders were either highly select Party cadres (in the case of Vneshekonombank) or high-status individuals with close ties to the bank (in the case of Kredobank).

Peculiarities of the First Russian Cards

My first encounter with Russian credit cards was surprising. Right at the beginning of my first interview in the summer of 1998, I discovered that despite being commonly referred to as "credit cards" (*kreditnye kartochki* or *kreditki*), Russian credit cards did not usually extend any credit to their holders.[10] On the contrary, as a necessary condition, banks required card applicants to deposit their own money into the bank. Not only did this include the money that the cardholders would access with their card, kept on a demand deposit account, but also a hefty security deposit kept in a separate account and used to provide an additional guarantee to the bank.[11] For instance, Kredobank asked for security deposits as high as $10,000 on its debit Gold Visa cards.

What was the role of the security deposit if these were essentially debit cards? Security deposits would protect the bank in case the cardholder overdrew his card account.[12] As indicated by their descriptive name, "cards with unauthorized overdraft" (*kartochki s nerazreshennym overdraftom*), overdrafts on such cards were strictly prohibited. Nevertheless, they were still possible, and card technology was to blame.

In the 1990s, the majority of Russian merchants used imprinters rather than the more expensive electronic point-of-sale (POS) terminals. Imprinters are still sometimes used in the United States when the computer connection is down or unavailable (such as for in-flight purchases), but they can only be used to process credit, not debit cards, which require PINs and electronic authorizations rather than cardholders' signatures. Thus, most store card charges in Russia resembled credit card transactions. Paper slips had to be filled out by the merchant and signed by the client. The slips were then submitted by the merchant to the acquiring bank, which reimbursed the merchant minus the amount of merchant discount. The slips were then forwarded to the processing company, which sent them along to the issuing bank. The issuing bank reimbursed the processing company and debited its client's account. Because slips were submitted only at the end of a business day (or once or twice a week for smaller merchants), there was a gap between the time of the purchase and the payment. Under certain circumstances, this gap could be as large as one month. For this reason, many banks specified in their card agreements that in the case of a card account closing, all remaining funds would be returned to the customer forty-five days later, to provide ample time for all, even the tardiest merchants, to come forward with outstanding slips.

Even with such inadequate technological equipment, overdrafts could still be avoided if the bank that issued the card authorized each and every purchase. In principle, during each of the card transactions merchants using imprinters could pick up the telephone and call the issuing bank to verify the availability of funds to cover the purchase (this is called voice authorization). But such authorizations are time-consuming and depend on the availability of telephone lines in both the store and the bank. (What if there are several cashiers who are trying to verify their buyers at the same time? How many lines should each store have? How many people should the bank hire to respond to such inquiries?)[13]

In reality, some purchases were not authorized at all. Many merchants (especially in the West) do not ask for authorization when the purchase price falls below a certain amount (known as a "floor limit"). This is because authorization is costly for the processing company and is simply not worth it for smaller purchases; where imprinters are used instead of electronic terminals, authorization is also time-consuming. Most Russian merchants had low or zero floor limits, but holders of Visas and MasterCards who traveled to foreign countries could encounter floor limits as high as $1,000 (especially in hotels).[14] In one of my interviews with a high-ranking security department employee, I was told of a popular fraud scheme consisting of four steps: 1) obtaining a card based on false information, such as a counterfeit passport or a stolen identity; 2) making a large number of quick purchases on prelimit amounts (usually $100 or less) in one well-known German department store; 3) taking the goods to Poland; and 4) selling them at one of the open-air markets.[15] The issuing bank was rarely able to find the perpetrators, while they walked away with several thousand dollars of profit in a matter of a few days. Since it could be easily abused, the size of a floor limit at a retail location was usually a closely guarded secret.

Moreover, the issuing bank approved only some of the authorized purchases. Instead, the processing company that the merchant called permitted or prohibited transactions using a database provided by the bank that issued the card. This meant that the authorization took place in an *off-line* regime. Thus, there was no immediate debiting of the cardholder's account in the issuing bank. The account was only debited when the merchant submitted the paper slips to its bank and the processing company passed these on to the bank that issued the card. Because the information about transactions was not transmitted immediately, it was possible for the sum of all authorized purchases for the day or for a several-day period to be larger than the balance on the account, thus resulting in an overdraft.

Contrary to off-line authorization, *on-line* (real time) authorization always occurred when money was withdrawn from an ATM machine or a cashier (both operations are quite expensive for the bank and thus on-line authorization could not be done at every point-of-sale). On-line authorization also took place when the authorization request went directly from the merchant to the issuing bank. This happened when the issuing bank was also a processing bank for a credit card network.

Unsanctioned overdrafts usually resulted in heavy penalties, which varied greatly between banks. In one bank, a five-day overdraft was free, but if not paid in full, the interest rate increased to 30 percent, and to 60 percent if not paid in full in one month. In another bank, the penalty for an unsanctioned overdraft was the full 120 percent APR. If asked in advance, however, banks sometimes opened temporary credit lines for valued customers (decisions were made on a case-by-case basis). For example, one of the banks called this occasional overdraft a "bonus" given to clients of particular significance to the bank (examples that I was given included well-known singers and actors). This bonus was applied to one's card account based on the signatures of two or three top managers and was provided free of charge.[16] One of the banks revealed that about 4 percent of its accounts with unauthorized overdrafts were currently overdrawn, most of them as a result of transactions conducted abroad. But the majority of such cardholders had been diligently paying off the interest accrued on their accounts.[17] We found only two banks in Moscow in 1998 that openly advertised and issued cards "with authorized overdraft" (*s razreshennym overdraftom*). One of them, Kredit-Moskva bank, demanded a security deposit that was twice the size of the card's overdraft limit.

Nevertheless, some cardholders managed to qualify for more than an occasional or even regularly authorized overdraft. A handful of banks admitted to issuing a number of cards with authorized overdraft and without security deposits. Such cards were never openly advertised in the 1990s and issued only as a VIP product to an extremely limited number of people: the bank's owners and top managers, owners and managers of their shareholders and large corporate clients, and in some cases, select politicians and top state bureaucrats. Such cards were issued as favors, kickbacks, and signs of loyalty. For instance, in an interview with a representative of one of the largest banks and a leading card issuer, I learned that the bank issued more than a thousand overdraft cards to VIP clients, and these cards, while yielding little direct profit, "benefited the bank in other realms, specifically in political and economic spheres."[18] Former Russian president Yeltsin was reportedly issued a card of a local STB brand by the now defunct SBS-Agro bank.[19]

Most banks distinguished their employees from other customers by offering cards to the former on much better terms. For instance, one of the largest issuers offered Visa Classic and Gold cards (both as debit cards with "unauthorized overdraft") to its own employees with lower fees than what the bank charged others. But whether employees could qualify for a card with authorized overdraft with or without a security deposit was a consequence of their positions within the organizational hierarchy, the most privileged cards being issued to those occupying the highest ranks.

Cards with unauthorized and authorized overdraft only accounted for a small part of all cards issued in Russia. A much bigger portion were straightforward debit cards, specifically, Visa Electron and Maestro, issued by Europay/MasterCard. These cards are not embossed and therefore are not compatible with paper technology (that is, imprinter slips). They can be serviced only through an ATM machine or POS terminal, as they always require 100 percent on-line authorization. By the end of 1998, the Visa Electron card accounted for almost 88 percent of all Visa cards, and Maestro cards for over 96 percent of all MasterCards issued in Russia. These cards were also the fastest-growing products in both credit card networks in 1998 (64 percent and 81 percent growth, respectively). Today, the situation is different. While debit cards still account for the majority of plastic cards issued in Russia, their rate of growth in 2005 was 50 percent, while the number of issued credit cards grew 82 percent (RosBusinessConsulting 2006).

Since none of the cards issued in Russia in the 1990s extended any credit to their holders, why is this period covered in such detail in a book on Russia's emergent *credit* card market? For several reasons. First, the emergence of debit cards signified the appearance of the card concept, multinational card brands, and card technology. They paved the way for both banks, which were learning the ropes of card technology and retail in general, and consumers, who knew little about cards or any other noncash means of payment and had little experience with banking besides the memories (among the older generation, mainly) of keeping their savings in local branches of Sberbank. In the words of the head of the plastic card department in one of the largest banks: "People were not used to having bank accounts and preferred cash; therefore we have been developing our ATM network. Now people have been [gradually] getting used to not only having bank accounts, but also cards. They are acquiring the taste for using [debit] cards—they do not have to carry lots of cash with them, it is safe, if they lose a card we will block it."[20] So banks viewed debit cards as the primary mechanism of compensating for the lack of consumer experience with banking and as the way to educate consumers about the techniques of card use. In this sense, they perceived debit cards as the logical precursors of the eventual growth of Russia's credit card market. This is how the head of the plastic card department in another leading issuing bank made sense of this transition: "First of all, we need to teach people to work with banks . . . Debit cards should come first, since they pose little risk . . . Credit [cards] will naturally come later."[21]

Second, a portion of the debit cards issued in Russia in the 1990s were regular Western-style credit cards with a void credit function. Because they could potentially lead to unwanted overdraft, banks treated them as credit cards, requiring security deposits and conducting verifications. Thus, the banks' organizational practices provided an insight into their handling of uncertainty, which is one of the key problems a credit card market faces.

Still, why weren't there any *real* credit cards (unsecured revolving cards, to which Americans have gotten so accustomed) in the 1990s in Russia? When asked this question, the Russian bankers were unanimous in their reaction, pointing at too much uncertainty and few means at any bank's disposal to handle it. In the words of the card specialists in one of the largest Moscow-based banks: "The problem is that we have to have confidence in the client [in order to issue a credit card]. This confidence should be based on the analysis of previous payments and fulfillment of the obligations before the bank."[22] This kind of information would comprise what otherwise is known as "credit history." But in Russia, credit reporting was not legislated until much later—December of 2004. Moreover, as the same banker explained (and many others would agree with his diagnosis), "It is difficult to obtain information about real incomes."[23]

What this banker meant was that it was close to impossible to verify what most individuals really earned. The main reason has been widespread tax evasion on the part of both businesses and individuals. As a result, only a portion of what individuals earned was paid to them officially, in the form of a "white," openly declared salary that could be confirmed by the employer. The rest was passed on as cash in an envelope, or dispensed through a variety of more complex schemes, existing due to the loopholes in the legal system and periodically closed off by the Tax Authorities, only to resurface in another form later. One such scheme involved opening up extremely high-interest bank accounts in the employee's name (the interest rate could be as high as 1,000 percent APR). Banks would charge a fee for what they well knew was a tax-evasion scheme. This fee would be negligible, however, compared to what the enterprise was saving on unpaid taxes.[24]

Today, faced with many more diverse applicants, Russian banks rely on several indirect indicators of one's real income. For instance, they base their assessments on applicants' patterns of consumption and life style, inquiring about monthly mobile-phone expenses, possessions (most commonly cars), and destinations for summer vacations. They favor applicants who vacation abroad, but may ask several simple questions about popular destinations to verify that applicants are not lying. Some even visit applicants at their homes in order to help them fill out the application forms while, no doubt, attentively looking around. In addition, banks compare the wages stated in the application with their own estimate of an average wage for the applicant's sphere of employment and position.

Conclusion

Circumstances in Russia were hardly ideal for the advent of a credit card market. Not only did Russians have little experience with consumer credit and commercial banking, but commercial banks also had little interest in developing retail business. Preoccupied with staying afloat in the turbulent waters of postcommunist reforms, they were busy flirting with the state; pursuing large-ticket deals with important corporate clients; and engaging in financial speculations with foreign currency, short-term interbank loans, and the State Treasury bonds. As a result, many of them were falling prey to periodic economy-wide crises, eroding the trust of the public in commercial banking. The credit card market had been developing alongside, suffering inevitably from all the blows to the banking industry, but also skillfully capitalizing on the two key socialist legacies: the importance of interpersonal ties and paternalistic relations between employers and workers. These legacies acted as useful social and organizational resources, coming to define the shape and the future of the Russian credit card market.

Thus, for the first several years, cards in Russia were issued almost exclusively as debit cards, and essentially as status symbols, both for the individuals on whom the cards conferred a high social status and for banks, elevating their standing among peer banks and attracting "important" customers. These first programs issued cards through interpersonal ties, and I now turn to their analysis.

CHAPTER FOUR

Inner Circles

Card Issuing at the Dawn of the Market

Unlike Bank of America and its followers that boldly mailed thousands of unsolicited credit cards to unsuspecting individuals, the first Russian card issuers did not even consider this to be a viable strategy. Part of a young and unstable industry, and in the midst of drastic economic reforms, Russian issuers were painfully aware of the uncertainties involved in card issuing, as well as their own vulnerabilities, and felt compelled to proceed accordingly. Where American banks skipped on screening, Russian banks paid great attention to the verification of prospective applicants. Where American banks issued cards *en masse*, Russian banks handpicked their future cardholders. Where American banks worried about attracting merchants, and indeed succeeded in jump-starting the market despite the devastating losses as a result of unsolicited mailings, Russian banks viewed cards as status symbols, mainly intended for those who would use them abroad. Last but not least, where American banks issued unsecured revolving credit cards, Russian banks carefully started with secured debit cards.

This chapter analyzes the strategies that Russian banks employed in assessing prospective cardholders at the dawn of the market, specifically when it came to issuing cards that posed any uncertainty: Classic or Gold card products with unauthorized and authorized overdrafts. These strategies helped the banks handle uncertainty, but did not bring them closer to solving the problem of complementarity because they only allowed for slow and selective cherry-picking from among a fairly exclusive group of potential customers. As such, these strategies had little to do with *market building*, which, in addition to card dissemination, presupposes a process of establishing a merchant acceptance network. Because these strategies were not calculative, they escaped the logic of economic rationality, and would perhaps be overlooked or disregarded by a mainstream economics observer as trivial and inconsequential. In fact, in such a highly uncertain and unpredictable environment as the one found in transitional Russia, it would have been entirely impossible to determine in advance what course of action or strategy would be rational (Beckert 1996). Perhaps not to issue any cards at all. The strategies I address in this chapter are emblematic both of the banks' initial approach to card issuing and of the dominant macroeconomic context in which they had to operate in the 1990s: banks were much more interested in short-term profits obtained from financial speculations, while card programs were viewed as good publicity for the bank and a way to keep and attract important clients.

Chapter One lined up multiple strategies of handling uncertainty: reduced exposure, guarantees, compensation, prescreening, and sanctioning. Here I rely on interview data to address the Russian banks' specific strategies within each of these categories.

Reducing Exposure

Those Russian bankers who read Nocera's book (1994) on the early days of the American credit card market must have been amazed at the American banks' audacity: sending ready-to-use credit cards to complete strangers. In Russia, card issuing has been inalienably linked with efforts to reduce banks' uncertainty at all costs (even at a cost to market growth and profitability). In the words of a security department employee of one of the largest card issuers, "Our bosses remind us daily that there should not be any [unsanctioned] overdrafts."[1] The primary way of achieving this goal was to painstakingly screen applicants prior to the issuing decision and to keep the pool of cardholders small. Some banks must have been so diligent in selecting their cardholders and eliminating any possibility of overdrafts that they were able to insist dismissively that while there were some cardholders who incurred overdrafts and were late on their payments, these rare cases were successfully negotiated and the bank had no losses due to nonpayment or fraud.

Under some circumstances some clients were able to incur overdrafts in their debit card accounts, sometimes even on a permanent basis, but more often temporarily. Recall the bank that extended occasional overdrafts on a case-by-case basis if asked in advance. This bank considered such one-time overdrafts a safer option than a regular line of credit: first, the overdraft was usually extended in particular circumstances, such as for a business trip or a vacation abroad, and second, it was provided for a limited amount of time, lowering the chance that the account would be compromised if the card were stolen and used fraudulently. When allowed, overdrafts were supposed to be paid off in a limited amount of time—usually within a month, and certainly in no more than two, underscoring again the "exceptional, out of the ordinary" nature of such one-time loans.[2]

So unlike American banks, which draw their highest profits from extended repayment of credit card balances because this allows for overall larger interest payments, Russian banks took the opposite approach.[3] Not only did they issue debit cards instead of credit cards for the first ten years, but where overdrafts occurred (or were allowed) they had to be quickly paid off. In the frenzy of limiting their exposure and reducing uncertainty, Russian banks passed on the opportunity to earn interest on credit balances, settling instead for clients' deposits as their primary source of profit.

Guarantees and Compensation

Although most of the cards issued in the 1990s did not allow for overdrafts, due to technical limitations they were still possible. As a result, banks tried to further protect themselves by requiring cardholders to procure separate security deposits and maintain minimum balances on their debit card accounts (essentially asking them to freeze a certain portion of their deposits as a cushion against unsanctioned overdrafts). Both security deposits and minimum balances would be used to compensate the banks' possible losses if overdrafts occurred but could not be repaid.

Asking to maintain minimum balances and security deposits in the 1990s amounted to shifting uncertainty from banks to clients because at that time deposits in Russian banks were not insured.[4] American credit card holders, even with secured cards or direct-payment systems, take virtually no chances, since deposits in U.S. banks are protected by the Federal Deposit Insurance Corporation (FDIC).[5] Russian customers, on the other hand, had good reasons to be nervous. Bank failures were frequent. When choosing a bank, consumers relied on gossip and hearsay, or followed the recommendations of friends. A common expression "too big (or, as an alternative, too important) to fail" indicated that despite the absence of formal deposit insurance, depositors considered some banks, including the state-owned Sberbank, unassailable, their right to the government's help in case of financial difficulties assumed and unquestioned.[6] Yet, this principle was violated before. The pioneer of Visa cards in Russia—Kredobank, a relatively large bank at that time, went under in 1995; other large banks with well-known card programs—Mytishchinskiy Bank and Tveruniversalbank—also went bankrupt and annulled their card programs. Many cardholders never saw their security deposits again.

The 1998 crisis put this belief to rest entirely. So large was its scale that only the state-owned Sberbank was indeed lent a helping hand by the government. None of the six largest private card issuers—Inkombank, ONEXIMbank, SBS-Agro, Mostbank, MENATEP, and Rossiyskiy Kredit—survived intact. Some were bankrupted; others managed to resist bankruptcy, restructuring their debts and transferring their assets to "bridge" banks and reopening under new names, such as 1st OVK, Rosbank, MENATEP-St. Petersburg, and Impexbank. Inkombank's story is particularly notable. It ceased to exist just two months before its widely anticipated tenth anniversary. Two years earlier, it had been the second-largest bank, and (with five other banks) it had controlled 95 percent of Russia's Visa market.[7]

Quite tellingly, however, banks did not consider security deposits a solid guarantee against losses. In the words of the head of a plastic card department of one of the large banks, "Any bank can be 'stripped naked' ['stolen from on a large scale'—in the original language, *lyuboy bank mozhno razdet dogola*] regardless of the size of a security deposit."[8] Similarly, in another interview, I was assured that even a $1,000 security deposit would not protect the bank from intentional fraud.[9] Moreover, as a result of competition in the mid-1990s, banks were gradually giving up requirements for minimum balances and security deposits for cards with unauthorized overdrafts, further under-scoring the crucial importance of prescreening.

Prescreening and Data Verification

Prescreening amounts to analyzing information about applicants to distin-guish those who would be desirable cardholders from the undesirable ones. In the 1990s, Russian banks had limited access to third-party information about the applicant. Credit bureaus were not founded until 2005, and it was not customary to collect information from the applicant's employer, friends, or acquaintances, perhaps because such information would not be trusted. Banks mainly relied on information provided by the applicant on the appli-cation form and on the visual inspection of the applicant by the bank officer at the time the application was submitted.[10] This information was frequently verified with the help of various databases—some public, some stolen from state agencies, and most sold on street markets—and with occasional in-quiries to other banks through informal embedded ties between the banks' middle management.

Information obtained from applicants at the time of application included a copy of their passport with stamped residential registration, local address if it was different from the one where the applicant was registered, home phone number, employment (including the name and address of employer, job de-scription, and direct phone number), marital status, education, whether the applicant was ever convicted of a crime, and the primary way the card was going to be used. Sometimes the question on the future uses of the card came up during a subsequent face-to-face meeting between the bank's staff and the applicant. If the applicant could not answer the question or did not give an answer that was reasonable, bank officers became suspicious. They also became suspicious if the amount of money that the client was offering to deposit in the bank was too high for their claimed occupation. The con-cern was that the person was applying for a card that then would be used by someone else. Card specialists used the following example to describe this type of fraud. A small company would hire a student. As his first task, he (because it was exclusively male students who were offered such a "job") would be asked to apply for a credit card in his name and given a couple of thousand dollars—enough to open a card account and to make a security deposit. The "employer" would then take the card and disappear. When the account is overdrawn, the student can easily be traced, but he knows nothing about the "employer" and has no money with which to reimburse the bank.[11]

This assortment of information helped banks assess two things: rule out fraud by ID-ing the applicant (for instance, making sure the passport was authentic) and establish reliable channels of communication with the applicant. In the mind of the bank, the two were often connected; making sure that the applicant was within reach was akin to fighting fraud and generally preventing future losses: "[T]he most important factor in screening is to make sure that the person could be easily located and contacted. . . . [This included having a set place of work and an authentic stamp in their passport about local residential registration.] This was our attempt to at least cut off intentional fraud."[12] According to another bank's estimate, "[I]n up to 4 out of 5 cases of incurred and unpaid overdraft, initial information turned out to be incorrect."[13]

Since preventing fraud was one of the main efforts of Russian card issuers, they often contacted other banks with inquiries about specific applicants. The goal was to investigate whether other banks had any negative information about the applicant (some banks maintained blacklists of cardholders suspected of or pursued for fraud). These channels of interbank communication were usually maintained at the level of "security departments" (*otdely bezopasnosti*)—special bank units with the responsibility for screening card applicants, tracking and investigating possible cases of fraud, solving interbank charge-back problems, and working with problematic accounts. Security departments usually carried a lot of weight in issuing decisions. They made recommendations to issue a card, which were used as a basis for the final decision made by the head of the card division of the bank. The bank could still reject the applicant in spite of the positive recommendation of the security department. But a negative recommendation was a serious barrier. In one bank, I was assured that in such a case even the head of the board of directors could not intervene.

Interbank information exchange existed courtesy of the interfirm mobility of personnel (Granovetter 1985), in part increased by the overall instability of the banking industry in the 1990s. Since banks were going under frequently, even big and well-known ones, former employees who found new positions in different banks could rely on already-established ties. In addition, and probably more important, security departments were staffed by former members of the security forces (police, military, or KGB), who either knew each other personally or could appeal to their shared alumni status to elicit cooperation and information exchange.

But information is only as good as it is verifiable. This includes, first of all, making sure that the applicant is not lying about his or her contact information or job status, and that there are no criminal convictions. Again, the professional roots of security department employees come in handy: "There is no centralized pool of customer information, and as a result, each bank verifies applicants in its own way. For instance, security department employees may use their contacts in police."[14] In addition, banks relied on various databases, which helped them fairly quickly to verify the factual data supplied by the applicants. For example, a common database frequently used for this purpose was the database of telephone numbers correlated with addresses of private residences and firms. With the help of these databases, the bank could check whether the applicant's phone number was registered to their stated address.[15] Bank officers could also run the applicant's passport number against a database of stolen passports, or conduct a quick criminal background check against available databases of legal offenses. Finding discrepancies between applicants' self-reported data and these databases would raise a red flag, in some banks leading to an automatic disqualification from further consideration.

In addition, bank officers were trained to look for inconsistencies in information stated by the applicant on the application form and the applicant's appearance or behavior. For example, some paid attention to how applicants were dressed, what brand of shoes or watch they wore, or whether female applicants had adequate manicures and hairdos. Since the first cards were typically issued to a fairly exclusive group, the unwritten standards of self-presentation were often quite high. The main goal of this verification was to assess the applicants' *honesty*, which was taken as a proxy for their general reliability, and thus for their future willingness to abide by the contract, repay the amount if the overdraft did occur, and be open to negotiating with the bank.

Yet the most important consideration that banks emphasized time and again was whether they would be able to easily contact the person in order to pressure them to compensate for a possible overdraft. To rest assured that the lines of communication worked, a few banks even resorted to a little trickery: they called the specified telephone numbers as if to ask additional questions, or perhaps inform the applicant that the card was ready for a pickup. A failure to speak with the applicant after three attempts signaled that the contact information was unreliable; this was usually a reason to stop pursuing the application. Bank officers preferred to call the work number because they believed that they were killing two birds with one stone: they were making sure that the person could be easily reached and at the same time confirming the applicant's employment.

To sum up, prescreening by Russian banks in the 1990s pursued three main goals: to prevent fraud, to assess the applicants' overall honesty, and to ascertain that they could be contacted quickly when necessary. The problem that these examples illustrate, however, is that it was difficult or often impossible to assess the quality of information on which banks had to base their decisions. For instance, informal databases were usually bought from street vendors after being stolen from state agencies, and their completeness and the extent to which they were updated with the most recent information, or even their authenticity, were questionable. On the other hand, informal interbank exchanges relied entirely on the benevolence of former coworkers, who, one should not forget, now worked for competing firms. These information exchanges were selective, bilateral, and entirely voluntary, their success depending heavily on the personal trust established between individual bank officials. Blacklists only contained information about suspected or confirmed fraud, and would be of little use in preventing possible overdrafts or defaults.

So third-party data was not reliable, but neither was the information coming from the applicant. Income data, for instance, was and still is extremely difficult to verify. In fact, this was the main reason that Russian banks downplayed the role of the applicant's ability to repay in their decisions. Better-off Russians, who initially were the primary audience for international cards, tried especially hard to conceal their real incomes from the state and tax authorities, from organized crime, and even from their business competitors. But most of the time applicants could not confirm their income because their employers underreported their salaries in order to reduce payroll taxes, or because they made much of their money in the shadow economy.

Reliance on Social Ties in Card Issuing

Since information was difficult or impossible to verify and security deposits were considered to be a weak protection, especially against intentional fraud, Russian banks had to carefully choose to whom they could issue cards. In line with Beckert's (1996) argument, banks experienced uncertainty in their decision making, and had to resort to social devices (in this case, social networks) in order to make decisions and carry out social action. Uzzi (1997) makes a similar argument about embedded relations among producers and supplies in the garment industry. Trust, which emerges as one of the benefits of embedded relations at the level of the firm, allows for reliance on heuristics in decision making, instead of engaging in systematic information search and rational calculation, and for this reason helps to speed up decision making and conserve cognitive resources. In addition, embeddedness also helps actors to solve problems on the fly by making them willing and able to renegotiate the terms (raise "voice" [Hirschman 1970]) in the name of future cooperation instead of immediately "running to lawyers" (Macaulay 1963) or quitting. Thus, the use of embedded ties is particularly beneficial when information is unavailable, incomplete, or distorted, and when the chances of successful legal recourse following breach of contract are slim—precisely the situation that prevailed in the Russian credit card market in the 1990s.

Reliance on embedded ties in card issuing made banks distinguish sharply between insiders who were connected to the bank in some way (as regular customers, employers of the bank's corporate clients, or through friendships and recommendations) and the rest, or "people from the street." It was insiders who were favored because, depending on their strength, the ties either gave the bank the best possible guarantee that the agreement would not be breached, or they at least made cardholders more transparent for the bank and more easily accessible. Most of the Russian banks started their card programs from actively issuing cards to their own employees and families and friends of their top bank executives (see also Ledeneva 1998, 211). Here the borrower-creditor relationship was intermingled with workplace ties or close social bonds. For instance, one interviewee was granted an American Express card by his friend, who at the time was a high-ranking employee of AmEx in Moscow. Furthermore, friends and relatives of the banks' top executives and long-term clients could recommend other potential cardholders, both formally and informally. But while information can travel great geographic and social distances, especially if transmitted through weak ties (Granovetter 1973), trust and influence diminish with each remove. For this reason, the rule of thumb for dealing with these recommendations was that there should not be more than one person between a bank officer and an applicant.[16]

In addition, banks eagerly issued cards to their existing customers, especially if their bank accounts demonstrated a significant rotation of funds. One of the very few banks that issued cards with real credit lines and offered them unsecured for the first $300 (applicants who desired a higher credit limit had to cover the remainder with a security deposit) was willing to issue these cards to the two types of existing clients: those who already had a debit card issued under a salary project or those who were authorized users of a corporate Visa or MasterCard.[17] Their status as current customers tied to the bank through their current employer confirmed, if not their overall honesty, then certainly their work status and the fact that they could easily be contacted when necessary.

If card issuing to bank employees, their friends and family, and existing customers provided for very slow growth of bank clientele, a strategy that successfully tackled uncertainty but ignored complementarity (as it was difficult to persuade merchants to accept cards if the banks' cardholders were limited in number), issuing cards to employees of the banks' corporate clients provided for a bigger market, and one that had potential for future growth. It did not, however, compromise on controlling uncertainty. For instance, while "the bank couldn't verify one's salary, it was, however, easier to do for those who worked for companies which were a bank's corporate clients or for those whose salaries were directly deposited to the bank as part of salary projects."[18] As a result, it was not uncommon for a bank to have an overwhelming majority of cardholders with "unauthorized overdraft" (90 percent in some cases) employed by the bank's numerous corporate clients. In addition to their salaries and the overall financial stability of their employer being transparent to the bank, these people could be contacted easily.[19]

The strategy of issuing cards to a bank's corporate clients illustrates one very important feature of the Russian card market: reliance on employing organizations. Full use of employers in facilitating card spread in Russia will be explored in detail in the next chapter, which discusses the role of salary projects in building the market. Here I would like to further elaborate on a particular case of using professional affiliations as a basis for card distribution.

While in the above example, card applicants were connected to the bank through the ties the bank had to its corporate clients, cards were also issued to applicants who were deemed sufficiently anchored in their own networks, not necessarily connected to the bank itself (Guseva and Róna-Tas 2001).[20] Anchoring networks did not have to be legally liable for the potential misdeeds of the applicant. Nor did they have to sanction the offender themselves. They only restricted the cardholder's exit and made it easier for the bank to contact him or her to check on a suspicious transaction or negotiate the terms of repayment or sanction.

Examples included issuing cards to people who were deemed anchored in organizations where they worked, even if these organizations were not tied to the bank via corporate relations; or issuing to people of high social standing, for instance, those holding positions of economic or political power. In the latter case, cards could be issued not just because such people tended to be affluent, but also because they were securely anchored at the top of the national social hierarchy. Since being in the public eye was a necessary part of their activities, they were unlikely to vanish without a trace. To streamline the process, one bank even compiled (as an internal bank document) a list of such positions, which made their holders eligible for credit cards without a security deposit (these cards were never openly advertised but offered to a very exclusive circle of customers; they provided credit lines up to $1,500). Notably, the bank issued such cards to positions rather than to particular people. When these cardholders left their positions, they were asked to apply for new cards, issued on different terms. By the summer of 1998, this bank had issued no more than one hundred such unsecured cards.[21] Occasionally such cards could also be given to famous artists and pop stars.

Exclusive reliance on embedded ties in issuing cards posed a dilemma: engaging in time-consuming, case-by-case decision making and monitoring slowed down the process of building the bank's customer base, solving the complementarity problem, and developing the market. But to be able to mass-issue cards, Russian banks needed to fundamentally alter their screening and decision-making strategies to allow for quick, yet secure processing of applications. While even by the second wave of interviews, in 2003–2005, almost none of the Russian banks (with two rare exceptions) had developed classic credit-scoring models based on a statistical analysis of the bank's past clients' financial behavior, many had been making attempts at standardizing and rationalizing cardholders' prescreening by developing rules, generalizations that served as shortcuts in screening and decision making.

Standardization and Rationalization of Decision Making

One bank that specialized in issuing secured credit cards developed a standardized questionnaire as a guide for its officers in screening prospective cardholders. Answers to eight questions were assessed:

1. Are the place of residence reported and the place of registration the same?
2. Is the telephone registered to the applicant?
3. Is the company where the applicant works located in an office as opposed to a private home?
4. Is the applicant's work phone registered to the company?
5. Are the workplace and the job title indicated correctly?
6. Does a secretary answer the work phone?
7. Is the applicant recommended (in writing) by another client with the bank's card?
8. Does the applicant already have a card from another bank?

Getting five positive answers was necessary for a favorable decision. In addition to assessing applicants' honesty (question 5) and the ease with which they could be contacted (questions 1, 2, 5, and 7), the questionnaire also attempted to evaluate their insider status (questions 7 and 8) and the prestige of their workplace (questions 3, 4, and 6).

Another way to standardize screening and decision making was to identify categories of applicants whose profiles raised immediate red flags. This helped banks (specifically, security departments) to optimize their limited resources by focusing attention on those applicants who required particularly close scrutiny. Some of these categories were arrived at as a result of extrapolation from past experience. For instance, staff at one of the banks developed a rule based on fraud patterns that they had identified previously. They had information that several residents of Petrozavodsk, a small suburb of St. Petersburg, were involved in card fraud. Subsequently, Petrozavodsk was put on a so-called "hot list of geographic regions." Anyone born and raised there automatically became subject to particularly intense scrutiny.[22]

Other generalizations were a result of the banks' experts exercising their common sense. Several banks developed guidelines about categories of risk groups, which included people without regular income (for example, artists working on commission), temporarily unemployed, students, retired, home-makers (which made it more difficult for women to be issued a card), citizens of other former republics of the Soviet Union, those in the military, and even entrepreneurs. Their applications were subject to particularly thorough verification.[23]

Entrepreneurs were viewed with so much suspicion because this was a no-toriously vague category encompassing not only small enterprise owners and managers but also currency speculators, crooks, and various wheeler-dealers with unstable, irregular, or perhaps even illegitimate incomes.[24] Those in the military could relocate to a remote geographical location (the same was true for people from other parts of the former Soviet Union, who might have migrated to Moscow for economic opportunities but maintained homes elsewhere) or retire from active service and move, making contacting them difficult and costly. Students were also suspect unless they worked; then they would be treated and evaluated as employed applicants rather than students. In fact, to avoid possible complications further on in the approval process, bank officers accepting applications would usually ask students to redo their applications, this time omitting the fact that they were students and only mentioning their employment status.

One of the banks categorized students further by gender because, as I learned during the interview, male and female students applied for cards for different reasons and presented different kinds of risk:

> Male students are riskier than female students because they are technically more literate [and could intentionally defraud the bank]. If they apply, we first ask why they need the card. If they say that [they] want to make purchases on the Internet, and they are not employed in addition to being a student, we reject their application. If they work, we ask them to rewrite the application to indicate that they work and omit the fact that they are also

students. . . . Female students often apply for a card because their parents are sending them abroad for a [sic] language study. In this case, we call their home and verify whether their parents could be easily reached at the phone number indicated.[25]

In both cases, before making any decisions, the bank's security department tried to find out if the students had well-off or well-positioned fathers. In other words, the students' parents rather than the students themselves were prescreened, and if the parents passed, the bank asked them to apply for the card and open an additional card for their child.[26]

It is important to emphasize that all these applicants were not considered high risk because of their low incomes. There were plenty of others who received notoriously low wages and experienced frequent wage arrears in the 1990s, including doctors, teachers, and college professors (called *byudzhet-niki* because they were paid by state or municipal budgets), who were not on this list. As one of my interviewees explained, this was because, despite their low or uncertain incomes, teachers and doctors were "squeezed (*zazhaty*) in an organization,"[27] or in my terminology, they were securely anchored. In contrast, the risk groups—retirees, homemakers, students, entrepreneurs, and others—were not anchored sufficiently.

Notably, while banks ruled that certain categories of applicants were high risk, they rarely rejected them outright, resorting instead to already familiar in-depth analyses of applicants' profiles. As the situation with students illustrated, banks tried to establish whether the applicant was part of a family who could meet the standards set by the bank for their cardholders. When faced with retirees, homemakers, and those in active military service, banks focused their attention on their family ties—children and spouses—and evaluated their status and the degree to which they were anchored.

In general, banks pointed out that they did not like to reject applicants; instead, for high-risk categories of applicants, banks conducted more thorough analyses. And even if they could not issue a requested card, they could usually still offer a card of a lower status and risk. For instance, they could decide that a person who did not frequently travel abroad did not need a Visa or a MasterCard and suggest a card of a local brand instead. Similarly, if based on the results of prescreening the bank could not issue a Visa Classic card, the applicant could instead be offered a Visa Electron card that required 100 percent authorization, making unauthorized overdrafts virtually impossible.

Thus, in a surprising twist, Russian banks were following the Western dictum of keeping customers happy. The reason for this, I think, was that the typical cardholder at that time belonged to a fairly small and exclusive group of people. Cards were considered status symbols, and banks believed that most of those who came into their branches to apply for a card were already preselected. Therefore, instead of rejecting them, the banks preferred to screen them in greater depth, perhaps hoping that the students would turn out to have well-positioned parents, homemakers—well-placed husbands, and the unemployed would appear to be top state functionaries in transition from one high appointment to another.

Inquiries about families were not an attempt to anchor applicants. Anchoring was done only in work-related structures, organizational hierarchies and professional communities, rather than in the systems of residential or kinship membership. Where applicants were not sufficiently anchored and banks inquired about family members, the goal was not to ascertain that these relations would prevent the cardholders' exit and make them available to the bank for negotiation or sanctioning. Rather, given their earning status, parents, children, and spouses would then become the target of the bank's attempts to negotiate in case of a problem with the account.

Ironically, despite the attempts to formalize decision making by formulating rules and articulating the categories of risk groups, the decision making was still ultimately based on a case-by-case evaluation. Rules and risk groups rarely called for the automatic disqualification of applicants from subsequent consideration, but rather provoked a closer look. In the words of one interviewee, in Russia, decision making and the verification that accompanies it called for "an individual approach at the level of art." This interviewee was emphatic that even if more formalized screening methods were introduced (like the credit scoring routinely used in mature markets), such "art-like" verification would persist because "bank customers [could not] be standard and remain standard throughout the year."[28] He argued that the methods of verification used by security departments were an undertaking akin to a craft as opposed to an assembly line.

Sanctioning

How did the banks handle situations when, despite their thorough and careful prescreening, the terms of the agreement were broken, an unsanctioned overdraft occurred, or the cardholder was late in payment? In these cases, as well as when an unusual transaction took place (for instance a charge from Greece or Thailand, which immediately raised the possibility of a fraudulent transaction), the banks first evaluated what they knew about this cardholder. If this was one of their special clients (a VIP or someone linked to the bank via social ties), the cardholder's contact at the bank was probed for any additional information. Especially with VIP clients, the bank did not want to create a problem prematurely. For instance, if the client in question was a friend or a family member of one of the bank's employees, that employee could casually be asked when they last saw the cardholder and whether they knew of the person's plans. If the cardholder's liaison in the bank knew that their friend was going on vacation, especially if they mentioned a foreign destination, this was often enough for the bank to not react immediately to the Thailand charge or overspending. This is a specific example of the propensity of embedded ties to solve problems "on the fly" (Uzzi 1997).

According to the banks interviewed during the first wave in 1998–1999, in the majority of cases of unsanctioned overdrafts or late payments that they experienced with their cardholders, individuals were sincerely unaware of their overspending, forgetful, or simply not organized to make a payment on time. Banks were willing to excuse such forgetfulness, considering this a minor offense, because on being reminded, cardholders either repaid the balance immediately or at least were ready to work out a repayment schedule. In rare cases, cardholders who incurred an overdraft (either accidentally or with the bank's prior permission) subsequently fell on hard times. In those cases, the bank was usually still hopeful that the repayment would be forthcoming, even if not immediately.

It was only when the cardholder could not be contacted, admitted that they passed the card to someone else, or essentially refused to pay claiming they had no money at all, that the bank turned to heavier tactics. Sometimes, bank employees had to exert extraordinary pressure on clients refusing or unable to pay (as one security department employee candidly put it during the interview,

"We scare and intimidate them"), but no one admitted to the use of brutal force in negotiations, which was allegedly commonly used at that time by notorious violent entrepreneurs collecting on company debts (Volkov 1999).[29]

It is important to emphasize that irrespective of the chosen tactics, when it came to dealing with delinquent cardholders, banks were entirely on their own. So if many of their strategies looked as if they favored "voice" over "exit" (Hirschman 1970), or that they avoided "running to lawyers" (Macaulay 1963), it was because they really did not have much choice. During the first wave of interviews, none of them considered the pursuit of legal action a viable strategy, citing long delays, inefficiency, and a lack of trust in a favorable outcome. And while the bank could close the account and put the person on the bank's blacklist, this measure had little effect on either compensating the bank or punishing the cardholders since there was no centralized credit agency, and the client was free to go to a different bank and open a new account there. In other words, in the absence of formal institutions, embedded ties not only helped banks prescreen but they also allowed them to negotiate with pressure, or otherwise sanction cardholders.

Conclusion

The Russian banks that issued cards in the 1990s relied on scarce information and had limited opportunities to verify it. In a situation of no credit reporting and widespread tax evasion, banks could only be confident in a small and select group of clients, mainly those linked to the bank through embedded ties (or better yet, known personally by the bank's administration). Embedded ties helped verify information and established the applicants' overall honesty. These ties also ensured that cardholders could be contacted quickly and easily and would not disappear.

But relying exclusively on embedded ties created natural limitations on the number of potential cardholders and thus on the size of the market, because a small and slowly growing pool of cardholders did not attract enough interest from the merchants. Thus, while issuing cards through embedded networks helped to manage uncertainty, it completely ignored the problem of complementarity.

Russian banks needed to find a way to manage uncertainty on a mass scale, otherwise credit cards would remain a boutique product. Besides, when state resources started to dry up, they had to look for other ways to attract financial resources. In the next chapter, I will explain how salary projects allowed banks to kill two birds with one stone: they helped to mass-issue cards in Russia while keeping uncertainty low, and they also allowed the banking system to expand its customer base to include millions of new depositors, whose earnings were previously kept under mattresses.

CHAPTER FIVE

The Stick But No Carrot

Disseminating Cards Through Employers

This chapter focuses on card issuing through employers, the first of the Russian banks' solutions that promised to solve the problems of uncertainty and complementarity simultaneously. These enterprises served as go-betweens in providing banks with instant access to hundreds or thousands of potential cardholders. In addition, they also helped banks handle uncertainty, as they had better and more immediate control over their employees. This arrangement eliminated the need to prescreen and significantly simplified the subsequent monitoring and sanctioning of cardholders.

What Are Salary Projects?

At this point it is impossible to trace the origins of the idea of salary projects, but by the time of my first visit to Moscow in the summer of 1998, my interviewees were unanimous in calling salary projects "the banks' central method of attracting new clients" and "the foundation of the card market in Russia."[1] Secondary literature confirms these claims: in 1997, as many as 70 percent of all cards issued in Russia were issued through salary projects. Many banks were issuing cards *only* this way (Salnikov 1997a). Although today Russian banks are engaged in a variety of other ways of issuing cards, experts argue that more than 80 percent of cards that are currently in circulation in Russia have been issued through salary projects (Logvinova 2005). Individual banks report similar figures: Vneshtorgbank admitted recently that salary projects provided up to 80 percent of its card issuance (Kuzina 2006).

A typical salary project involves an agreement between a bank and a company to issue cards to all of the company's employees (from the top manager to the janitor), while their salaries are directly deposited in the bank (Russian employees have been traditionally paid in cash). The bank's fees (as a rule, no more than 1 percent of each salary) are usually paid by the company at the time that the salaries are transferred to individual employees' accounts; or in some cases, the same 1 percent can be paid by the employees at the time of withdrawal. The bank's possible losses from unauthorized overdrafts or misconduct in relation to the card would be paid by the next month's salary, and the company would be obliged to notify the bank as soon as the employee is fired or quits. In the overwhelming majority of cases, the bank, not the company, initiates salary projects.

Companies acquire both rights and responsibilities in connection with the salary project. One of my interviewees indicated that "[t]he company has a right to cancel someone's card services or make the employee reapply for a card as an individual applicant (usually when that employee quit or was fired)." This usually means that service fees for the card would be raised in accordance with the bank's policy regarding the cost of individual cards. Furthermore, he explained that "the company shoulders the risk of nonpayment, but only to a certain extent. For instance, if the company notified the bank that a particular employee has been fired, and the bank took several days to update its stop list (a list of cards that are no longer valid and should not be accepted), it is the bank, not the company that would be responsible for the unauthorized charges during this time."[2]

Overall only 20–30 percent of the corporate market has been tapped by salary projects so far, according to Dmitry Osipov, deputy head of the board of SDM bank (Logvinova 2005). But in areas of high bank concentration, competition allows companies to demand that cards be issued and serviced free of charge. For instance, Transcreditbank's salary project for Uralvagon-zavod, the Ural carriage-building plant, involved issuing cards with a customized design and developing a card-acceptance infrastructure, which now allows workers to use cards in the plant's numerous stores and canteens. Among the perks that Bank Soyuz provided to its salary cardholders were Internet banking, discount purchases in partner stores, and even nominally priced Bolshoy Theater tickets (Zaslavskaya 2005).

Although the main goal of the banks in promoting salary projects was to speed up card dissemination and to stimulate the growth of the merchant acceptance network, they pursued other goals as well (Gorokhov 2005). Prior to the 1998 crisis, the majority of banks scoffed at retail, chasing after the state budget or the accounts of large corporate clients. But the crash of the State Treasury bond market in August of 1998 put a sobering end to the Russian banks' financial bonanza, and this reformulated priorities for the banking community. Soon after, many banks realized that the next big pie to divide would be household finances. Salary projects allowed banks to acquire new individual depositors and widen their clientele base. In the words of a high-ranking manager of one of the largest regional banks, "Salary projects [were] the only way to extract people's money from under their mattresses" and get them accustomed to saving in the bank rather than keeping cash at home.[3]

This is how many of the banks, which initially specialized in corporate banking, started to enter the retail market and get themselves involved in salary projects. For corporate banks, this was a natural transition, as they administered their first salary projects for their existing corporate clients. Eventually, when all of their corporate clients were served, banks turned to other companies treating salary projects as "bait to attract new corporate clients with high turnover on their accounts."[4]

What banks are after when it comes to salary projects are the balances on payroll accounts. Although in the first 3–6 months people use the cards to withdraw almost 90 percent of their salaries, stipends or pensions (Andreev et al. 1998), later around 30–40 percent tend to be left on the accounts, for which banks pay low or no interest at all. This is why banks are especially on the lookout for subsidiaries of large international conglomerates, joint ventures, and other companies with potentially well-paid employees.

In addition, in a surprising marketing move, salary projects are also providing a testing ground for banks' new services (Internet banking, utility bill payments, and so on) (Zaslavskaya 2005). This means that salary cards often provide their holders with the fullest line of services that their bank currently offers, and rather than being viewed merely as a compensatory strategy of card distribution in the absence of credit reporting and the weakness of traditional marketing channels, salary cards are the ones driving the technological sophistication of the Russian card market forward.[5]

Market Structure

Mass consumer markets consist of a variety of producers, retailers, and consumers. Producers may be retailing independently (for instance, Gap, ECCO,

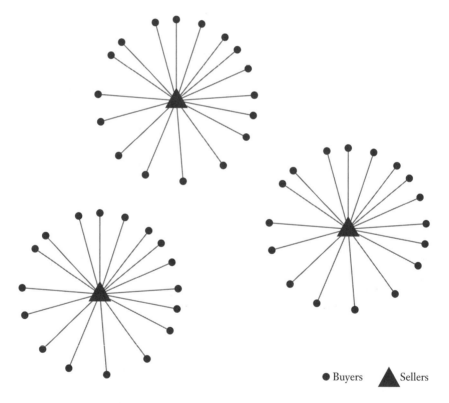

● Buyers ▲ Sellers

Figure 5.1 "Hubs-and-Spokes" Market Model
Source: Guseva 2005, p. 445.

or Toyota) or through designated or nondesignated retailers. For instance, Circuit City sells a number of consumer electronics brands but does not have an exclusive right to their distribution, while certain brands of cosmetics are only sold at a limited number of department stores. Retailers and consumers are connected through numerous direct ties so that a mass consumer market looks like a series of "hubs-and-spokes" (Figure 5.1).

While retailers frequently resort to various methods of personalizing customer experience in order to increase consumer loyalty (for instance, by offering frequent-buyer programs, mailing personalized catalogues, or providing bonuses tied to consumers' birthdays), retailer-consumer relations in mass markets remain at an arm's length because of a large number of "spokes" originating in one hub. A curious exception to this rule is a model of distribution perfected by Tupperware and Avon cosmetics representatives, who usually recruit "hostesses" to sell products at home parties to their friends (Biggart 1989).

Retailer-consumer ties in mass credit markets generally follow the same logic except that these markets must deal with the additional problem of uncertainty inherent in lending. Mature credit markets have solved this problem of lenders' uncertainty about future repayment of loans with the help of formal institutions. The U.S. credit card market is a "hubs-and-spokes" market, where banks submit data about existing customers to credit bureaus, which aggregate, classify, and quantify it before feeding it back to the banks to aid in prescreening (Figure 5.2). Had it not been for credit bureaus, banks would have had to keep the number of borrowers small, investing in the relationship with each of them. This is precisely the way that Russian banks started to issue cards: by limiting their customers to the ones they know, can trust, and monitor. U.S. credit bureaus promote market growth because they make embedded lender-borrower relations unnecessary and allow banks to reach for a wider consumer base. Notably, the success of credit reporting depends greatly on banks' willingness to cooperate by making their customer data available to their direct competitors.

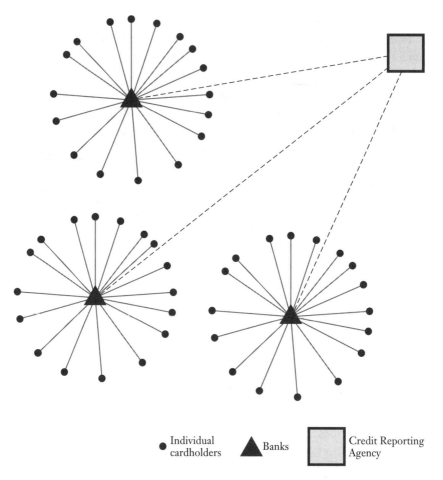

Figure 5.2 "Hubs-and-Spokes" Market Model (American Credit Card Market)
Source: Guseva 2005, p. 452.

Relational Benefits of Bi-Level Networks

Russian salary projects provide a surprising variation on the "hubs-and-spokes" model. Since banks issue cards to individuals through their employers, the Russian market resembles "snowflakes" (Figure 5.3). Each bank is connected to a limited number of companies, each of which is linked to their employees (direct links represent cardholders that applied for cards on individual terms). Banks reduce uncertainty by keeping the number of direct ties small. A smaller number of ties allow banks to control and monitor them better, but this does not limit the market, as each such tie connects the bank to an employer and provides access to hundreds or thousands of individual cardholders. Moreover, since the customers with whom the banks have direct ties are not individuals but large companies, they are easier to screen than individual card applicants and can also be held accountable better since they cannot disappear overnight (and their assets may serve as collateral). Thus, bi-level networks that combine individuals and organizations help compensate for the lack of cooperation and information sharing between banks. The benefits that banks derive from these networks cannot be overestimated: they provide banks with access to new depositors and cardholders, and also replace the need to prescreen these people individually because of their relationships with their employers. In short, bi-level networks allow the card market to grow even in the absence of formal prescreening mechanisms and any significant interbank cooperation.

Unlike "hubs-and-spokes," which usually consist of fleeting arm's-length ties and are devoid of social context, "snowflake" relations are embedded—contextualized and long-term, and they are also multiplex and interconnected. A buyer of an iPod™ at a Best Buy store is just that—a "buyer." But

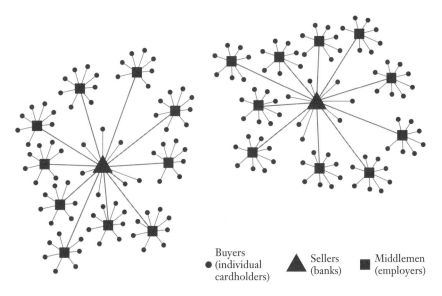

Buyers
● (individual
cardholders)

▲ Sellers
(banks)

■ Middlemen
(employers)

Figure 5.3 "Snowflakes" Market Model (Russian Credit Card Market)
Source: Guseva 2005, p. 454.

a salary card holder is simultaneously a customer of a bank, an employee of a company, which is this bank's corporate client, and perhaps even the company's consumer who uses the card to pay for lunch in the corporate canteen (in the latter case, the company is both an employer and a retailer). One social role, that of an employee, makes the person eligible for another, salary cardholder, which in turn enables one to act in the third scenario: charging one's lunch in a factory cafeteria to a card. Moreover, workers' employee roles restrict their behavior as cardholders: for instance, they could not easily disappear because their employment would be at stake. Bi-level networks produced an informal institutional mechanism for governing relations between issuers and holders of cards. They helped banks manage uncertainty while at the same time allowing them to standardize and routinize their prescreening practices. The fluidity of roles and multiplicity of ties in bi-level networks exemplify the fundamentally social nature of the Russian card market. This complex social skeleton is particularly unexpected in the context of a mass market.

How Do Banks Manage to Get Organizations Interested?

Salary projects greatly benefit banks, providing them with hundreds and thousands of new depositors and cardholders without the need to pay for advertisements and to open retail branches. But what are employers gaining from providing banks with access to their employees?

The key to the banks' success with salary projects stems from their ability to reformulate the initial configuration of bank → company → employee into company → bank → employee (Figure 2.1, p.40), inserting themselves between the company and its employees as an indispensable middleman. Banks promise to take on functions (storing and dispensing cash wages) that companies gladly relinquish. What is an additional headache for the companies, ill-suited to their main purpose, is at the same time a core function of the banks' professional activity and their source of profit: namely, servicing the financial needs of wage-earning individuals. With the salary project arrangement, the company no longer needs to worry about the secure delivery and storage of large amounts of cash, and dispensing of salaries to employees. According to RosBusinessConsulting, expenses for transportation, security, and dispensing of cash wages can account for as much as 2 percent in larger enterprises (2004). A large metallurgical company, "Severstal," reported that in 1997 it saved more than 2 million rubles monthly (approximately $300,000) by directly depositing employees' salaries ("Severstal" press release from April 10, 1998, cited in "Plastikovye kartochki v Cherepovtse" 1998). In addition, salary projects reduce tensions and loss of productive time by eliminating long lines in front of cashiers' windows on paydays, and since cash is not immediately available, may even prevent the celebratory payday drinking popular among workers.

The benefits for the employer were even more pronounced in regional industrial towns centered on a single company (or a few companies belonging to the same industry) where a large proportion of the adult population worked.[6] What made these towns especially suitable for salary projects were the severe problems of cash availability and chronic wage arrears in the early-to-mid-1990s (for a detailed analysis of Russia's monetary problems during this period see Woodruff 1999). In some cases, it was a direct consequence of the lack of paper money in the town; in other words, there was money on salary accounts, but it could not be paid in cash. For instance, in 1992 in Cheboksary, a city of 450,000 people on the Volga River, there was a shortage of small-denomination banknotes. One 50,000-ruble banknote paid the salaries of every two workers, which the unlucky pairs then frantically tried to change all over town (Yevtyushkin 1996).

More often, it was not merely the lack of cash that was the problem but rather chronic nonpayments between companies, as a result of which there was no money left at all to pay salaries. A common solution was to pay workers "in kind": in a better scenario, the workers would be paid with an assortment of various consumer goods and foodstuffs; in a worse case, the company would pay workers with its own output, which the workers would then try to sell themselves (Ildemenov and Harchenko 1999). Stories abounded of employees advertising women's boots, glasses, bikes, or china sets through their social networks or desperately trying to sell them at flea markets. This practice created "gray" markets where the company output was sold at a much lower price, undermining the company's standing in the regional economy. Provincial salary projects solved the problem of liquidity through a system of mutual clearance, as cards could be used for transactions in the factory cafeterias or in the town's stores, laundries, and gas stations.

The success of card distribution in regional towns greatly depended on the presence of three main factors: very large employers, wage arrears and/or shortage of cash, and a bank monopolist. One large-scale distribution of salary cards was carried out by Metallurgic Commercial Bank (Metkombank) in the town of Cherepovets, located in the northwest part of Russia (population 321,400). The very first Meta-cards (Metkombank's own brand) were issued in 1996, initially to the bank's own employees and their families (around one thousand cards), then to the employees of "Severstal," providing work for 49,000 people, and then to those working at the Cherepovets Steel-Rolling Factory, Cherepovets confectionary factory, and a few other smaller enterprises (an additional six thousand cards). The case of "Severstal" is particularly instructive. The company was able to preserve its leading position in the domestic metallurgical industry throughout the economic downturn of the 1990s. For several years, "Severstal" had been occupying a position among the top twenty companies with the largest amount of output sold, and among the top forty companies with the largest capital. The average wage at "Severstal" was the highest in the industry. Nevertheless, the company did not avoid the problem that plagued most of the Russian economy in the 1990s: namely, wage arrears, which in 1997 were more than two months long. This was most likely one of the primary reasons that "Severstal" management became interested in implementing the salary project ("Plastikovye kartochki v Cherepovtse" 1998). By the beginning of 1998, 149 merchants' outlets in Cherepovets were accepting Meta-cards, which were issued to about 25 percent of the employed population, and about a third of the transactions were cashless (the rest involved ATM cash withdrawals) (see also Egorova 1996; Salnikov 1997b; "Chelyabinskaia oblast" 1997; "Kartochki v Sverdlovskoy oblasti" 1997; "Plastikovye kartochki v Permskoy oblasti" 1998).

Another successful distribution of salary cards took place in the town of Magnitogorsk, located on the eastern side of the Ural Mountains. This town also has one large enterprise: the Magnitogorsk Metallurgical Plant (MMK), with persistent wage arrears in the mid-1990s. The difference between the situation in Cherepovets and that of Magnitogorsk was that compared to "Severstal," MMK's overall economic standing was much more precarious, resulting in the Magnitogorsk population having little disposable cash. As a result, retailers in Magnitogorsk were even more enthusiastic about accepting cards than those in Cherepovets; Magnitogorsk stores agreed to pay the merchant discount, while those in Cherepovets insisted on free service and additional perks.

The town of Vologda in the northeastern part of European Russia experienced much greater difficulties with card distribution than Cherepovets or Magnitogorsk because it did not have an enterprise as large as "Severstal" or MMK. While Metkombank enjoyed a near-total monopoly in Cherepovets, in Vologda there were several branches of large Moscow banks in addition to local banks, and as a result there was greater competition between the card brands ("Plastikovye kartochki v Cherepovtse" 1998).

It was not only employers who were interested in salary projects. The Pension Fund (an equivalent of the Social Security Administration) picked up the idea of salary cards; the Fund was also unable to pay pensions on time because many of the companies were behind on their payments. In 1997, the Municipal Department of Social Protection of the small town of Angarsk (in the Irkutsk region in Siberia), in agreement with the regional office of the Pension Fund and the "Sibcard" company, implemented a social program in the form of a "pensioner's" card. In a format very similar to salary projects, cards were offered to local recipients of retirement benefits, albeit with one important exception: at least in this pilot project, pensioners were entirely free to choose whether to have the cards issued or not. Each month, the Angarsk Department of Social Protection would credit the pensioners' cards for the full amount of monthly benefits, and the cards could then be used in a number of local stores and other establishments, such as post office branches. Most of the stores belonged to the same industrial companies that were behind on their payments to the Pension Fund (for instance, many were owned by the local bakery "Karavay"); therefore, when retailers sold on credit, they also reduced the amount of their debt to the Pension Fund. This enabled a more convenient continuous pattern of Pension Fund payments by the companies, as opposed to the regular one-time contributions of previously accumulated funds. Given the social nature of the project, pensioners even received 5 percent discounts on card purchases. According to the organizers of the program, over time the number of pensioners' card users increased directly with the increase in pension benefits arrears (Samovarshchikova 1998).

Today arrears in salaries and payments of social benefits are for the most part a thing of the past. Nevertheless, salary pension cards continue to be popular all across Russia. For instance, in 2002, through collaboration between the Bank of Moscow and Visa, the Moscow municipal government issued Visa

Electron Moscow Social Cards to 2.5 million Muscovites who received some 350 types of subsidies from 60 agencies. As a result, in addition to bank branches, ATMs, and Visa merchants, the cards can be used to pay for public transit, health, and medical insurance and to make government-subsidized purchases at participating stores.[7]

From Debit to Credit

In the mid-1990s, salary projects almost exclusively distributed debit cards. But even then, temporary credit could be extended on a case-by-case basis. For example, if there was a delay in payment from the distributors or the municipality, the bank could credit the payroll account of the company and essentially open credit lines for the employees. In addition, as a loyalty perk, some organizations could request that the salary cards of their high-level managers have an overdraft feature. In this case, the company was required to provide the issuing bank with security deposits for such cards (Kulagin 1997; this information was also corroborated in interviews with several banks). In the latter case, salary projects shifted banks' uncertainty onto companies, which were, however, in a much better position to control their employees and pressure them to pay if necessary.

Starting in 2001–2002, overdrafts extended through salary cards became much more common. Many banks were offering credit lines of up to 70 percent or more of an individual's monthly wage not just to upper management but also to holders of ordinary salary cards (Fedorov 2003). The stipulation was that the outstanding balances should usually be paid within the next month.

Were "snowflakes" going to stir a real credit card blizzard? It seemed so, because for the first time since the start of the postcommunist transition, instead of courting only those of extraordinary status and wealth, banks started to offer credit lines to the mass consumer, an average Ivan toiling at metallurgical and manufacturing plants, confectionary factories, and oil refineries. In part, this was a result of the rise in personal incomes and the banks' increased interest in promoting retail banking services. In addition, the state contributed as well: in 2003–2004 legislation on deposit insurance and credit bureaus removed considerable obstacles for further development of both Russia's retail banking and credit card market.

Uncertainty and Complementarity

Bi-level networks helped banks to solve the problem of *uncertainty*: employers were in a much better position than banks to control and monitor their employees. The financial arrangement between the bank, the company, and the holder of a salary card was such that even in the case of an unauthorized overdraft on the card account, the employee's continuous employment would ensure that the company would post the salary to the card account, enabling the bank to pay off the negative balance. In the words of one bank's security department employee: "Salary projects pose less risk for the bank because card accounts are replenished regularly by the employer. In other words, even if [an] overdraft occurred, it would not stay on the account for long. When next month's salary is posted to the account, it first pays for the accrued interest, then for the outstanding balance, and finally debits [the] account for the remaining sum. . . . Besides, there is little risk of not finding the client."[8]

Salary projects allowed banks to move away from case-by-case evaluations of individuals considered for a card. When cards are offered in bulk, individual circumstances become irrelevant. Instead, banks focus on companies. Those employers that are related to the bank as its founders, stockholders, or business partners are not evaluated at all, and the rest are evaluated based on several criteria regarding their economic activity. "It is much easier to do than to prescreen individual cardholders," explains one of my interviewees, because company-level data are more immediately available and better verifiable, and one such verification yields not just one but hundreds or thousands of new cardholders.[9]

In addition to helping banks to manage the problem of uncertainty by issuing cards to those firmly anchored within an organizational structure, salary projects also opened an unprecedented opportunity for banks to issue cards *en masse*. This was a dramatic change from the previous era of slow and exclusive elite card issuing. Bi-level networks provided banks with much-needed access to otherwise elusive and reluctant individual consumers, promising to solve the problem of *complementarity*. Unlike the direct mailing practiced by American banks, this mass issuance of cards was as safe as it can be: individual prescreening was replaced with the screening of companies and monitoring of cardholders by employers, while the predictability of directly deposited wages provided banks with guarantees that both unauthorized overdraft and allowed credit balances would be paid off. It seemed that the Russian banks managed to have their cake and eat it too: they managed to issue cards wholesale, but without losing control over the uncertainty inherent in card granting. Moreover, they solved the problem of uncertainty without resorting to marketwide interbank cooperation and formalized information sharing. The only price that the Russian banks had to pay was the revenue that the market was able to generate. As opposed to the American card market whose main source of profit comes from finance charges on revolving credit card accounts, until recently Russian banks have been predominantly issuing debit cards and relying on cardholders' directly deposited wages (on which the banks paid very low or no interest) and various miscellaneous fees as their main source of revenues. As one card specialist admitted, "Salary projects do not bring super profits, but [they nevertheless] allow the bank to receive stable income from commissions."[10] This is changing, however, as more and more Russian banks provide routine overdrafts (and charge interest rates) on salary cards secured by cardholders' directly deposited wages.

Coercion as a Factor of Building Consumer Demand

Generating demand for novel goods and services is not a trivial matter, especially for those products that revolutionize accepted ways of doing things: paying for purchases, transmitting information, or transporting. Not only do entrepreneurs in such circumstances offer a new way of satisfying a need, but they also have to justify and legitimize this need to consumers. Consumers are pragmatic: they desire products and services to solve real problems at hand: loans to enable immediate rather than delayed consumption, drugs to alleviate present pains, and devices to increase safety. But the credit card is a novel, technologically sophisticated product, and unlike other known forms of consumer credit, its ability to deliver benefits might not be immediately apparent to potential consumers. For instance, installment credit is tied to a particular retailer, and it is reasonable to suggest that it appeared in response to the customers' desire to buy more from a particular merchant than they could afford at the time. Similarly, an auto loan or a mortgage are both tied to a particular product and serve the clear purpose of helping consumers to afford large-ticket items few of them would be able to pay for up front. So while these types of loans are constrained by the product or merchant location, credit cards are truly liberating: ideally, they can be used in any location that accepts them, for any type of product. They are also universal: they can help us afford luxuries we cannot afford to pay for in cash at the same time that they are a means of everyday convenience, used to pay for the most mundane purchases such as groceries, gas, and dry cleaning. In other words, if consumer loans and mortgages facilitate the purchasing of particular products, credit cards enable the consumer lifestyle. They deliver more to consumers than consumers themselves could ever imagine, and therefore, more than they know how to demand.

Russian card issuers could not wait for individuals to learn about the usefulness of credit cards at their own pace because, in order to attract merchants, banks had to quickly sign up a substantial number of individuals. Thus, banks resorted to coercion. Today, neither American consumers nor Russian companies need to be convinced of the advantages of cards. Because of the increased competition between card issuers, they are now in the position to choose between multiple offers. While American consumers are bombarded by preapproved offers, and often opportunistically switch from one card to another, large Russian companies organize tenders between banks in the search for the best conditions and rates. It is the majority of Russian consumers, forced to deal with whatever bank managed to woo their company, who still have no say in these matters. In the words of a vice president of a small Moscow-based bank heavily engaged in salary card programs, "Employees might not want [to have cards], but nobody asked for their opinion."[11]

The banks' position is understandable. Given the reliance on cash, informal borrowing, and overall distrust of commercial banks, they stood little chance of evoking mass demand for cards among the Russians without such a coercive element. Bi-level networks came in handy here as well: instead of enticing, attracting, and convincing each prospective cardholder individually, banks went after companies: enticing, attracting, and convincing them. Companies saw the benefit in this arrangement and were eager to free themselves from the same kind of tedious bi-level financial relationship (organization-individual) that banks were desperately longing for but could not easily achieve without the companies' help. And a seal of a happy marriage had transformed individual workers into card-carrying customers of the bank.

Salary projects are not unique to Russia, however. Issuing in a "snowflake" fashion drives card issuance in other postcommunist transitional economies, such as Ukraine, the Czech Republic, Bulgaria, and Hungary, where banks also use their corporate clients as an entryway to signing up individual cardholders. Even in China, as early as 1988, in a more exclusive version of salary projects, American Express made cards available only to employees approved by their employers.[12]

But the extent to which salary projects are instrumental in cardholder recruitment should differ. They were perfect for a post-Soviet economy such as Russia's, which featured a large urban population (73 percent of Russians were urbanites in the mid-1990s [Nezavisimy institut sotsialnoy politiki. Undated.]) and an industrialized workforce employed mainly at large or medium-size enterprises (82 percent of the labor force was employed in large enterprises alone in 1992 [Gimpelson and Lippoldt 2001]). Large industrial enterprises are particularly attractive to banks as a platform for salary projects because of the volume one salary agreement can yield. In contrast, in China in 1994, 54 percent of the labor force was still employed in agricultural production, while small and medium-size state-owned enterprises accounted for 60 percent of overall SOE employment (Cao, Qian, and Weingast 1999), and new private businesses were small, family-based companies—not as fertile ground for a salary project concept as post-Soviet economies.[13]

Conclusion

In the absence of formal institutional means to manage the prescreening, monitoring, and sanctioning traditionally found in mature consumer-credit markets (credit bureaus and collection agencies), Russian salary projects gave rise to an alternative institutional mechanism of governing bank-cardholder relations. Bi-level networks helped reduce uncertainty because bank-to-enterprise and enterprise-to-workers ties channeled information, while the organizational structure tethered workers down, restricting the flexibility of their behavior as cardholders. But reliance on ties does not inhibit market growth since hundreds or thousands of cardholders could be signed up at one time.

Are salary projects a transitional phenomenon in Russia? And if they are, will they be forgotten as an evolutionary dead-end when the center of gravity in card issuing shifts toward consumer lending and credit bureaus are established? It is likely that the distribution of cards through salary projects will eventually slow down, and there are signs that this process might have already started. But rather than being directly related to the rise of credit bureaus or competition with consumer lending, it signals that the salary-card market is reaching a saturation point, where most of the large and medium-size employers have already affiliated themselves with particular banks.

In the next chapter, I am going to test the argument I have put forth so far, that salary projects delivered an effective solution to the problem of complementarity, and will focus on the third and currently the most promising way of issuing credit cards in Russia—in connection with consumer loans.

CHAPTER SIX

The Carrot, at Last

Will Consumer Lending Lead the Way for Russia's Credit Card Market?

Salary projects, the Russian banks' second approach to card distribution, were much more successful than their predecessor, elite-issuing strategies, which issued cards through the embedded ties connecting banks and cardholders. Salary projects provided Russian banks with instantaneous access to a large number of potential cardholders with companies serving as middlemen, and sometimes even guaranteeing coverage of expenses on employees' overdraft cards. This meant that salary projects had not only solved the problem of uncertainty, but they had also tackled the issue of complementarity. Or had they?

With the rise in popularity of salary projects, both the number of cardholders and the volume of transactions were steadily increasing (Figures 6.1 and 6.2) as more and more people obtained and used cards. Starting in 2003, Russia has remained in the lead with the number of cards issued in the CEMEA region.[1]

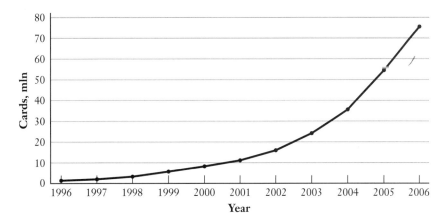

Figure 6.1 Cards Issued by Russian Banks from 1996 to 2006

Source: Data from *Platezhi. Sistemy. Kartochki.* (1998, p. 10; 1999, pp. 6–7), Central Bank of Russia (www.cbr.ru). Data are missing for 1999 and 2000.

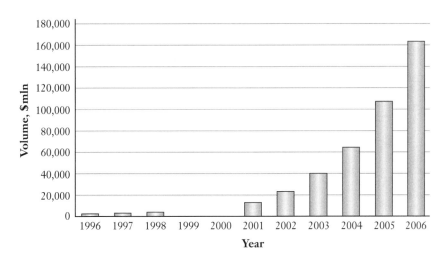

Figure 6.2 Volume of Card Transactions in Russia from 1996 to 2006

Source: Data from *Platezhi. Sistemy. Kartochki.* (1998, p. 10; 1999, pp. 6–7), Central Bank of Russia (www.cbr.ru). Data are missing for 1999 and 2000.

There was only one little nuance that was rarely making headlines in the self-aggrandizing accounts of card issuers, credit card multinationals, and bank associations: almost all of the impressive transaction volume was from cash withdrawals rather than store purchases (Figure 6.3). Even after a year of receiving salaries directly deposited to their card accounts, people tended to use them to withdraw cash. Across the country, only 15 percent of all card transactions were cashless, and only 6–7 percent of the total volume of card transactions were from retail sales. Even though the number of merchants who accepted cards had been growing, cardholders, about 80 percent of whom had received cards through salary projects, would stubbornly head to ATMs first, and then, armed with cash, to stores.[2] It turned out that implanting cards in consumers' wallets did not equate with having them used in merchants' outlets.

Banks hated this. Cash withdrawals in the banks' own ATMs were free of charge for cardholders (and most of the cardholders did just that), so unless banks found a way to bring cardholders to stores, where merchants would pay merchant discounts (a percentage of the value of the purchase that is paid to the acquiring bank and is shared with other banks through an in-

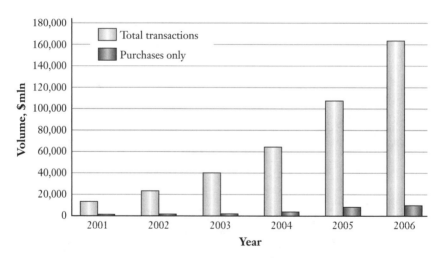

Figure 6.3 Total Card Transactions (Including Cash Withdrawals) and Retail Card Purchases in Russia from 2001 to 2006
Source: Data from the Central Bank of Russia (www.cbr.ru).

terchange system), banks would be making little money on card programs. After all, "[T]he meaning of plastic cards' spread is to rid people from the need to use cash and to make their payments easy and convenient," said Lev Gorfunkel, deputy head of the board of Interregional Investment Bank (Zaslavskaya 2005).

Multinationals hated this, too. Visa evaluates its success by its "ability to displace consumers' use of cash and checks" (Visa International 2004, 11). Cardholders' resistance to using cards signaled an unpleasant fact: despite the seeming ingenuity of salary projects as a mass-issuing strategy that also solved the problem of uncertainty, Russian banks had not managed to solve the complementarity problem after all. While they did attract cardholders, the latter preferred cash, bypassing merchants. Banks kept on cheerfully reporting increases in the number of cards, but without merchants they could not stimulate the future demand for cards, having to continue the tried-and-true method of forced dissemination of cards through salary projects.

Did Salary Projects Fail to Build the Foundations of a Self-Expanding Market?

The idea behind the initial mass issuing of cards was that the rapid increase in the number of cardholders would provide an incentive for merchants to sign up to accept cards in their locations. This would provide the market with a self-expanding quality rooted in the complementarity principle: the availability of merchants accepting cards would attract other prospective cardholders, while the growing population of cardholders would persuade new merchants to join. The history of the U.S. credit card market attests to this. American banks did not halt unsolicited mailings of cards by choice, but instead were pressured to do so by the legislation in the late 1960s. Yet the market continued growing thanks to the number of cardholders and merchants that had already signed up by that time. So if Russian salary projects generated enough card-carrying consumers, Russian banks would not have to continue with their coercive practices forever. Why didn't this plan work in Russia?

One of the main differences between the American and the Russian cases is that while for the Russians both cards and consumer credit were entirely new, the American consumer credit revolution had already occurred by the time that credit cards arrived in the mid-twentieth century. The Americans gained their experience in consumerism from buying Singer sewing machines and Model T Fords in the 1910s and 1920s. By the 1950s, many of them had already experienced consumer credit, albeit often extended to buyers directly by merchants. While credit cards brought banks directly into the picture, they became a new variation on an old tune, a greatly improved version of an already familiar product. Unlike the Russians, American consumers already knew what to say when they bought on credit ("Charge it!"); all they had to do differently was to flash their card. And unlike Russian merchants, many American merchants were also already experienced in selling on installment credit, so that accepting bank credit cards did not require such a big cognitive leap.

In addition to being inexperienced with cards, Russian consumers also exhibited a deep distrust of banks and their services. In the early-to-mid-1990s, a large number of Russians lost a significant amount of their private financial resources as a result of hyperinflation, several government-initiated currency denominations, frequent bank failures, and financial pyramid debacles, and with them, they lost a great degree of trust in private banks. Historically, cash has been the only means of payment available to Russian consumers. But distrust further contributed to Russians favoring cash over bank deposits and foreign currency, usually dollars, over rubles, apparently trusting the U.S. Treasury more than their own. While the majority of Russians were wary of banks, banks were equally cautious about prospective cardholders whose standard of living had plummeted as a result of the decade-long recession and collapsed welfare state, making lending to them a highly uncertain pursuit.

Banks found a way to control uncertainty by issuing debit rather than credit cards, that is, spreading cards but not credit, but individual consumers had no choice. If their company administration signed an agreement to have their salaries deposited in a bank, they had to accept this arrangement despite being suspicious about this bank's stability. What they could do was head straight to the ATMs. Over time, however, cardholders learned to trust banks: they did not cash all of their wages at once but withdrew money more gradually. So while cards were used more frequently, they were mainly used for trips to ATMs rather than stores. Incidentally, banks also learned to trust their cardholders, eventually offering generous overdrafts on salary cards.

Is it possible that the reason for the predominance of cash withdrawals over store purchases has to do with economic rationality? In the United States, credit cardholders are given strong incentives (grace periods and lower interest rates, as well as various perks such as cashbacks, bonuses, miles, and insurance, including on purchases) to use the cards for purchases instead of cash advances. Debit card users, on the other hand, do not usually have any special incentives; both card purchases and cash withdrawals are free if cardholders use their bank's ATM, except for some similar competition-induced perks and promotions tied to cashless transactions.

In Russia, grace periods were not available until January 1, 2005, after an amendment to Russia's Tax Code was passed making short-term loans taken during interest-free grace periods exempt from taxation.[3] It was argued that being taxed on credit card balances during grace periods made it prohibitive to use credit cards to pay for purchases, and that it prevented their wider use. But this should not have mattered for the use of debit cards, which have always been the predominant type of cards issued in Russia.

A look at the fees charged by the leaders of the Russian card market in 1997 and 1998 on various Visa and MasterCard transactions (Table 6.1) suggests that only one bank, Kredit-Moskva, charged more for using cards in stores than for cash withdrawals from their ATMs (1.5 percent versus 0 percent). Another bank, Dialog-bank, charged the same percentage on purchases (0.5 percent) as it did on cash withdrawals in rubles, and so did Sberbank, for which both purchases and cash withdrawals were free of charge. The rest of the banks charged cardholders *more* to withdraw money from the ATM than to use cards directly for purchases.[4]

In 1997 and 1998, two card monthlies, *Mir Kartochek* and *Platezhi. Sistemy. Kartochki.*, published regular tables comparing transaction fees on Russian cards. These tables further confirm the trend. In 1997, *all* of the banks with one exception had purchase fees lower than their cash withdrawal fees.[5] By 1998, the majority of banks in the sample did not charge any fees at all for using cards in the stores.[6] In other words, there were *no* economic barriers to using the cards for retail purchases; on the contrary, there were clear advantages.[7] By the end of 1997, desperate to get cardholders to buy, a few Russian banks offered discounts on card store purchases. For instance, Rossiyskiy Kredit offered a 0.2 percent *bonus* on each store purchase ("Za kazhduyu pokupku po plastikovoy karte 'Rossiyskiy Kredit' nachal platit dengi" 1998). Banks also periodically ran promotional campaigns promising prizes for card users in retail locations.

If the fee structure favored store purchases, perhaps another explanation for cardholders' resistance to using the cards in retail locations is that there were simply not enough merchants who accepted cards. This was a regular complaint of the 1990s: in the haste of issuing cards through salary projects,

TABLE 6.1

Fees Charged by Russian Banks for Cash Withdrawals and Noncash Transactions on Visa and Europay/MasterCards in 1998

	Visa Classic, MasterCard Mass, Visa and MC Gold			Visa Electron/Plus and Cirrus/Maestro		
	Store Purchases, %	Cash from Own ATM, %	Cash from Another ATM, %	Store Purchases, %	Cash from Own ATM, %	Cash from Another ATM, %
Dialog-bank	0.5	0.5 (RUR) 1.5 ($)	1.5 (min $3 - max $10)	0	0 (RUR) 1 ($)	1 (min $3)
Sberbank	0	0*	0.5	0	0*	0.5
Bank Moskva	0	1	1 (min 20,000 RUR or $3)	0	0 0.5 ($)	0.5 (min 20,000 RUR or $3)
ONEXIMbank	0	1	1.5 (min $3)	0	0.5	1.5 (min $1.5)
Toribank	0	1–1.5	na	0	1	na
Kredit-Moskva	1.5	0	1.5 (min $3)	0	0	1.5 (min $3)
Mosbiznesbank	0	1	na	na	na	na
Avtobank	0	1	1	0	1	1
Alfabank	0	1.5	na	na	na	na
Inkombank	0.5	1	na	na	na	na
MENATEP	0	1	na	na	na	na
Mostbank	0	0.5	na	na	na	na
Rossiyskiy Kredit	0	1	na	na	na	na
SBS-Agro	0.3	1	na	na	na	na

Source: Data from banks' brochures and advertising materials, *Mir Kartochek* 15 (1997), p. 13.

*0.5% for cash withdrawals from Sberbank ATMs or branches in other service zones than the one where the card was issued. Sberbank's branches are located all over the country. The city of Moscow and Moscow region are considered to be one service zone.

banks were "forgetting" to also invest in expanding the network of merchants, which was especially problematic in the regional towns. The Russian magazine *Finans* reported on one bank that issued salary cards to the oil field workers located in a remote area of Siberia. That bank ended up sending a once-a-month helicopter with an ATM connected to a satellite to assist with cash withdrawals (Logvinova 2005). Needless to say, there were no opportunities there at all to use cards for noncash purchases. In 2006, when the number of issued cards passed the fifty million mark, there were only 120 thousand retail locations nationwide that accepted cards as a means of payment. While most of them were located in Moscow (where the number of cards per capita was also the highest), as many as two-thirds of Moscow stores did not accept them, including some large supermarkets and chain stores, such as the French Auchan or the homegrown Pyatyorochka and Kopeyka ("Kreditka nedoveriya" 2006; "Obyazatelnaya karta" 2006).

Those merchants who accepted cards in the 1990s tended to be high-end stores that attracted foreign tourists and a limited number of well-to-do Russians but not common folk, who continued buying at cash-only markets and from street vendors. While the number of merchants who accept cards has been growing steadily, new ATMs are being added faster than new POS terminals in merchants' locations. In 2005, the number of merchants' locations accepting cards grew 12 percent, while the number of ATMs grew 23 percent (RosBusinessConsulting 2006). The ratio of ATMs to card-accepting merchants worldwide is 1:24. In 1997 in Russia it was 1:13, meaning that there were too few POS terminals in merchants' locations compared to the number of ATMs. ATMs grew even further to one ATM for every six POS terminals in 2004.[8]

The reason that retail locations that accept cards are in short supply is not only because of the banks. Merchants often exhibit their own strong preference for cash. Even large merchants sometimes resist accepting cards, which they see as more of a drawback: in addition to having to pay a merchant discount fee on all card transactions, electronic record-keeping would make their sales immediately transparent. Anecdotal evidence suggests that many stores, including big supermarkets, lower their reported turnover by paying some of their suppliers in cash and retailing these goods on cash, without any official receipts. This allows retailers to claim lower taxes.

President Putin recently implemented a number of measures intended to reduce the size of Russia's underground economy. These measures include the introduction of a 13 percent flat income tax rate in 2001, a significant reduction and simplification of business taxes, increased sanctions for tax evasion, and a widely announced amnesty on previously unreported savings. But despite these efforts, Russia remains a cash economy. A large portion of wages in Russia are still being paid in cash to reduce taxes for businesses, and subsequently, income taxes for employees.[9] In the words of Valery Nikitin, card department head from Avtobank: "It is difficult for Russian people to get out of the habit of using cash. It is tied to many things: tax evasion . . . , [an] underdeveloped card acceptance network, lack of experience among people of using bank accounts, and simply the basic habit of always relying on cash" ("Kak Avtobank rabotaet s plastikovymi kartochkami" 1996). In other words, a cultural and historical preference for cash is reinforced by strong practical reasons to favor cash over electronic transfers. An obvious link between cash and illegal trade even led a radical politician to suggest that the Russian government delegitimize cash altogether (Zhirinovskiy and Jurovitskiy 1998). Duma's committee on Banks and Banking Activities has recently announced that it is going to put forward a draft proposal that would mandate card acceptance in large retail locations (those with a monthly turnover of more than $20,000). If made law, this proposal would contribute greatly to expanding the merchants' card-acceptance network in Russia and promoting the development of the card market.

Another possible explanation for the overwhelming resistance of Russian cardholders to cashless transactions has to do with the essence of salary cards, which comprise the overwhelming majority of cards issued in Russia. Salary cards are issued to *employees* at their workplace, rather than to *consumers*. Therefore, using salary cards as a means of payment requires connecting these two different social roles, making a cognitive leap from being an employer to being a consumer, from being compensated for one's labor to shopping, and from the productive context of a workplace to consumption and the mall. Perhaps, salary cards' descriptive name contributed to this difficulty as well: it signaled the primary function of the cards and limited their use to accessing salary accounts. Salary cards became earmarked in exactly the way that Zelizer describes the earmarking of money (Zelizer 1994), when the source of monies determined (or at least, severely limited) their uses. The same way that gift money cannot usually be used for mundane purchases such as groceries, salary cards do not translate well into the means of consumption.[10] While I cannot test this assertion with the data I collected, this is a plausible argument which would underscore the role of cultural repertoires in shaping economic action.

To sum up, there are three possible explanations for the dominance of cash withdrawals over store purchases: a strong cash preference among both consumers and merchants, insufficient development of the merchants' acceptance network, and the earmarking of salary cards as a means of compensation rather than consumption. These are the barriers to the successful development of the Russian credit card market. What I am going to argue in the rest of the chapter is that consumer lending, the third and most recent method of distributing credit cards in Russia, has been able to address all three of these problems.

Russia's Consumer Credit Boom

If salary projects were the stick (which, incidentally, did not work as intended), consumer lending is undoubtedly the carrot. Where the former forced, the latter lures. Russia is believed to be in the middle of a consumer credit boom, which is shared by other Eastern European transitional countries, such as Bulgaria, Romania, and Ukraine. Lending to households in Russia has been increasing on average about 90 percent each year starting in 2000, from just $1 billion to more than 1 trillion rubles (about $34 billion) by January 1, 2006 and more than 2 trillion rubles a year later (Figure 6.4) (Bush 2004; Prokop'ev 2006). So popular has consumer lending become in Russia that its annual growth rate during the last several years has been surpassing that of household deposits held in banks and of banks' lending to enterprises, a long-time banks' favorite (Figure 6.5). A quarter of Russians took out consumer loans in 2004, and 39 percent did so in 2005 (Kopylova 2006). Lending to households now comprises more than 10 percent of banks' assets. And the experts predict exponential growth for the next few years. Separate geographic regions show an even more impressive dynamic of growth. For instance, in

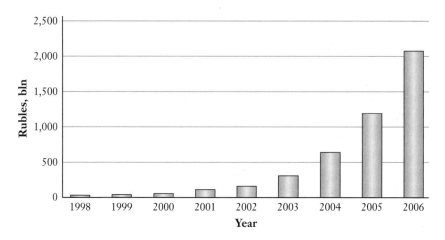

Figure 6.4 Bank Lending to Russian Households from 1998 to 2006
Source: Data from the Central Bank of Russia (www.cbr.ru).

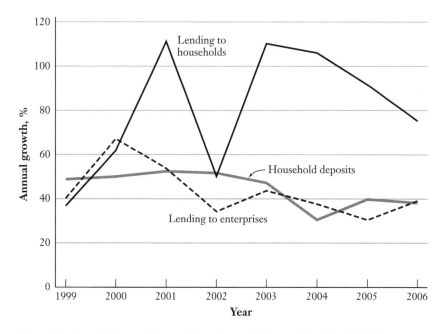

Figure 6.5 Annual Growth Rates of Lending to Households, Household Deposits, and Lending to Enterprises in Russia from 1999 to 2006
Source: Data from the Central Bank of Russia (www.cbr.ru).

the Sverdlovsk region in the Ural Mountains, the consumer credit volume grew more than fifteen times in just three years: from 2 billion rubles in 2002 to 32 billion rubles in 2005 (Starkov 2005). Credit cards are playing a major role in this consumer revolution. No longer viewed exclusively as status symbols, or as a means to expand the banks' deposit base, they are now an integral part of Russian banks' broader strategy in household lending.

What contributed to the spectacular growth in consumer lending? Why has it been expanding so dynamically starting in 2000–2001? There are several reasons that explain it:

- Banks' search for new sources of profits and the rise in popularity of retail banking
- The need to lure clients lost as a result of the 1998 crisis of the state-owned Sberbank
- Overall economic growth that translated into higher incomes and higher demand for credit
- The rise and spread of large consumer chains and shopping malls, many of them owned by foreign or multinational corporations

As explained in Chapter Three, the 1998 financial crisis coincided with the disappearance of banks' old sources of profits: state budget resources were being withdrawn from all but a few specialized banks, accounts of large companies were already divided, and the corporate banking market was getting very competitive. Many banks previously specializing in corporate banking started to diversify their services to include retail operations. Some newly organized banks focused entirely on catering to individual clients, developing mass products such as credit cards and consumer loan programs. Others were actively getting into the retail market, undoubtedly attracted to the very high rates of returns on household lending, as some of the household lending leaders end up charging 40–50 percent interest a year, if one accounts for various additional charges and fees, often not stated upfront (Table 6.2).

Commercial banks that survived the crisis had to win back the depositors they lost as a result of the crisis of the state-owned Sberbank. To compete, commercial banks had to develop new services that the sluggish and unwieldy Sberbank was not able or willing to offer. Mass consumer credit, especially

TABLE 6.2

*Advertised and Real APR on Consumer Loans
in Select Banks in Russia in 2005*

	Advertised APR	Account maintenance fee, % per month	Real APR
Home Credit&Finance	28.5	1.99	52.38
Russkiy Standart	23	1.9	45.8
Citibank	24–28	1.5–1.84	42–50
Deltabank	28	1.8	49.6
Impexbank	18	0.8	27.6

Source: Olga Kuzina, "Credit Card Market in Russia," talk given at the Hungarian Academy of Sciences, Budapest, December 16, 2005. Used by permission.

express loans and credit cards, became such a draw for Russian consumers. Despite being the leader of the consumer credit market, Sberbank's application procedure is reportedly very cumbersome; at the time of writing this book, it was not offering express loans or revolving credit cards.

The after-crisis period also saw the subsequent steady growth of the economy, an increase in incomes and consumer purchasing power. After a decade-long recession, Russia's GDP grew 6.4 percent in 1999, and since that time averaged 6.7 percent annually (Figure 6.6). The average real monthly earnings of workers rose 19.8 percent in 2001, following an increase of 23 percent in 2000 (Tennenbaum 2002). Real incomes have been rising by an average of 11 percent a year, and the consumer sector as a whole has doubled in size over the last decade. Mikhail Terentiev, an analyst with Moscow's Troika-Dialog, claims that "Russia has one of the fastest-growing income and consumption rates in the world" (Mainville 2007). One of the secrets of a seemingly insatiable consumer demand is that, despite relatively low average income (about $300 in Russia overall, but at least twice as much in Moscow), an unusually high proportion of it—70 to 80 percent—is discretionary thanks to continued government utility subsidies, low flat-rate income tax, and housing privatization, which allowed millions of Russians to own their Soviet-era apartments outright, without the need for mortgages (Bush 2006).[11]

The growth in the living standards was met with the intensification of consumer desires. Writing on the rise of consumer society in the post–World War II United States, Gelpi and Julien-Labruyere (2000) argue that consumption enabled members of the growing middle class to acquire a social status that would otherwise have been unavailable to them. These people could not base their status on any ascribed characteristics such as their cast position, an aristocratic title, or possession of property. They were the wage earners who borrowed in order to consume for their personal pleasure rather than to invest in business. The acquisition of consumer goods, therefore, "became the symbol of the middle-class style of life" (Gelpi and Julien-Labruyere 2000, 106). One can draw interesting parallels with the transitional society, which emerged out of the socialist period virtually classless, with suppressed income inequality, and with endemic shortages on most consumer goods. Consumption appears to be one of the most obvious means of social differentiation and status achievement available to a growing number of wage earners in today's Russia.

Retailers enthusiastically welcomed the growing consumer demand and purchasing power (Figure 6.6). The after-crisis period saw the emergence of numerous retail chains, among them those specializing in groceries, consumer

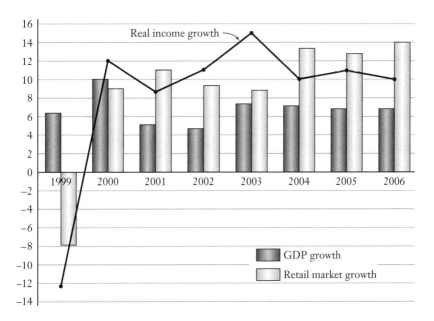

Figure 6.6 GDP, Retail Market, and Real Income Growth Rates in Russia from 1999 to 2006

Source: Data from the Russian Federal Statistical Service (www.gks.ru).

electronics, and home goods. Fourteen new shopping centers (many of them built by French, German, and Turkish retailers and developers) opened in 2001 alone (Thorne 2002). The Swedish furniture retailer IKEA recently opened a $400 million, 230,000-square-meter (almost 2.5 million square feet) MEGA-2 shopping mall in the northern suburb of Moscow, the largest and busiest shopping mall in Eastern Europe, which in 2005 was frequented by more than 50 million people (Mainville 2007). This was the second such mall built by IKEA in Russia; the first one opened in 2002 in the southern suburb of Moscow. As of December 2006, eight MEGA malls were open in Russia.

Shopping mall culture familiar to Western consumers is also developing in Russia. Many consider shopping to be quality family time and visit the malls weekly. At MEGA-2 mall, some visitors come primarily to relax, walk around, eat, or skate at a free skating rink rather than shop: "Where else could we go in this area?" A group of three female consumers explains, "Here it is nice, warm, and clean in a European way. Our winters are terrible. And here one can wear light clothing. Kids are running around. A person that is dressed lightly feels differently, don't you think?" (Kozul'kova 2006). Shopping, even if just window shopping, is becoming a way of life. And Moscow, the largest European city with 8.5 million inhabitants, is becoming the shopping Mecca of the postcommunist world. IKEA boasts that its two Moscow stores have three times the sales level of the stores elsewhere in Eastern Europe, surpassing IKEA's own projections.

Down the road from MEGA-1 is the Rolf car dealership, where daily sales average fifteen to twenty Mitsubishi and Hyundai cars. Overall, sales of foreign cars in Russia grew 57 percent in 2005 (a sixfold increase since 2001) and reached 600,000. The number of cell phones in use jumped from 3 million in 2000 to 150 million in 2006, according to the Minister of Information and Communication Leonid Reiman. At least 20 percent of households own a computer, a fourfold increase from 2001 (Bush 2006). According to A. T. Kearney's 2005 Global Retail Development Index, Russia is the second-most attractive market for international retailers after India.[12]

Consumers enjoyed higher incomes, merchants had more goods to offer and were interested in attracting consumers, and banks were looking for new sources of profits. The timing seemed to be perfect for banks to promote consumer lending. They jumped at this opportunity, seeing that it also helped promote the credit card market.

Express Lending as a Way to Promote Credit Cards

The fastest-growing segment of the consumer credit market are express loans, small short-term loans extended in stores and shopping malls to finance consumer purchases (electronics, furniture, and computer equipment). To reach consumers, banks open up makeshift booths with one or two representatives that accept applications. Consumers are approved while they wait and can walk home with the goods they have chosen. According to the Russian national pollster VTsIOM's 2006 opinion poll, 59 percent of all borrowers obtain their loans in stores, while only 38 percent obtain them from bank branches (Kozul'kova 2006).

Express loans are becoming a direct vehicle of promoting the credit card market. For instance, DeltaBank, recently purchased by GE Consumer Finance, extends express loans in the form of revolving credit cards, Visa Electron Instant Issue cards, that can be used anywhere Visa is accepted. The cards are issued to finance the purchase or to provide cash advances up to the specified limit. "Customers are learning how to use credit cards as they are tied to a relatively familiar concept of installment credit," explains Deltabank's Deputy Head of the Board Dmitry Ishchenko.[13] This is how the process of applying for a card usually works:

> It's a Tuesday morning in Moscow, and Konstantin Savelyev, a twenty-nine-year-old security guard, is shopping with his family at the huge IKEA furniture store at Khimki, north of [Russia's] capital. He and his wife want to buy toys and bedroom furniture for Artyom, their eighteen-month-old son. But before making the purchases, Savelyev has to complete another task. He sits for twenty minutes in the office of Delta Bank, located inside the store, giving personal information to a sales assistant. She types the data into the bank's computer. After a few minutes, good news. He is approved for a Visa credit card with a $500 limit and an interest rate of 24 percent a year. Savelyev is pleased. "The amount you have to pay back is miniscule compared to what you earn, so it doesn't have a big impact on the family budget," he says (Bush 2004).

By the end of 2004, the bank had issued 140,000 Visa Electron Instant Issue cards, worth $40 million in credit.

Russkiy Standart, the leader of the Russian credit card market, was established in 1999, and by the middle of 2004, it had made 3.2 million express loans worth $4.1 billion (77 percent of the consumer loan market). Its growth has been spectacular, in just three years since its birth becoming one of the five most profitable banks in Russia. In 2004, Russkiy Standart showed a profit of $59 million, which prompted *The Banker* to name it one of the most profitable banks in the world (Bush 2004). But unlike DeltaBank, it issues credit cards to those who have already successfully repaid their express loans (such borrowers become automatically eligible for a credit card). The majority of Russkiy Standart cards are revolving credit cards, and the bank considers express loans the main way of increasing their credit card holder clientele. Of more than three million cards the bank had issued by 2005, only about one hundred thousand (less than 3 percent) were issued through bank branches.[14] To attract potential customers for express loans, Russkiy Standart works with large stores, such as household electronics retailer M-Video, which reports that 30 to 50 percent of their sales are now done on credit ("Bytovaya tehnika—eto ne pirozhki i ne yogurt" 2002).

The founder of Russkiy Standart, Roustam Tariko, a fantastically successful Russian entrepreneur previously known as the manufacturer of "Russkiy Standart" vodka, was named by *Business Week* in 2004 among the twenty-five "Stars of Europe: Leaders at the Forefront of Change." Bold and unconventional, Tariko recalls that all the newspapers were making fun of his choice to name the bank after the vodka brand. But in fact, he jokes, vodka and banking have something in common: they both make your wishes come true ("Roustam Tariko" 2004). There is at least one other obvious similarity between drinking and buying on credit: both can become addictive and lead to ruin if not controlled.

Will Consumer Lending Succeed Where Salary Projects Failed?

Consumer lending, or more specifically, express lending, might be that long-sought magic wand that would turn cash-loving, salary-card-holding Russians into avid credit card users. According to Visa International, 55 percent of credit card holders in Russia obtained them through retail locations, either in connection with an express loan or following a successful repayment of such a loan.[15] This card marketing strategy seems to have a better chance of succeeding than the salary projects.

What makes it different? Both salary projects and consumer loans have been viewed as powerful tools of card dissemination in Russia, but while salary projects were firmly associated with the spread of cards in the mid-to-late-1990s, consumer lending spearheaded the card issuance of the twenty-first century. Salary projects targeted workers at their workplace, while consumer loans are extended to shoppers at retail locations (Table 6.3). If one of the problems with salary projects was the missing link between compensation for one's labor and consumption, consumer lending took care of this: prospective cardholders are approached while they are consuming, the cards now being firmly associated with leisure and pleasure rather than work. Moreover, while salary projects failed to bring merchants into the picture, consumer lending starts with the merchants: they and their merchandize are used as bait for prospective cardholders. Instead of encouraging cardholders to take their cards into stores and expecting merchants to sign up, the banks unite with merchants to encourage consumption, which they make possible with express loans. Finally, while salary projects were seriously challenged by cash preference, consumer lending addressed this problem head on: merchandise that would be unaffordable on cash alone lures consumers to turn to the help of loans and credit cards. As in a classic consumer society, wants are reinterpreted as needs, which consumer credit helps satisfy. As one of our interviewees put it: "People would not have come to the bank [to apply for a card], but are eagerly coming to stores . . . Retail lending is most actively developed through the system of retail stores. This is where customers get [the] burning desire to buy, and this is when they are most likely to want to apply for cards." [16]

While being instrumental in card distribution, both salary projects and consumer loans made it possible for banks to achieve another goal: they allowed banks to significantly expand their retail operations without additional investments in the development of branches. If salary projects supplied banks with scores of new depositors, card distribution in retail locations enabled banks to increase the volume of retail lending.

Still, salary projects and consumer lending were more different than similar. While both facilitated card distribution as a result of forming bi-level networks and tying banks to organizations (employers and retailers, respectively), and through organizations—to potential cardholders, these bi-level networks performed differently in the two cases.

In the case of salary projects, bi-level networks provided banks with *relational* benefits: since employers have ongoing control over workers, they facilitated both access and screening. Ties with retailers, on the other hand, only endowed the banks with *locational* benefits: merchants enabled the banks to have access to potential cardholders, therefore solving the problem of complementarity. Banks were able to approach the retailer-consumer relationship and make themselves indispensable to both parties by providing

TABLE 6.3

Signing Cardholders Up: Stick Versus Carrot

	Salary Projects	Consumer Loans
Target audience	Workers	Consumers
Method	Force	Lure
Location	Workplace	Point of consumption
What location provided	Access to potential cardholders and ability to control uncertainty. Employers as middlemen. But merchants are not part of the picture.	Access only. Banks as middlemen between consumers and merchants. Merchants as bait.
Other incentives	Growth of the number of customers and volume of deposits without investments in branch development.	Growth of consumer credit without investments in branch development
Benefit of bi-level networks	Relational	Locational
Problems solved	Uncertainty, but no complementarity	Complementarity but no uncertainty
Starting point	Card	Credit
Next Step	Switching cardholders from cash withdrawals to card purchases.	Switching from special-purpose purchasing credit to general-purpose revolving credit cards, from a one-shot deal to a long-term relationship.
Main Problem	How to take the next step? How to link cardholders to merchants? How to make them bypass ATMs and take their cards to stores?	How to reduce uncertainty at the consumer credit stage? How to prescreen quickly and effectively?
Solution	Hinges on changes in cardholders' behavior. Depends on transferring salary cards from the work context to the consumption context.	Hinges much less on cardholders' behavior, more on changes in banks' own strategy.

the often-missing element of a successful transition: financing. But consumers are not tied to retailers in the same way that workers are anchored in their employers' organizational hierarchies. Unlike employer-employee relations, which are long-term, mutual, contractual obligations, consumer-retailer relations are fleeting, usually anonymous, and for this reason they cannot help prescreen, monitor, or sanction. What makes retailers attractive for banks is that shoppers flock to stores, and they do not have to be convinced to buy—this is the main reason that they are there. Therefore, rather than struggling to create consumer demand for cards, banks ride on the wave of a quickly growing retail market capitalizing on the success of retailers in shaping demand for the symbols of the middle-class life-style: new furniture, consumer electronics, and computers. Moreover, retailers have the power of escalating consumers' desires to make them want more than they can afford at that moment, and thereby open up possibilities for bank financing. But when it comes to consumer lending, banks get no help in handling uncertainty. They and they alone have to devise means to screen, monitor, and sanction borrowers. Thus, while retailers are useful in attracting consumers, they cannot help banks in solving the uncertainty problem.

Salary projects helped banks to reach individuals and arm them with cards while containing uncertainty. They were successful in and of themselves (the concept was solid), but to be useful for the burgeoning credit card market, banks had to find a way to make the leap from salary cards to credit cards and solve the problem of complementarity: to send cardholders to the stores and switch them from bimonthly salary withdrawals to regular card purchases (Figure 6.7a). Consumer lending, on the other hand, promotes the credit card market in a direct and unimpeded manner, as cards become instruments of lending. But unlike salary projects, consumer lending as a concept is itself built on a shaky foundation: unless the problem of uncertainty is successfully handled, the increasing volume of lending may result in a crisis of mounting defaults (Figure 6.7b).

A comparison between all four strategies of card distribution (U.S. unsolicited mailings, Russian elite issuing, salary projects, and consumer lending) reveals that none of them managed to successfully solve both problems at once (Table 6.4). Elite issuing was limited, and therefore, while secure, could not saturate the market with enough cards to attract merchants. Salary projects, again, were a low-uncertainty strategy that also failed to reach complementarity

(a)   (b)

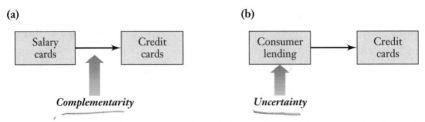

Figure 6.7 Barriers in the Transition from Salary Cards and Consumer Lending to Credit Cards

TABLE 6.4

Comparison of Different Solutions to the Uncertainty and Complementarity Problems

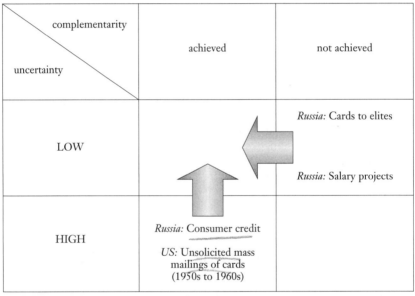

uncertainty \ complementarity	achieved	not achieved
LOW		*Russia:* Cards to elites *Russia:* Salary projects
HIGH	*Russia:* Consumer credit *US:* Unsolicited mass mailings of cards (1950s to 1960s)	

despite distributing cards wholesale. Using consumer lending to promote credit cards is a strategy very similar to the one employed by American banks. Both U.S. unsolicited mailings and Russian consumer lending were each in their own way successful in solving the problem of complementarity, but in the haste to saturate the market with cards, banks exhibited a profound disregard for uncertainty. U.S. banks mailed cards to millions of people without any screening, not even name verifications. Russian banks issue cards with very basic and quick verification, and little attempt at testing the effectiveness of their screening methods.

Growing Defaults

Because decisions on express loans are made on the spot within thirty to forty minutes, bank officers usually have little to rely on besides the information supplied by the applicant. At best, application information is run through a basic scoring or point model (many of them were developed in the West but "adapted" to the Russian reality), but often without even verifying whether the information used is valid because of time constraints. In some cases, all that is needed to successfully obtain an express loan is one's passport. So even when the decision-making process is routinized, data is limited or its quality is questionable: it mainly comes from one source—the applicant, who undoubtedly has an incentive to conceal damaging information, and it mainly covers issues pertaining to the present rather than reflecting on the applicant's past behavior.

What is surprising is that while 76 percent of banks consider credit risk their biggest problem, according to Russia's Central Bank, they express a profound disregard for screening (Central Bank of Russia 2006). Several of the interviewed banks claimed they were much more concerned about attracting new customers and increasing their market share, preferring to worry about uncertainty and developing screening techniques later. This is clearly the opposite of the banks' old strategy of anchoring cardholders in personal networks.

One possible explanation for such seemingly reckless behavior has been voiced a few times during the interviews. Currently, the rate of foreign ownership among Russian banks remains quite low, lower than the equivalent in several other post-Soviet states, such as Ukraine or Georgia ("Krupneyshie banki SNG" 2006). The prevailing sentiment is that once foreign banks arrive (perhaps when the last barriers are removed with Russia's ascendance to the WTO), domestic banks will not be able to successfully compete. Those Russian banks that most aggressively develop their retail clientele base are suspected in the banking community of "preparing for the big sale" because claiming a large portion of the retail market might be one way to attract foreign buyers.[17] In 2004, Russkiy Standart was going through sales negotiations with the French BNP Paribas bank (which was going to buy a 50 percent interest in the holding that controls 90 percent of the bank), but the deal fell through ("BNP Paribas Let Russian Standard Go" 2006). The Austrian

Raiffeisenbank recently purchased Impexbank, ranked twenty-first among the banks by assets in Russia, with 190 branches and 350 retail loan outlets. This puts Raiffeisen in the fourth place in Russia's retail loan market.[18]

Needless to say, a strategy that disregards prescreening can lead to disaster. What is particularly troubling is that in the absence of reliable information sharing in the lending market, banks are in the dark about the extent of their borrowers' other debts.

Some warning signs of a possible crisis with nonpayments are already appearing in the Russian market. While overall the rate of defaults remains low (less than 2 percent, according to the Central Bank of Russia, across all the banks and all kinds of credit), in express lending it is much higher.[19] Individual banks that most actively specialize in express lending report rates as high as 6.94 percent in Russkiy Standart, 7.85 percent in Finansbank, and a staggering 15 percent in Home Credit&Finance ("Noveyshaya kreditnaya istoriya" 2006; Samotorova 2005). Viktor Sorin, director of the Consumer Debt Collection Agency, reflecting on his experience of working in Russkiy Standart, claims that more than 50 percent of borrowers of express loans delay their payments (Starkov 2005). Moreover, during the first eleven months of 2004, the default rate grew faster than the volume of credit to households (102.2 percent and 72.6 percent, respectively) (Papernaya 2004). Currently, according to Andrei Kashevarov, deputy head of the Federal Antitrust Office, defaults are growing at twice the rate as that of consumer lending (Prokop'ev 2006).

In response to the market frenzy surrounding express lending, Sberbank also decided to test the waters in 2005. It opened experimental express-lending offices in three retail locations, but quickly discovered that 90 of their 359 borrowers (25 percent) fell behind in their payments (Zarshchikov 2006). As a result, the experiment was halted. The bank publicly announced that while it was planning to issue revolving credit cards, it would do so in a traditional fashion, in bank branches, because it concluded that express lending was too risky. "It is impossible to ensure control over loan repayment in such circumstances," admitted Andrei Kazmin, Sberbank's president and head of the board ("Sberbank ne verit klientam v magazinah, nadeyas uvidet ih v svoih otdeleniyah" 2006).

Central Bank officials started to express concern that if the growth rate of household borrowing continues, in a few years the population won't be able to pay debts back. According to an independent Russian market research company, ROMIR, almost two-thirds of borrowers spend 25 percent of their family income to pay off debts, 15 percent of borrowers spend between 25 percent and 50 percent, and 5 percent, more than half of their monthly family income (2005).

Three Market Logics and Three Channels of Card Distribution

Over the last fifteen years, the dominant distribution channel of payment cards in Russia shifted from the bank branch, to the enterprise, and finally, to the shopping mall, focusing first on the VIP client, then on the worker, and finally, on the consumer.

In the early-to-mid-1990s, the majority of Russian banks viewed card programs as part of their publicity campaign or an attempt to satisfy the needs of their VIP clients. The consensus was that the mass consumer was not yet ready for a card. Those banks that lacked any real interest in expanding card issuing beyond the reach of embedded ties, therefore, relied on their branches as the main vehicle of card distribution. They did so not because anybody can walk in, apply for a card, and be approved. On the contrary, at that time, a frequent confession common among banks was, "We do not work with people from the street." Branches were there to accept applications and to establish those ties and links that made applicants eligible for a card, even if applicants were not linked to the bank, but were evaluated as part of their own embedded and stable networks, i.e., anchored (Guseva and Róna-Tas 2001).

The rise in the popularity of salary projects signified the banks' increased interest in expanding the market further and spreading cards wider (and a related interest in attracting additional financial resources by increasing the number of depositors). The enterprise became the primary channel of card distribution for the next several years. But as I argued previously, salary cards did not do the trick. While they did transform thousands of workers into cardholders, they could not complete the magic by turning them into consumers. And the Russian card market probably would have remained underdeveloped (with cardholders mainly using their cards to withdraw cash) had it not been for the rise of consumer lending.

Consumer lending allowed banks to move card distribution closer to where the cards were intended to be used: in stores. The shopping mall became the main locus of card spread, both physically and philosophically. What this signaled, for the first time in the history of the Russian credit card market, was that banks were targeting mass consumers. The mall replaced the branch and the enterprise, but, of course, not entirely. Branches still accept applications, and salary projects are there to stay as well. But the action in the card market is now in malls, and that includes the profits.

The move from the branch to the enterprise and to the mall was accompanied by a similar move from prestigious Visas and MasterCards with large security deposits affordable to the affluent and well-connected few, to cheap debit Cirrus/Maestro and Electron or Russian local-brand cards, to a still small but growing number of Visas and MasterCards with revolving credit lines that are targeting Russia's growing middle class.

This switch is particularly illustrative in the case of Visas. Prior to 2004, the most popular places (judging by the sales volume) accepting Visa cards to pay for goods and services in Russia were high-end hotels, airline ticket counters, expensive boutiques, and restaurants. In 2004, for the first time, they gave way to large retail chains, such as M-Video, Ramstor, Perekrestok, Tvoy Dom, Starik Hottabych, and others.[20] This illustrates two tendencies. On one hand, a change in card users, from mostly foreign visitors (thus hotels and airline counters) using cards issued by foreign banks, to Russians using cards issued by domestic banks. On the other hand, the fact that among the leaders in card sales are popular grocery store chains such as Ramstor and Perekrestok suggests that this is also a change in what cards can pay for and how they are perceived. Cards are increasingly viewed as a means to pay for day-to-day household consumption rather than only infrequent and expensive purchases. Correspondingly, the size of the average card transaction has been declining. Visa, for instance, reports a decline from $130 to less than $80 ("Lou Naumovski: 'Uspeh bankovskoy roznitsy opredelyaetsya masshtabom biznesa'" 2005). This is corroborated by Russia's Central Bank: while the share of the retail sales volume in the total volume of card transactions has changed little since 2001 (from 6.93 percent in 2001 to 5.95 percent in 2004), the share of the number of retail transactions among all card transactions grew from 10 percent in 2001 to 15 percent in 2003 (Euromonitor International 2004). That the size of card purchases is getting smaller suggests that cards are increasingly being used to pay for everyday needs, transforming them from a symbol of luxury and prestige to a means of daily convenience.

Why did some banks decide to become pioneers in card issuing, even in an abridged form that hardly resembled mainstream Western credit cards, while others refrained? Can the resulting variation in strategy be explained by any of the banks' characteristics? For the most part, the banks that were actively promoting the market in the early-to-mid-1990s were the largest, well-known, and politically influential ones.[21] For instance, the first Russian bank members of Visa were Sberbank and Kredobank (since 1989). In 1992 they were joined by MENATEP, in 1993 by Mostbank and Inkombank, and soon after by Rossiyskiy Kredit, Avtobank, SBS, and others. These were the same banks that fiercely competed for the status of authorized banks, for privatization tenders, and for the loans-for-shares program, as detailed in Chapter Three. These banks viewed card programs as a way to maintain their status with their elite customers and among peer banks, while their size and reputation helped them negotiate memberships in international card networks.

These pioneers managed to preserve their leading market positions when the center of gravity of card issuing moved to salary projects. Here, the main characteristic that determined the banks' success was an already developed corporate line of business because salary cards were initially issued to employees of existing corporate customers.[22] This group was significantly larger, including not only Moscow-based banks, but also those from St. Petersburg and large regional centers.

The composition of the group that is leading the latest strategy of issuing cards in retail outlets is quite different since many of the largest banks active in card issuing in the 1990s heavily invested in the State Treasury bonds, and as a result, took the hardest hit in the August 1998 crisis. Few of the previous leaders survived unscathed, and a lot of new banks entered the market in 1999–2000. This third group is also the most heterogeneous of the three, in terms of banks' size, ownership, and age. Some of the banks, such as Russkiy Standart, were founded after the 1998 crash, but others were experienced foreign-owned banks that did not appear in Russia until then (like Home Credit&Finance and Raiffeisen). Unlike the promoters of VIP and salary cards, many of the leading issuers of credit cards positioned themselves as retail banks from the start.

Because each subsequent strategy did not replace the previous one but was added to it, many banks now issue cards via three strategies at the same time: the most prestigious cards through personal networks (usually to VIP customers), debit cards with or without overdrafts as part of salary projects, and revolving credit cards as part of consumer lending in retail locations.

Conclusion

Salary projects solved the problem of uncertainty, but cardholders, while numerous, stubbornly headed to ATMs to withdraw cash rather than to stores to use the cards to pay for purchases. Thus, salary projects failed to attract merchants and solve the complementarity problem. Consumer lending helps banks to promote cards because through shopping malls and big stores they can simultaneously reach prospective cardholders and merchants.

Unlike salary projects that managed to produce a stable mechanism of control over a cardholder-employee but essentially failed to turn cardholders into consumers, consumer lending successfully bundles the cardholder and consumer roles together and promotes the credit card market. But consumer lending also walks on thin ice: contrary to employers, retailers cannot help banks solve the uncertainty problem. As a result, while Russia is experiencing a consumer credit boom, and there is evidence that cards are being transformed from status symbols into a means of everyday payment, the main concern is over the growing default rate. The future success of the Russian credit card market depends on the ability of banks to find a way to reliably and effectively prescreen cardholders, which means formally institutionalizing credit reporting. In the next chapter I will detail the process of legislating credit reporting in Russia, which culminated in 2004 with the Law on Credit Bureaus, and also analyze the Law's shortcomings.

CHAPTER SEVEN

The Missing Piece of the Puzzle

*The Struggle to Institutionalize Interbank Information
Sharing and Create Credit Bureaus*

In the late 1990s, the South Korean government had been encouraging the
spread of credit cards in an attempt to increase consumer spending. The
goal was to help the economy recover after the 1997–1998 financial crisis
and to increase economic transparency and tax revenues. Consumers were
enticed to spend by being offered tax breaks on loans. Banks and card companies saw few restrictions on the issuance of cards, as neither their risk-
management strategies nor the adequacy of their reserves were closely monitored by the state regulatory agencies. Fiercely competitive banks desperate
to increase their market share peddled credit cards on street corners without
much or any verification of the applicants' backgrounds or their current indebtedness. The South Korean economy responded with spectacular growth
in consumer lending, spending, and increased tax revenues. Credit card use
had been rising at a rate of nearly 90 percent each year, with the average Korean owning at least four credit cards. Between 1998 and 2002, the total
value of credit card transactions jumped tenfold, the household savings rate

declined from 23 percent to 10 percent, while household debt nearly doubled (Korea Economic Institute 2004). The Korean credit card market modeled itself after the American "hubs-and-spokes" market, where banks lend to consumers directly, rather than through employers or other mediators. Korean banks inexperienced in consumer lending overlooked the imperative of relying on credit bureaus to prescreen prospective cardholders, falling into the same trap as Bank of America did forty years ago. The number of delinquent accounts started to rise, and in late 2002 the South Korean household credit market collapsed under its own weight, sending the entire economy into a downward spiral, calling for government bailout, and teaching the rest of the world a grim lesson in risk management (Day 2002; Min 2003; "Finance and Economics: Snap! Credit Cards in South Korea" 2004).

This is a story of caution for Russian lenders, many of whom are familiar with the Korean boom and bust. But better, more effective screening of applicants, although crucial to banks, is not entirely up to them. Even big players on the Russian market scene, such as Russkiy Standart, which claims to use several scoring models, at least one of which was purchased from a foreign company with the rest developed in-house, need to first verify information before the models can be run. Although banks do resort to using various databases, such as lists of registered telephones or criminal convictions, because these lists are often obtained illegally they might not be complete or up-to-date. Credit bureaus are designed to make this verification a one-stop process. What consumer credit lenders would also like to know is how many other loans the applicant has. And this is something the banks cannot learn on their own unless the individuals volunteer this information. Therefore, no matter how much a particular lender has advanced in developing decision-making tools, to be able to expand beyond their existing circle of clients, banks need to access information from other lenders. Accumulating information about borrowers' past performance takes time, so that even after the bureaus are established, they will need a year or two or three to collect these data before becoming fully operational. However, other kinds of information, such as passport specifics, residency, work, income, and taxpaying status, can be gathered and verified right away.

In other words, lenders' success in screening is based on the availability of information-sharing mechanisms. So while Russian card issuers readily agreed, even during the 1998–1999 wave of interviews, that credit bureaus were necessary for a more mature and stable market, and that their decision making would be greatly aided by the information credit bureaus could collect and distribute, they (and the state) until recently had fallen short of taking practical steps to organize one. This chapter follows the process and the debates of legislating credit reporting in Russia, which resulted in the passing of the Law on Credit Bureaus in December 2004, and evaluates the practical effects of the law on the state of credit reporting.

Barriers to Creating Credit Bureaus in Russia

Literature on interbank information sharing (Pagano and Jappelli 1993; Miller 2003) identifies two main obstacles to the creation of credit bureaus: market competition and the existence of privacy laws. Russia's privacy laws have strictly prohibited the sharing of financial account information with third parties until the amendment was passed in December 2004 together with the new Law on Credit Bureaus.[1] This formal barrier to credit bureaus was frequently evoked by my interviewees in the 1998–1999 wave of interviews. But my sense then was that it was offered as a smokescreen to conceal other, deeper problems. Since changing the law was not up to the banks, they placed the blame on the state for failing to create conditions for viable information-sharing mechanisms.

Market competition can also create obstacles to the creation of credit bureaus. Credit bureaus are more likely to emerge in countries where competition between lenders is restricted by some form of government regulation (Pagano and Jappelli 1993). This was the case in the United States, home to the oldest and one of the most advanced credit-reporting institutions. There, the National Banking Act of 1864 prohibited national banks from opening branches, "confirming the general attitude, carefully cultivated by local monopolist bankers, that branching only existed to drain funds from the countryside to finance growth in the cities" (Doti 2003). Individual states differed on their position with respect to branching by state-chartered banks. For instance, California legislators did not ban branch banking, but such restrictions existed in Texas, Wyoming, Montana, New Mexico, and Colorado until late in the twentieth century. American banks were also prohibited from interstate banking by the McFadden Act of 1927.[2] Consequently, until recently, U.S. consumer banking and by extension consumer lending were largely local in character.

Whereas nothing precludes banks from competing nationally, as in Russia, they are much more resistant to the idea of sharing "positive" account information because they fear this will intensify the competition further as other banks would glean information about their best clients and could lure them away. Restricting the access of other banks to their customers' account information allows Russian banks to charge information rents and limits competition (Pyle 2002). This tendency to bring competition under control to promote market stability is, according to Fligstein (2001), a usual goal of market development. But while obstructed information sharing prevents competitive credit markets from becoming even more competitive, both banks and customers miss out. Good borrowers are locked into their banks, which have no incentive to offer them more competitive terms on loans since their quality as borrowers is not apparent to anyone but their current bank. Banks, on the other hand, may suffer from occasional bad borrowers because, in a market without interbank information sharing, defaulters can simply move to another bank and borrow there. Russian banks know about this, and to protect themselves they engage in informal exchanges of negative information about borrowers. Sharing negative information alone can greatly benefit credit markets and help increase lending rates, and in some countries, such as Belgium, Australia, Norway, the Philippines, Singapore, and Finland, banks share only negative information (Jappelli and Pagano 2002; Miller 2003). But negative information will not protect banks against clients who have no prior strikes but who assume too much debt by borrowing simultaneously from different lenders. Nevertheless, some Russian banks even resist blacklists, arguing that this would prevent defaulters from borrowing elsewhere in order to pay their primary creditor; subject banks to doubts about their professionalism, stability, and ability to control risk; and damage the banks' public reputation. Moreover, in extremely competitive environments, banks might consider it to be in their best interest not to inform their competitors even about cases of fraud.

The Russian context presents a few more obstacles in addition to those specified above. Besides being competitive, the Russian retail-banking/consumer credit market is also very concentrated: two banks with the largest consumer credit programs in Russia, Sberbank and Russkiy Standart, together account for 60 percent of Russia's overall consumer credit market (54 percent and 6 percent respectively) (Kuzmenko 2005; Buzdalin 2004). Large lenders are particularly reluctant to share their account data with credit bureaus because they believe that by making information available to other banks they will immediately lose their market advantage. They can clearly see that a system of interbank information exchange would put them in the position of donors: they would lose control over their clients, but gain very little in return.

Another obstacle particular to the Russian context is the lack of trust in one another on the part of Russian banks. In the words of one of the bankers, "Banks do not trust each other, they are stealing each other's customers; any personal information about their customers is considered to be confidential."[3] Commenting on the prospects of the creation of a credit bureau in Russia, another one of my interviewees confided that banks "are afraid that someone powerful would take control [of the bureau]. They are afraid that other banks would use the bureau to get information on their customers and lure them away, or that it would make information about fraud available and this would discredit reliability and [the] public image of banks."[4] The lack of trust in each other stems, in part, from the history of commercial banking in Russia. Mindful of the days of internecine bank wars, bankers believe other banks will not stop at anything to gain market advantage. They sense that information is power, and they try to keep as much of it as possible inside their bank's walls. This widespread attitude of secrecy was especially pervasive in the banking community in the mid-to-late-1990s, during my first field visit, and it accounted for many of the difficulties I experienced with gaining access to my interviewees.[5]

Banks are also suspicious of the intentions of the state and its agencies. They feel they have fiduciary responsibility toward their clients and are protective of their account data. One of the commonly evoked concerns is that the Tax Authorities would gain access to customers' account data. This is a real fear given the ubiquity of unreported personal income and widespread tax evasion.

Finally, and most important, banks are apprehensive about the state of data protection in Russia, where the most confidential databases have made their way to the black market, and are doubtful of the ability of any prospective credit bureau in Russia (whether state-run or private) to secure the data from being stolen and used to their or their customers' detriment.[6] They have reasons to be suspicious since in their own verification of prospective cardholders or borrowers most of them have been relying on databases illegally obtained from state agencies and sold on the street.

As a result, although appreciative of the importance of credit bureaus for the future of consumer credit in Russia, banks have been resisting the idea of sharing account information with other banks.

Debates Around the Credit Bureau Law in Russia

The first attempt to organize a credit bureau in Russia dates back to 1995, when a number of leading Russian banks/issuers of credit cards and several processing companies worked on the creation of the Interbank Bureau of Credit Information. The purpose of the bureau was to accumulate information about holders of domestic and international bank cards. The database was to be accessible to members only, and new membership was to be extended only with the agreement of all the current members. Clearly, it was designed to be more of an exclusive data pool than a commercial enterprise. Starting in 1997–1998, a few professional journals dedicated to bank cards started to publish articles educating the professional community about the benefits, principles, and history of credit bureaus in mature markets ("Kreditnye byuro—vchera, segodnya, zavtra" 1998; Guseva 1999; Kuznetsov and Spiranov 1999). In 1997, the need for organizing interbank information sharing was acknowledged at the international banking congress devoted to risk management, held in St. Petersburg.

At the same time, the Duma's banking committee, chaired at that time by Pavel Medvedev, an enthusiast of the credit bureau idea, also started to actively discuss these issues. In the fall of 1997, Medvedev authored a draft law "On the Federal State Archive of Credit Histories." As follows from the title, the draft law called for a single, centralized credit bureau to be closely supervised by the Central Bank. But Russia's government and the Bank of Russia concluded that the draft law required further conceptual revision. An alternative to Medvedev's draft law, written by another member of the Duma,

Ivan Grachev, suggested instead that numerous private credit bureaus should be created and that the role of the Central Bank should be limited to that of the regulator. Neither of the two draft laws passed even on the first reading. Medvedev's draft law was revised numerous times, but to no avail. Why were they not successful? The most immediate reason was the lack of consensus between the Parliament members as reflected in two almost diametrically opposite conceptions of credit bureaus.[7] In addition, the administration of most banks perceived plastic card or consumer credit programs as little more than pet projects but not real moneymakers (real money was made on trading state bonds and on short-term loans to large enterprises and other banks).

In 1998, the government and the Central Bank issued a program called "On the measures to restructure the banking sphere of the Russian Federation," expressing the need to create a system that would accumulate and distribute information about borrowers' credit histories (Bogdanovskiy 2005). But in the summer of 1998, Russia was hit by a severe financial crisis, which for several weeks paralyzed the entire banking sphere. This was followed by a marked economic downturn and a period of heightened political uncertainty in 1999, when the banking community, sensing political changes on the eve of the December parliamentary elections and the impending replacement of President Yeltsin by a successor, offered no new initiatives and generally took a "wait-and-see" approach. In addition, several of the largest banks got tangled up in prolonged bankruptcy proceedings following the 1998 crisis. Some of them were eventually liquidated, and their card programs were closed. Rather than actively pursuing the program to build credit bureaus, the government was preoccupied with saving the national banking industry, handling the political crisis brought about by massive defaults, and in general stabilizing the economy. Momentum was definitely lost, though it is difficult to say whether the law could have been passed had the crisis not happened.

Two years after the 1998 crisis, the Russian economy started to recover: incomes were increasing; consumers were buying with more and more confidence; and banks were offering multiple forms of credit, from overdrafts on bank cards to revolving credit cards, from installment credit to credit cards cobranded with merchants, and from auto loans to mortgages. In line with Pagano and Jappelli's argument (1993), the need to develop credit reporting institutions emerged once the consumer market got larger. The absence of credit bureaus in Russia was declared one of the main obstacles to further development of consumer credit markets and to improved access and affordability of consumer loans. Popular press engaged in active discussions and debates about the benefits and drawbacks of various forms of credit bureaus, contributing to the legitimizing of the concept among laypeople. Other lenders, including retailers who sold or had considered selling on credit, joined the credit card issuers openly expressing the need to develop an institution of credit reporting in Russia. Besides, the conditions unexpectedly became ripe for finally removing the formal obstacle to the creation of credit bureaus: privacy laws. After almost seven years, several draft laws, and endless task forces, round tables, miniconferences, and initiatives dedicated to the topic, the Russian Parliament seemed to be ready to seriously consider the passage of the credit bureau law.

In 2001, the Russian government and the Central Bank approved the Joint Strategy of the Development of the Banking Sector, which included a provision for the preparation and passing of the credit bureau law. For the next two years, the Ministry of Economic Development, in consultation with bankers, members of the Parliament, and experts, worked on the government-sponsored draft law "On Credit Histories." The draft law was mainly based on Grachev's earlier version but viewed as a compromise of the two alternatives. Some experts even suggested that the main reason for the emergence of Grachev's draft law was to stall the passage of Medvedev's idea of a single federal credit bureau. In the latest revision, credit bureaus were to be organized as private organizations designed to collect, store, and distribute credit histories of both individuals and firms. In addition to private credit bureaus, the Central Bank of Russia was going to organize the Central Catalogue of Credit Histories, which would store credit histories of organizations with more than a hundred employees and hold databases of liquidated or closed credit bureaus. In addition, the Central Bank would create an archive of title pages of consumers' credit histories, indicating their location in the private credit bureaus.

Boris Gryzlov, the Duma's speaker and the leader of the pro-government party Yedinaya Rossiya, sponsored the draft law in May 2004. It was to be evaluated by Arkadiy Dvorkovich, head of the expert group in the administration of the president, and coincidentally the first author of the draft law written while Dvorkovich was deputy minister of Economic Development and Trade. The draft law was brought into the Duma as part of the national program "Affordable Housing," a collection of more than thirty laws, among them regulations on mortgage lending. By official estimates, 77 percent of Russians would like to improve their housing conditions. President Putin has taken up the problem personally; it was a part of his re-election platform during the last presidential election, which he won decisively in March 2004 with more than 70 percent of the vote. In his May 2004 address to the Federation Council, Putin emphasized the importance of solving the housing problem and developing mortgage lending in Russia as one of the strategic directions for the development of the Russian economy. He also mentioned credit bureaus as key in facilitating mortgage lending. If earlier the task of building credit bureaus in Russia was considered to be important, after Putin's address, analysts agreed, it became clearly inevitable (Moiseev 2004). It was no longer a question of "if" but "when," especially since the Duma's current majority is pro-presidential. Even the supporters of Medvedev's ill-fated draft law favoring the model of a state-run credit registry changed their minds, started to actively advocate for commercial bureaus, and announced an impending recall of Medvedev's proposal.

As predicted, the federal law "On Credit Histories" was swiftly passed in December 2004. The Duma also passed amendments to Russia's Civil Code regarding the privacy clause, enabling credit bureaus, in addition to borrowers and their representatives, to have legal access to bank account information. The law has subsequently been approved by the Federation Council and signed by the president. The law took effect on June 1, 2005, when all credit organizations had to begin accumulating credit histories. They had to sign an agreement with at least one bureau and start submitting credit account information by September 1, 2005. Just a few days before June 1, the Ministry of Economic Development and Trade, whose experts authored the final version of the law on credit histories, finally named the Federal Financial Markets Service (FFMS) to be a supervisory body for the credit history bureaus and to officially register and license the newly formed bureaus ("RF Economic Development Ministry Picks Out Credit History's Supervisor" 2005). But soon it became increasingly clear that the deadline would not be met (largely, because FFMS was not identified as a regulatory agency until very late in the process), and it was rescheduled for March 1, 2006. In the following two months, FFMS registered the first ten bureaus. The process of formally institutionalizing interbank information sharing in Russia had begun.

Bank Cooperation Versus Market Competition

From the very beginning of the political debates surrounding the creation of the credit reporting institution in Russia, its proponents often could not see eye to eye. If a potentially heated argument about whether to create a single state-run bureau under the auspices of the Central Bank, or instead, to have a market for credit reporting with a number of competing private bureaus ended quickly and peacefully, with the private model gaining an incontestable advantage, other details of market architecture continued to be hotly debated. One aspect discussed by the members of the Duma was the limitation on the size of the ownership share in the statutory capital of credit bureaus. The initial version of the draft law did not call for any limitations, but right before the second reading, a provision appeared for a 10 percent limit on each ownership share. This limitation meant that at least ten participants were necessary to create one bureau. The rationale behind this condition was to foster cooperation and information sharing between banks and prevent the creation of "pocket" bureaus by large banks, a situation that could have negative consequences for borrowers. The Association of Russian Banks (ARB), a longtime supporter of the idea of institutionalized interbank information sharing and a participant in some earlier attempts to legislate it, had already conceived of such a collaborative model. Before the law was even passed, ARB had already organized the National Bureau of Credit Histories. Among its other founders were the U.S. credit bureau TransUnion and more than a dozen Moscow-based banks, enough to satisfy the 10 percent rule. In retrospect, the 10 percent limitation was intended to overcome the biggest obstacles to the creation of credit bureaus in Russia: banks' unwillingness to cooperate because of the lack of trust and fierce competition, and the particularly staunch opposition of large lenders to sharing their data.

But the 10 percent limit was not destined to prevail. In fact, it was the main reason that the draft law was returned to the second reading in the beginning of December 2004, instead of proceeding to the third and final reading (only minor changes are allowed between the second and third readings). During the preliminary discussion, the Duma members briefly favored a 20 percent limitation on ownership share for credit organizations and none for other organizations. But a group of parliamentarians reacted very negatively to this provision, arguing that it would still allow banks to control credit bureaus through nonbank companies they could organize. The final reading of the draft law approved the increase of the maximum share to 50 percent for everyone, which meant that a bureau could have only two owners. Thus, large credit providers such as Sberbank did not need to join several smaller banks, but could pair up with just one other partner.

Why was the 10 percent limit removed? According to the experts' explanations, it was removed because of the concern that it could have discouraged market competition. In a swift reversal of alliances, Pavel Medvedev, deputy head of the Duma's banking committee and author of the single state-regulated public bureau model, supported the elimination of the 10 percent quota, arguing that the quota would lead to the creation of a monopoly bureau or a small number of bureaus because there were allegedly only a limited number of banks interested in participating. Medvedev and other proponents of the quota elimination reasoned that credit bureaus require large up-front, long-term investments, and so there should be no limitations for those willing to invest in their development. Having many bureaus would stimulate competition and drive prices down. Thus, the lawmakers appeared to be much more concerned with promoting *competition among bureaus* than they were with fostering *cooperation among banks*.

The debate over the minimum number of credit bureau founders and the competition-cooperation dilemma revealed the market participants' alliances. Medium-sized banks' interests have been represented mainly by the ARB, the founder of the National Bureau of Credit Histories (NBCH) and one of the few outspoken proponents of the *cooperative* credit bureau model. ARB's position is that a bureau with many owners would be more efficient in collecting information. Notably, most of the banks that joined the NBCH are not market leaders, but are challengers with recently initiated but already ambitious credit card programs. Lacking a large database themselves, they favor cooperative information sharing with banks in a similar position (Buzdalin 2004).

Large lenders and foreign credit bureaus favor a market-competition model, albeit for different reasons. Both of them prefer a 50 percent limitation to a 10 percent one because with fewer founders they can control a bigger share of the bureau. Additionally, with a 50 percent limitation, large lenders do not have to enter into an essentially unequal information exchange, where they would be forced to share data with at least nine other banks, and ultimately offer much more than they would receive in return. Foreign bureaus, for their part, welcome market competition because they are confident that their expertise and reputation will ensure their success.

The Role of Foreign Credit Bureaus

One very important question is why the draft law did not prevent foreign parties from participating in the creation of credit bureaus in Russia. After all, Russian banks have been actively lobbying for a restriction on the presence of foreign banks in Russia, fearing intensified competition (Johnson 1997). Their reasoning is that foreign banks are bigger, more stable, more experienced, and would perhaps be more trusted; besides, they have access to cheaper resources so they could offer loans on better terms. Unrestricted access to the Russian markets by foreign banks has been a thorny issue in the prolonged Russian negotiations on the WTO membership. So, the willingness of the banking community and the lawmakers to embrace foreign credit bureaus is at least notable.

Unlike foreign banks, foreign credit bureaus are not competitors but service providers to Russian credit organizations. Besides, there are no domestic credit bureaus already functioning in Russia; therefore foreign bureaus could be viewed as sources of much-needed expertise and legitimacy. In addition, they are perceived as more capable than domestic organizations of guaranteeing fair storage and distribution of banking information and of protecting it from unauthorized use.

In 2003–2004, representatives of several foreign credit bureaus—the UK-based Experian, American TransUnion, and German Schufa and Infoscor—made numerous trips and gave multiple presentations to Russian banks, experts, and politicians offering expertise and support, but certainly looking for a way to capture the untapped market. Infoscor even invited three members of the Duma's banking committee to learn about the work of their company in Germany, Switzerland, and Poland.[8] Their aggressive courtship must have sold the idea of a pluralist, market-based model of credit reporting to Russia's lawmakers, professionals, and the public. Professionals were attracted to their technical knowledge and experience of running bureaus in mature markets, while the promise of market efficiency and reduced costs of loans was intended to appeal to the public.

In addition to the spread of these ideas, foreign credit bureaus might have produced another, more specific, but also more nuanced effect on the future of credit reporting in Russia. The controversial removal of the 10 percent limitation on the size of the share in a credit bureau was not incidental. One of the suggestions that did not make it into the final version of the draft law was to raise the limitation to 20 percent for banks (thus lowering the minimum number of founders to five), but eliminate it altogether for other organizations. The eventual change to 50 percent came a few days after Russia's Interfax Information Agency announced that it had launched a new credit bureau together with the leading U.K.-based consumer credit bureau Experian (Experian Interfax Credit Bureau), each party with a 50 percent stake in the joint venture ("Experian Launches First Consumer Credit Bureau in Russia with Interfax Information Services Group" 2005). Unlike the initial 10 percent limitation, both the 20 percent and the 50 percent were in perfect legal agreement with the Experian-Interfax joint venture (it would be exempt from the 20 percent limitation because neither of the two founders are banks). Commenting on the announcement, Russia's Deputy Prime Minister Alexandr Zhukov said: "The creation of a Russian credit bureau with the participation of the Interfax Group and Experian company, a major global player in this market, can be considered a kind of 'confidence' vote in strengthening the Russian financial system" ("History collectors" 2004).

Thus, large foreign bureaus influenced the general framework for credit reporting in Russia, helping to establish it as a competitive market enterprise rather than a nonprofit cooperative service. But they did not stop there. In addition, they also shaped the final version of the law in a way that directly benefited them, as well as large domestic lenders and card issuers such as Sberbank or Russkiy Standart who cringed at the thought of sharing their customer data with smaller banks.

Practical Outcomes

By the time the Law on Credit Bureaus had finally been passed, there were already two registered credit bureaus that claimed to operate on a federal level: Experian-Interfax and the National Bureau of Credit Histories (NBCH) under the auspices of ARB. NBCH claimed fourteen banks as its founders, but as I mentioned earlier, those were medium-sized and small banks, not the leaders of the credit market. And what about the large banks? Sberbank with its share of slightly more than 50 percent of the consumer credit market has always been looked upon as a golden calf: any bureau that is lucky enough to have Sberbank's database would immediately become an unsurpassable leader in credit information. For a long time, preceding the passage of the law, Sberbank was listed on the NBCH Web site as one of its prospective founders. NBCH's management never failed to stress the fact of Sberbank's participation in their frequent public statements. But in a surprising change of heart, Sberbank recently announced that instead of joining any existing bureaus, it will organize its own ("Sberbank sozdaet kreditnoe byuro" 2005). The announcement had the effect of an exploding bomb. The biggest shock was undoubtedly felt by NBCH, which already considered Sberbank's database its own. As a consolation prize, Sberbank's officials promised to provide NBCH with negative information on their borrowers. Sberbank's announcement about founding its own bureau came a day after Russkiy Standart, another leader of the consumer lending market, issued an identical statement ("Russkiy Standart sozdaet svoe sobstvennoe kreditnoe byuro" 2005).

The move to create "pocket" credit bureaus on the part of the leaders of the credit market illustrates the point I made earlier: large players essentially refuse to donate their account data and relinquish their hard-earned source of market advantage. In addition, Sberbank is particularly concerned about the prospect of having to compete for its own customers, because it is largely outmoded but inflexible due to its socialist legacy and enormous size. To comply with the law, each of the two banks had to find at least one unaffiliated partner.[9] Currently, among the nineteen credit bureaus officially registered so far, there are five clear heavyweights (the rest are small regional bureaus). These are NBCH, Experian-Interfax, and the proprietary credit bureaus organized by three leaders of consumer lending in Russia: Sberbank's Infokredit, Russkiy

Standart credit bureau, and Global Payments Credit Services bureau of Home Credit&Finance bank.

It had not even been a year since the system of credit reporting was officially launched before both bankers and lawmakers were already heard complaining. The department head of the social credit program of Rosselkhozbank, Alexei Khomko, argues that it is technologically very difficult to work with nineteen bureaus because they may use entirely different protocols for data storage and sharing. Senior vice-president of BINbank Sergei Gorashchenko seconds him by saying that "It is bad having many bureaus. Bureaus are created to centralize information about multiple banks' borrowers. So the fewer bureaus there are, the more concentrated the source of information is" ("Kreditnye byuro nachali ploho" 2006). Roman Vorobiov, head of the retail department of Bank of Moscow, agrees that if the number of bureaus is too high, it might mean that their "main goal . . . is not to help banks minimize credit risks, but to extract more money from lenders" (Dementyeva 2006).

But an even bigger problem than the sheer number of bureaus is the fact that the market model without a 10 percent limitation on ownership share failed to promote bank cooperation. The caveat is that the three leaders of the credit market that have accumulated the largest databases are not required by the current reading of the law to share them with other banks. Neither the price of service nor the response time have been specified by the law, and as a result, owners of pocket bureaus can effectively discourage inquiries about their clients from other banks by making their service too slow or too expensive. In their apparently blind faith in the virtues of the market, the lawmakers believed that competition would bring about the most efficient forms of information sharing, the highest quality at the lowest price. Boris Voronin, an official of the Ministry of Economic Development and Trade, voiced this position in connection with the contested issue of the 10 percent limitation: "We should not destroy alternatives; let the market choose. Market participants themselves will choose the necessary model" ("Eksperty sklonyayutsya k otkazu ot ogranicheniy na dolyu v kapitale kreditnyh byuro" 2004). The problem, as it is obvious today, is that large lenders can easily refuse to treat their customer data as a commodity, forming storefront bureaus to formally satisfy the law, but operating in a monopolistic manner.

This prompted the Ministry of Economic Development to officially ask Sberbank to share information about its borrowers not only with its own credit bureau (Infokredit) but also with at least one of its competitors. While the government cannot make Sberbank do this, experts believe that without its database being accessible to other participants, the system of credit reporting in Russia would be defunct. Andrei Sharonov, deputy minister of economic development, in his letter to Sergei Ignatiev, Sberbank's chairman of the board, and Andrei Kazmin, its president, indignantly pointed out that "If Sberbank creates its own bureau, a large amount of information would not be available at an affordable price to other banks." After all, credit bureaus are supposed to guarantee that a large volume of "bad" credit does not lead the economy into a banking crisis, "the possibility of which cannot be ruled out at this moment," reminds Mr. Sharonov in his letter.[10] Mr. Sharonov urges Sberbank to choose one competing bureau with which to share its information ("Sberbank vedut na rynok" 2005). Several Duma members supported this position in an initiative addressed to the state to prohibit banks from supplying information to their affiliated bureau only. But the Central Bank and presidential administration apparently do not support this initiative ("Kreditnye byuro nachali ploho" 2006).

The fact that the Ministry could not force Sberbank but merely asked demonstrates that despite its unique market position, Sberbank should not be viewed as an extension of the Russian state in the way that it is now common to refer to state-owned Gazprom, the world gas monopolist and the largest Russian company. So Sberbank should not be expected to do what is best for the market; it is busy guarding data on millions of its customers from competitor banks in an attempt to preserve its current market share.

Others continue to voice support of the "market knows best" position. "Russia" Aleksandr Khandruev, former deputy head of Central Bank and vice-president of the banking association, is one of them. Reacting to the request that Sberbank share its customer data with a bureau other than its own, he reportedly said: "This is not Sharonov's or the state's business to intrude into the market. Should they now send similar letters to Russkiy Standart and other large banks that are creating their own bureaus?" The deputy head of the Duma's banking committee, Pavel Medvedev, believes that even if Sberbank agrees to supply their data to another bureau, it will not necessarily drive prices down. A more effective measure is to legislate the maximum price that bureaus are allowed to charge for inquiries ("Sberbank vedut na rynok" 2005).

The continuing debates suggest that the process of institutionalizing credit reporting in Russia is far from being consolidated. Despite hopes and expectations, the law did not remove all the barriers to the creation of credit bureaus in Russia. It mandated the supply of account information by banks, but it stopped short of helping banks solve the collective action problem. The system that was created essentially closed access to the most comprehensive databases for the majority of market actors ("Kreditnye byuro nachali ploho" 2006).

By not pursuing the version of a public credit registry, which would mandate data submission from all the banks and accumulate it in one centralized location, the Russian Parliament missed the opportunity to overcome the barriers that have been precluding Russia from forming bureaus (distrust, competition, and high market concentration). Rather than mandating cooperation *by force*, they attempted to provide market participants with *incentives* to cooperate and share information (albeit, up to this point, unsuccessfully). Moreover, by removing the 10 percent requirement and replacing it with a 50 percent one (and essentially opening the door to the formation of pocket bureaus by the market leaders), Russian lawmakers bought into the market competition mantra. They expected that a large number of credit bureaus would prevent monopolies and promote competition, which would ensure the tandem of lower prices and a higher quality of service. While the law was successful in removing the formal obstacle (privacy) of credit information sharing, it did not address the root of the problem, the lack of interbank cooperation. The story bears an eerie resemblance to the overall course of the postcommunist reforms of the 1990s. Both followed an ill-conceived neoclassical recipe: remove the obstacles (in this case privacy barriers) and the market would miraculously flourish.

Ironically, the lack of interbank cooperation in sharing customer data means that existing credit bureaus are struggling. Banks are not ready to actively use the information from credit bureaus because, they argue, it is scarce. Instead, banks prefer to use tried-and-true methods of applicant verification developed by their security departments. Nevertheless, credit bureaus are optimistic about the prospects of the market in consumer credit data. They are currently trying to replenish their databases with information obtained from nonbanking organizations such as cell-phone service providers; gas, hot water, and electricity companies; leasing companies; retail stores that sell on installment credit; collection agencies; insurance companies; and pawnshops (Dementyeva and Chaykina 2006). For instance, according to an independent Russian market research company ROMIR, 53 percent of Russians used cell phones as of September 2005, putting mobile-service providers in possession of a potentially large database.[11] At the same time, many mobile phone companies complain that they suffer from dishonest phone users who do not pay their bills, but instead switch to other providers. Their willingness to pool their databases together may be enough to lift the credit information market off the ground. Besides, if gas, hot water, and electricity providers follow suit and start supplying information about their customers, such diversification of the sources of credit information can in theory help form the credit histories of virtually every Russian citizen, thus eventually making credit bureaus attractive to lenders.

Conclusion

The attempts to carry out the organization of credit reporting did not gain momentum until after the consumer credit boom started in 2000–2001. The decisive push for the creation of credit bureaus came when they were framed as a key element in the presidential housing-and-mortgage program. This allowed for a new draft law to be quickly passed by the Duma and for spill-over of the discussion about credit bureaus into the popular press and public sphere.

Although the law established credit reporting as a competitive business and specified the functions of credit bureaus, it failed to remove barriers that have been preventing banks from cooperating on information sharing. Market leaders such as Sberbank and Russkiy Standart, which have been especially resistant to the idea of sharing their customer data with smaller banks, have managed to create their own affiliated bureaus. The recent attempts of some government officials to appeal to Sberbank's sense of responsibility and to urge it to share its customer data with a bureau other than its own have likely fallen on deaf ears.

The outcome of the new legislation exposed a rift between formal and informal institutions. Legislating credit reporting was no doubt necessary: the law removed the privacy clause, which most of my interviewees blamed for the lack of interbank information sharing. However, laws that clash with informal practices, belief systems, and actors' interests may fail in their attempt to bring a desired effect (Nee 2005). The Credit Bureau Law did not explicitly mandate banks to cooperate on information sharing, only to submit their loan data to a bureau of their choice. Thus, it did not recognize that the largest lenders would continue their informal practice of protecting their customers' account data from competitors. Therefore, contrary to what institutional economists suggest, formal institutions may never emerge as efficient solutions to market failure (Williamson 1975), since competition and power inequality between market actors can be a source of continuous resistance to institution building even when the state steps in.

CHAPTER EIGHT

The Russian Credit Card Market Through the Lens of Continuity and Change

Credit card markets are not easy to build; their success requires much more than the earnest desire of their creators. As markets where transactions span a period of time, they are subject to uncertainty. As two-sided markets, they suffer from the problem of complementarity: the imperative of signing card-holders and merchants simultaneously. Uncertainty and complementarity call for contradictory solutions underscoring the challenges of building markets for credit cards. But the task that the Russian card issuers undertook was truly formidable: market building in the context of postcommunist transitions accompanied by macroeconomic instability, institutional weakness, and resistance to private banks, noncash payments, and borrowing. Yet, despite the laundry list of obstacles, the Russian credit card market survived the most turbulent period of its history, the 1990s, and it continues to surprise observers with its resourcefulness and resilience.

In this final chapter, I suggest that the Russian credit card market is the site of both change and continuity with the past, and it is also a force bringing major changes to society. It is not a mere replica of mature Western markets (the American one, most notably) despite the widely held notion that payment cards are offering standard and predictable services across the world, ideally to the point of a single card replacing the need for local currencies. In contradiction to the convergence hypothesis (Meyer et al. 1997; for a detailed review see Guillén 2001), the development of the Russian credit card market did not follow an imported blueprint. Instead, the resulting market architecture was a compromise between ideal goals and local realities and resources. It was constrained by the patterns of relations carried over from the Soviet past, yet it also managed to transcend them to become a transformative force, weakening or repatterning old ties and creating new ones. In this sense, it is both coming from the past and leading into the future.

The Credit Card Market as a Site of Change

The last two decades have brought a great many changes to the Russian political system, economy, and society. A new generation of Russians is growing up amidst consumer abundance that resembles little of the times when there were shortages on many basic goods. Instead of saving for years to buy state-rationed cars, furniture, and electronic appliances, individuals and households can now buy these goods in the open market. And those with little cash do not have to wait as dozens of banks across Russia offer various forms of consumer financing to help individuals and households make their dreams come true.

The Russian credit card market has also changed substantially since its inception. Starting with just a handful of cards issued to high-profile politicians in 1989, the Russian credit card market grew to more than seventy million cards by the end of 2006. Although initially viewed as an elite status symbol and issued exclusively to executives and high-ranking party functionaries, cards have eventually found their way into the wallets of ordinary citizens. Salary projects in particular helped promote cards among people who would be neither eligible nor interested in applying for them individually, such as blue-collar workers or pensioners. The phenomenal success of the most recent trend—issuing cards through retail locations—indicates that unlike bank branches and enterprises, shopping malls and chain stores artfully combine all the three necessary components of a successful lending relationship: cardholder, card issuer, and merchant. The popularity of card issuing in conjunction with consumer purchases reinforces the notion that credit cards are becoming a truly mass product.

The geography of card issuance has also been changing as cards are spreading from the capital to the provinces, and from larger cities to smaller towns. Initially, the majority of all cards were issued in Moscow, with St. Petersburg coming in a distant second. Today, the share of cards issued in Moscow is down to about one-third, while larger cities, smaller regional towns, and small towns in oil-rich territories (such as the Tyumen region) are catching up. Again, due to their capacity for mass-issuing cards to employees of large enterprises, salary projects have been key to promoting cards in the regions. In addition, regional towns have been increasingly viewed as a new frontier of consumer credit by many banks. For example, in the case of Russkiy Standart, the share of consumer loans issued in Moscow declined from 100 percent in 2000 to just 43 percent in 2003 (Russkiy Standart 2003, 24). Russkiy Standart bank now offers consumer credit in more than one hundred cities and towns all over Russia.

There have also been changes in the types of cards issued. Numerous local brands that dominated the Russian market in the 1990s (such as Zolotaya Korona, Union Card, and STB) gave way to international brands, specifically Visa. In 2003, one in three cards issued in Russia had a Visa logo, and 40 percent of all card transactions in Russia were with Visa cards.[1] Starting in 2003, for the first time, more than half of the cards issued in Russia were international-brand cards (Visa, MasterCard, AmEx, Diners, and JCB).

Despite the rapid growth in the popularity of revolving credit cards (their number jumping from 4,800 in 2001 to close to 300,000 three years later), debit cards continue to dominate the market, while credit cards comprise less than 2 percent of all cards issued. Nevertheless, it is the credit cards that show the most dynamic growth. They are forecast to reach 7.9 million in 2008 (Euromonitor International 2004). At the same time, debit card growth is predicted to slow down. Most debit cards have been issued as part of salary projects, and this market has already been largely divided among banks, at least in large cities and regional centers. Large banks that previously actively promoted debit cards through salary projects have recently started to shift their focus to offering revolving credit cards, following the example of market leaders in this segment, such as Russkiy Standart and Home Credit&Finance bank.

The conditions on which cards are issued are also changing. Reflecting intensified competition, procedures are becoming simplified, which further increases the popularity of cards among mass consumers. Many banks no longer require an official confirmation of income from the employer and are willing to accept indirect proofs of income (such as mobile phone bills or even receipts for large-ticket purchases). The requirements of collateral and guarantees, which prevented many consumers from being eligible for credit lines in the past and significantly slowed down the process of application and decision making, are also being abandoned in favor of unsecured credit lines. Most commonly, these are issued to consumers as part of express loans or to people whose previous banking history can be traced—those who already took out and repaid loans or used salary cards

The composition of issuers has also changed. Throughout the 1990s, the Russian banking industry successfully lobbied the state for protectionist policies seeking to deter foreign banks from operating in Russia (Johnson 1997). Although the Russian lobby was successful in keeping branches of foreign banks away, foreign banks and financial companies are promoting their brands through locally registered companies (such as Citibank ZAO) or acquiring existing local banks. As an indication, with the notable exception of the state-owned Sberbank, most current leaders in consumer lending and card-issuing markets are foreign-owned: American Citibank, Austrian Raiffeisen (which has recently acquired Impexbank and significantly increased its market share), Czech Home Credit&Finance, and Deltabank, recently purchased by GE Consumer Finance. For at least two of them (Deltabank and Home Credit&Finance), consumer lending has always been their primary line of business. Although the state-owned goliath Sberbank has been gradually losing its monopoly, its market concentration remains high: Sberbank still issues 25 percent of all cards, extends 30 percent of all consumer loans, and collects about 50 percent of all household deposits (Sberbank 2005).

A dramatically increased volume of lending and simplified screening and decision-making procedures are bringing inevitable changes to the banks' risk-management strategies. They are no longer able to invest time and human resources into thorough in-depth verification of prospective borrowers. Instead they are introducing further formalization of decision making, the most advanced of them tinkering with credit-scoring models, acquired abroad or developed in-house. But the main problem remains: despite the recent legislation and establishment of several credit bureaus designed to accumulate and verify information on borrowers' past histories and current indebtedness, leaders in the consumer credit market continue resisting information sharing with other banks. Yet the value of effective prescreening cannot be overestimated. Even the recent growth in the market for debt collection would not be able to substitute for the importance of obtaining verified information about prospective applicants as part of prescreening.[2] It remains to be seen whether a competitive market in consumer credit data prevails.

The Credit Card Market as a Site of Continuity with the Past

A close look at the two decades of card issuing in Russia demonstrates a particular pervasiveness of socialist legacies in market building. Socialist legacies served as a resource pool, from which market actors could pick elements of their solutions, preshaped a certain way, but insufficient until someone put them together. In the absence of formal institutional and cultural bases (or while they are being debated or developed), banks resort to the informal social ties ubiquitous in socialist societies and to the intermediation of companies. In particular, reliance on bi-level networks allows banks to reach a large number of consumers and even reduce the uncertainty inherent in card issuing. Banks reach into their cultural tool kit (Swidler 1986) and pull out the elements of social structure that are intelligible both to them and their potential customers because these elements stem from their shared socialist past.

Credit Cards as an Agent of Change

In addition to being a site of change and a vehicle of historical continuity, the Russian credit card market is undoubtedly a transformative force as well. For instance, card programs helped mitigate some of the most destabilizing effects of the postcommunist transition on the Russian economy. Specifically, they played a key role in helping to solve the problem of wage arrears and cash shortages prevalent in Russia in the 1990s, enabling local governments and businesses to settle accounts without resorting to barter. At the time when individuals were reluctant to trust commercial banks with their savings, salary projects also allowed banks to attract significant additional financial resources and increase their customer base.

Moreover, the Russian economy has been suffering from chronic underreporting of personal incomes and corporate profits and from widespread tax evasion. According to the poll conducted by the Russian National pollster VTsIOM in 2006, 27 percent of working adults in Russia receive salaries in under-the-table payments, 18 percent partially, and 9 percent fully ("Pochti tret' rossiyan poluchayut zarplaty v konvertah" 2006). One of the positive consequences of the increasing popularity of cards would be greater transparency and traceability of economic transactions and the legalization of "black" and "gray" segments of the economy. Salary projects have already contributed to this end, albeit modestly, since they reportedly have accounted for only a portion of salaries while the rest have continued to be paid in cash. Although a recent draft law proposed by the Duma's Banking Committee to require all large retailers to accept cards for purchases would undoubtedly be a boost to the Russian card market, it would also be a major step toward legalizing the turnover of retail companies. Some of them have been resisting card acceptance because trading in cash has allowed them to underreport their turnover to the Tax Authorities. Besides, with the greater popularity of credit cards and consumer credit, it will be in the best interest of applicants to legalize their real income to be eligible for a larger line of credit.

Greater popularity of bank-procured credit might also have an effect on personal relations and social integration. It has been argued that transitional countries in general and Russia in particular exhibit a low level of basic trust that allows strangers to transact without being tied together through an interpersonal relationship (Sztompka 1999). This kind of trust serves as lubricant for economic transactions and is essential for a viable civil society (Seligman 1992; Putnam 1993; Gellner 1994). The spread of credit reporting should contribute to the constitution of this basic trust to the extent that credit bureaus will be able to promote transparency, rationality, financial responsibility, and thus predictability in individual behavior. This is what has happened in the United States, where interpersonal trust was largely replaced by institutional trust (Zucker 1986), and where credit reporting emerged as a new form of social control. One's credit score is now used as a proxy of one's character: not only banks but also landlords, employers, and even insurers consider credit scores to be good predictors of personal reliability.[3] Ironically, the institutionalization of credit reporting in Russia might play a role similar to the one that was played during the Soviet period by local Communist party bureaus (enterprise-based units called *partburos*), a role that has remained essentially vacant since the collapse of the system. Just like party loyalty once upon a time made Soviets eligible for a myriad of goods— from hard-to-obtain-in-open-trade consumer goods to cars and housing, high credit scores would open doors to virtually unlimited consumer purchases as long as borrowers continued to behave in a prescribed way. Certainly, party control was much more near total control than credit reporting would ever be. For instance, besides procuring for one's "material conditions of life" in a perfect following of Marxist ideology, *partburos* also considered it their responsibility to control the moral foundations of one's private life. They could provide recommendations for job promotions, continuing education, and trips abroad, as well as attempt to stop an alcoholic from drinking and a husband from philandering, undeniably fulfilling much broader functions than those performed by credit bureaus in the United States.

It is the fact that credit scores in the United States are increasingly used by employers that makes institutionalizing credit reporting in Russia particularly attractive to labor markets. So far, hiring background checks in Russia are done by the employers' security departments (Yakubovich and Kozina 2007) in a similar way to card issuing decisions made by the security departments of banks. Russian credit bureaus would be able to provide employers with much easier access to job applicants' background information.

At the same time, the further spread of formal consumer borrowing can have a negative disintegrating effect on informal interpersonal relations in extended families or among friends. After all, the most common form of borrowing until recently had been informal borrowing from friends and family, including intergenerational money transfers, such as from elderly parents to their adult children (Clarke 2002a). The terms of such loans were notoriously vague, with some of them subsequently recategorized as gifts, reinforcing norms of reciprocity and strengthening social bonds (Polanyi [1944]

1957; Granovetter 1985; Uzzi 1996). Bank borrowing, on the other hand, can result in an increased financial independence from one's kin.

What is the effect of the spread of credit cards on inequality? Even more important, if new markets emerge using social structures established in already existing markets, are old inequalities reproduced? At each of the three stages (issuing to elites, salary projects, and consumer lending) one needed to belong in a particular category to be eligible for a card: during the first stage a member of an elite or someone personally linked to the bank, then an employee, and now a consumer. At each of those stages, people who were neither members of elites nor insiders, people without formal labor affiliations (such as retirees, unemployed, homemakers, and self-employed), and those without the means to consume have been automatically excluded from the pool of prospective cardholders. Although the current mode of card dissemination through retail locations seems to be the most inclusive of all three stages (one only needs to come to one of the places where the cards are offered with a desire to make a purchase), the expanding boundaries of consumer society are likely to be impenetrable for those without means. According to official estimates, close to 20 percent of Russians lived under the poverty line in 2004, and a large number of others only managed to make ends meet, spending all their income on bare necessities.[4] It is likely that inequalities in consumption (both in terms of *what* is consumed and *where* it is consumed—in a glittering Western-style shopping mall or at an open-air cash-based market) will be perpetuated by credit cards' unequal availability and use, as consumption is becoming the main engine of growth of the Russian credit card market.

Even despite the uneven penetration of credit cards among different demographic groups, they are profoundly changing the culture of consumption in Russia. Certainly, compared to elite issuing, the current mode of card dissemination makes cards available to a wider and more diverse group of people who are given an opportunity to own things they would not otherwise be able to afford without saving first. While consumer goods lure Russians into signing up for cards and taking on the burden of credit, are they transforming consumers into incorrigible spendthrifts running up bills and living beyond their means? Not necessarily. In Calder's (1999) account of the rise of consumer credit in the United States from 1890 to 1940, the central argument is that consumer credit "regulates and ultimately limits the hedonistic qualities of consumer culture" (294) because having a loan and living with a schedule of monthly payments is essentially a form of forced savings. Calling it a form of "budgetism," Calder argues that bank-procured "installment credit imposes on borrowers financial regiments requiring discipline, foresight, and a conscious effort to save income in order to make payments on time" (301–302), illustrating what he believes is the main cultural contradiction of American capitalism: that people are required to be both self-indulging consumers and disciplined workers.

Covering a more recent period in American consumer history (from the early 1980s), Manning (2000) paints a much more troublesome picture of consumer credit in America: rising consumer indebtedness, stemming from unrestrained access to too many lines of credit and resulting in financial and personal ruin. Manning places particular blame on the aggressive marketing campaigns by credit providers, which resulted in a sharp rise in the supply of revolving credit lines and their newfound ability to finance "employment disruptions, family emergencies and personal crises" (Manning 2000, 131) among the already heavily indebted middle class and the working poor. As a result, an average consumer in the nation that invented and perfected credit cards holds three or four credit cards (plus about four more retail and one travel and entertainment card, such as American Express or Diners) with a total outstanding debt of $4,000.[5]

In Calder's account, installment credit is considered a means of ensuring the middle-class lifestyle and the fulfillment of the American dream. Preserving that middle-class standing and all the possessions that reflect it compels borrowers to continue working and to budget their earnings rationally to satisfy timely bill payments. Manning, on the contrary, argues that the rise in revolving credit cards sets consumption free from the internalized discipline of continuous labor in order to meet the rigid schedule of repayments. The reason for this, in my interpretation, was that revolving credit severed the tie between a specific purchase and the loan used to finance it. This tie was clearly present in installment credit, helping borrowers connect their subsequent self-denial (budgeting and restrictions on future spending to assure the timely payment of bills) with the enjoyment of the item for which the loan paid. Which America, then—Calder's or Manning's—will be Russia's future?

In Russia, many of the credit cards are currently issued in connection with express loans to finance particular household purchases, such as furniture or electronics, which suggests that what Calder describes about installment credit in the early twentieth-century United States might apply in Russia too. However, Russian banks that are actively involved in express lending already report default rates of 7–15 percent, which is several times higher than the market average for household loans, evoking the gloomy reality described by Manning. The main difference between Calder's America and today's Russia is that in the early twentieth-century United States, installment credit was approved based on time-consuming in-depth screening of prospective borrowers, while in Russia these decisions are frequently arrived at on the spot, while shoppers are waiting. The speed of decision making and its effect on the quality of decisions, as well as the overall pace of growth of consumer lending in Russia brings back disturbing memories of the South Korean consumer credit debacle, where unrestrained distribution of credit cards on street corners led to a major market crash several months later. It is my conviction that the only way to avoid this is to stress prescreening, which naturally presupposes a need to formally institutionalize effective credit reporting. Not only will credit bureaus provide banks with information that will help them distinguish reliable borrowers from less than reliable ones, but the bureaus would also serve as a powerful deterrence mechanism. Failure to repay would jeopardize one's chances of getting another loan or credit card in the future, and thus the possibility of continuing to furnish one's middle-class dream.

Yet, one should not ignore the key lesson in Manning's account, however, that unrestrained competition and predatory marketing strategies by banks can lead to overcrediting. Although the Russian credit card market with its 0.4 bank cards per capita is a far cry from the four bank cards plus an assortment of department store, gas, and travel-and-entertainment cards owned by an average American household, the rate of growth in the Russian household-lending market and increasing competitiveness suggest that the scenario described by Manning is not entirely impossible in Russia. The high interest rates and profits prevailing in retail lending in Russia today make it extremely attractive both for foreign banks hoping to expand their operations in emergent markets and for domestic banks previously involved only with corporate lending.[6] This competition may drive banks to oversaturate the society with revolving credit lines, bringing closer the grim reality of the credit card nation (Manning 2000).

In addition to developing and strengthening the means of prescreening prospective cardholders and borrowers, and in anticipation of the increasing popularity of consumer lending, Russian lawmakers need to address the issue of debtor and consumer protection. Consumer lending and the institutionalization of credit reporting and collections leave consumers vulnerable to various forms of harassment from lenders, credit bureaus, debt collectors, and identity thieves. The measures necessary to extend such protections can include:

1. Personal bankruptcy legislation (still under debate in Russia) and effective consumer education about the "dark side" of consumer debt, including assistance in dealing with collection companies and their representatives;
2. Greater control over financial-data protection (recent cases of several public data leaks including the one from the Central Bank suggest that at this point the state seems to be losing this battle), and specifically, protection against identity theft;
3. Control over advertised loan terms that often hide real interest rates from inexperienced borrowers, and the sanctioning of offending banks.

To sum up, the credit card market is Janus-faced as it brings both virtues and sins. In one case, it glorifies consumption but can tame hedonism with the notion that one has to work and budget one's future income to pay the debts off; in another, it promises instant fulfillment of desires and dreams at the same time as it pushes borrowers deeper into financial demise. Card use can both promote legalization of the economy with a potential for higher tax revenues and serve as a vehicle for bribing and therefore promote corruption. Finally, while consumer credit encourages a rational and responsible attitude toward one's earnings and expenditures, it can also make borrowers the prisoners of Weber's proverbial "iron cage."[7] Weber warned about the increasing power that the pursuit of wealth emblematic of the modern economic order can have on people once its spiritual and ethical foundations are gone. The spread of consumer credit and credit reporting takes economic compulsion to a new level, where diligent rational labor is necessary not to finance one's insatiable quest for new worldly goods, but to preserve the lifestyle already acquired. For Russians, such a form of social control could strike a surprisingly familiar cord as Communist Party control would be replaced with the uncompromising red ink of debts.

Thus, the Russian credit card market serves as a link between the past and the future: having been initially built on many of the Soviet legacies, it fearlessly charges forward, reshaping itself in the process, capable of effecting profound changes in culture, social relations, and ideology, bringing Russians from the communist past into the capitalist consumerist future, out of the red and into the red.

Reference Matter

Appendix: Data and Methodology

In the first wave of the project (1998–1999), I conducted semistructured interviews with representatives of seventeen Moscow-based banks, including the Central Bank of Russia, one large regional bank, as well as the Association of Russian Banks (ARB) and four credit card networks. I also interviewed managers in two card-processing companies, as well as journalists and independent analysts who specialize in writing about card markets. All in all I conducted interviews with thirty-six individuals. With several people I conducted two or even three interviews. Repeat interviews were conducted during the second trip to the field a year later to inquire about the changes in trends. I was particularly interested in the effect on the Russian card market of a dramatic economy-wide banking crisis that occurred on August 17, 1998, the day after I returned from my first field trip. All the interviews were face-to-face, with the exception of one, which was conducted on the telephone, and all lasted between one and three hours. Of the face-to-face interviews, the majority was conducted at the interviewee's workplace, five took place in the foyer of the bank, and three in a park or a café.

In addition, I carried out participant observations at several training seminars where bank employees and store cashiers were taught procedures for accepting applications for cards, servicing cards, and identifying fraud and counterfeit. I also attended the Second International Payment Cards Forum, organized by the ARB in Moscow in October 1999. Finally, I gained full access to the archives of all three Russian specialized plastic card publications (two monthly journals and a daily electronic bulletin) for 1995–1999.

The second wave of the project (2003–2005) was supported by the American National Science Foundation grant to Ákos Róna-Tas (University of

California, San Diego). During this period, my Moscow-based collaborator Olga Kuzina (Higher School of Economics) and I conducted sixteen interviews, this time more closely following an interview guide developed by the project team. Fourteen of the interviews were with representatives of Moscow banks, one with representatives of the Association of Russian Banks, and one with a representative of a credit card network. All of the interviews were face-to-face, all but two were conducted at the interviewee's workplace, and all lasted between one-and-a-half and two-and-a-half hours. I further supplemented my analysis with materials from specialized trade outlets and general Russian periodicals, including Internet-based publications.

In both waves of the project I used the interview method to generate narratives about card issuing at the banks studied (including information verification and decision making, monitoring of cardholders, sanctioning of defaulters, development and marketing of new card products, and demographics of cardholders and card department employees), and about institutional and cultural aspects of the card business in Russia (specifically, the issues of interbank information sharing, the role of the state, legal sanctions against fraud or defaults, consumer culture, and building demand for card products/consumer credit). None of the interviews in the first wave of the project were recorded; instead, I took detailed notes during each of them, and wrote down even more detailed elaborations immediately following each of the interviews. In the second wave of the project, half of the bank interviews (seven) were audiotaped (while detailed notes were taken on the rest of them) and later transcribed. Where I quote my interviewees, I write their words *verbatim* and then translate them into English to the best of my ability.

As part of the initial agreement to an interview, our informants were guaranteed privacy: we promised that neither they personally nor their employer could be identified in the resulting publications. For this reason, we catalogued all of the interviews and assigned each a number. Direct quotes in the text are referenced in the endnotes with this number and the date on which the interview was conducted.

One of the biggest obstacles I encountered while carrying out this project was getting access to banks. Russian banks have been very protective of any information that concerns their customers or their products, ready to declare everything a "banking secret." In part, this probably stems from their history of internecine warfare described in Chapter Three, when banks bad-mouthed each other in public smear campaigns, apparently not stopping at anything to get ahead. This could also be a consequence of their highly uncertain environment, where the dominant strategy is divulging as little about oneself as possible. This was especially noticeable during my first two visits to the field in 1998 and 1999. Despite my quasi-native status, I was perceived as an outsider, my affiliation with an American university and my keen interest in mechanisms of financial decision making rendering me particularly suspect. On one occasion it was my academic discipline that was perceived as a red flag. I was told that sociologists were no better than spies (so more dangerous if they were Western sociologists), since this was what Soviet sociologists did (snooping around and reporting to the authorities).[1] On another occasion, I had a frustrating interview with a bank employee who refused to answer any question that contained a "how much" in it.[2] This was apparently the policy of their bank, which would not let their rank-and-file employees tell media sources how many cards the bank had already issued.

Needless to say, these circumstances made my task of finding people willing to talk to me quite challenging. I started by contacting banks, card networks, and processing companies whose contact information I found in a Moscow business directory distributed through a limited number of high-end hotels and business centers. Only two of my cold calls yielded interviews, however (and those were not with banks). In other cases I was either advised to contact the media relations department, where I was furnished with publicly available press releases, or told that the manager I was trying to reach was busy, away, or otherwise unavailable. In such a situation the best strategy was to use the snowball-sampling technique (Lee 1993; Maxwell 1998, 87–88): to make initial contacts and after interviewing them ask for referrals to their friends and colleagues who work in other organizations. Introductions proved invaluable, but even they could not always guarantee an interview; in several cases my persistent calls to recommended colleagues and/or friends remained unanswered.

So this is how I generated my sample during the first wave of the project (1998–1999). Snowball sampling has been used in studying rare, vulnerable, or highly stigmatized groups. This method has built-in "security features … because the intermediaries who form the links of the referral chain are known to potential respondents and trusted by them" (Lee 1993, 67). It was appropriate for my study because bankers considered the issues we discussed sensitive, and viewed "outsiders" with suspicion. Establishing my link to them through a mutual acquaintance (who, most likely, had already been interviewed) made me an "insider" and in most cases gave me the opportunity to get my questions answered.

One of the drawbacks of snowball sampling is that it tends to produce samples that are relatively homogeneous, as social relations are largely built on a homophily principle (Lazarsfeld and Merton 1954). This precludes internal comparisons, and can make overall conclusions biased (Lee 1981). A certain degree of homogeneity was present in my case: at least in the group interviewed in 1998–1999 all were males in their late 30s to early 50s, most with technical or security forces backgrounds. But this reflected the state of commercial banking in Russia at the time and career trajectories that brought individuals into banking and the card business. Another reason that homogeneity among interviewees should not be problematic is that the population in my study is not individuals but banks. I was only interested in the individuals I interviewed because they could provide information for me about organizational practices at their workplaces. Some homogeneity among banks is unavoidable too because at least initially banks that issued cards were predominantly larger Moscow-based banks.

By the second wave of the project, I was part of the research team, which had the support of the National Science Foundation, several American academic institutions, VISA, and two Eastern European banking associations. I was also no longer a Ph.D. student but an academic with a regular appointment at an American research university. That did not immediately make me an insider, but certainly gave more weight to my persona. Besides, I still had some of my old contacts, which I also put to use. Prior to going into the field, I put together a database of about forty Russian banks, including the largest ones, the ones listed as Visa Principal Members, and the ones mentioned in the periodicals in connection with their credit card programs. Of these, I selected twenty banks that were either the leaders of the plastic card market or stated on their Web sites that they were issuing credit cards. I also included all three foreign-owned banks that were included in the original group. All of the twenty sampled banks were sent formal invitations to participate in the project, and lengthy negotiations ensued in several cases. Six of the twenty banks rejected our invitation and we were left with fourteen banks. Out of this group, two banks are foreign-owned, one is state-owned, and domestic financial and nonfinancial organizations and individuals own the rest. While nonrandom, my sample is also diverse with respect to size: five of the banks are among the top twenty Russian banks ranked by the size of assets (three are among the top ten), another five occupy positions between twenty-first and fiftieth, and the remaining four are not ranked among the fifty largest banks. Notably, in the second wave of the project, our interviewees included a few women and several people with degrees in finance.

Notes

INTRODUCTION

1. Details of sampling, data gathering, and analysis are addressed in the Appendix.

CHAPTER ONE

1. The epigraph to this chapter is drawn from Joseph Nocera, *A Piece of the Action: How the Middle Class Joined the Money Class*. New York: Simon and Schuster, 1994, p. 15.

2. Not all the banks that were testing the waters of credit card lending were as reckless as Bank of America. New York–based Chase Manhattan Bank, which started its credit card program in the same year as Bank of America, sought to behave in a more cautious way: it only issued cards to those who applied for them, and then after a scrupulous credit check with as many as 50 percent of applicants rejected. But ironically, the conservative issuing of cards turned out to be hardly superior to mass mailing in terms of preventing fraud and delinquency, which ran higher than expected. And what is more important, it did not lead to success. With a slow growth in the number of cardholders, large merchants were particularly resistant to signing up for the service, driving down the bank's sales against projected targets and accumulating the bank's losses ($1.5 million in the first two years of operations). As a result, Chase Manhattan sold its credit card program in 1962, after fewer than four years in the market (Wolters 2000).

3. The losses that were a result of indiscriminate mass mailing had another—unintended—effect on subsequent market development. Other banks were fooled by Bank of America's initial losses and kept out of entering the credit card business until after they realized, sometime in the mid-1960s and with a considerable delay, how profitable the program had become. But by that time Bank of America already enjoyed an enormous competitive advantage (Wolters 2000).

4. The Russia of the 1990s could hardly have been more different from the United States at the time when credit cards were introduced there. The American

credit card market was born in the 1950s into an extended family of a stable economy, mature banking, and consumer credit; a long-standing tradition of collecting credit histories; and a developing field of credit scoring. On the other hand, the Russian credit card market was ushered on stage in the late 1980s–early 1990s by the country's young and unstable banking industry, and in the absence of credit reporting, credit scoring, debt collection, or even a noncorrupt and efficient legal system.

5. This process is nicely illustrated with the rate spiral currently being experienced by the American health-care system. As insurers raise premiums, they essentially encourage the youngest and the healthiest to drop their coverage: 26 percent of those between ages 18 and 24 are uninsured compared to 16 percent nationwide (Weitz 2006). However, as healthier individuals leave, the cost of providing health care for those who remain insured increases, prompting insurance companies to further raise premiums. Soon, another group drops the coverage, which becomes too expensive for their self-perceived health status, leaving those who are desperate to have insurance at virtually any cost, and raising overall expenses even further.

6. This approach suffers from a twofold problem of endogeneity. First, there is a selection bias. For those who do not get approved, there is no data on the dependent variable (defaulting versus not defaulting on the loan). Moreover, past approvals for loans are counted as signs of creditworthiness and past rejections as red flags. This approach can lock people into virtuous or vicious circles that are independent of their exogenous characteristics.

7. For a discussion of credit scoring in Britain, see Leyshon and Thrift (1999); Batt and Fowkes (1972).

8. One of the early and successful attempts to develop a scoring model (on a limited scale) was made by a banker who wanted to replace his loan officers drafted during World War II (Lewis 1992, 19).

9. Numerous presentations by and conversations with Ákos Róna-Tas.

10. I am indebted to Ákos Róna-Tas for initially making this point.

11. In 1937 it was reorganized into the Associated Credit Bureaus, Inc.

12. The fourth credit bureau, Innovis, has been in operation since 2001 (http://www.innovis.com/).

13. The percentage of the sales that acquiring banks charge merchants, usually to be shared in some proportion with issuing banks for taking part in the interchange system.

14. Yet another side of this tension is the competition between credit card brands.

15. For an overview of approaches to markets in neighboring disciplines and current research on markets in economic sociology, see Lie (1997); Swedberg (1994); and Swedberg (2005).

CHAPTER TWO

1. The title of the article, "With Little Choice, Stalinist North Korea Lets Markets Emerge" (*Wall Street Journal—Eastern Edition*, 6/20/2003, 241[120], p. A6), is symptomatic of this approach.

2. In addition to being viewed through the prism of their structural properties, markets are also considered sites of cultural production: they maintain and perpetuate cultural beliefs (Bertrand and Mullainathan 2004) and market activities are perceived by actors in cultural terms (Abolafia 2001), while market actors construct social values and prices of products (Zelizer 1978; Smith 1989; Velthuis 2005). Markets are also sites of institution-building efforts (Zucker 1986; Greif 1993), which create "conceptions of control"—stable and shared understandings of how markets work—that help mitigate competition and assure market stability (Fligstein 2001). The most recent trend is to account for performativity of markets (MacKenzie and Millo 2003), as it is argued that markets and market actors are not just embedded in social relations but are also actively constructed by society, more specifically by the discipline of economics.

3. This suggests that besides their traditional function of reducing uncertainty (by assisting in screening, monitoring, and sanctioning of borrowers), credit bureaus also help banks gain access to groups of borrowers.

4. Many international financial organizations like the International Monetary Fund (IMF) provide financial assistance to nations on the condition that their governments carry out certain reforms.

CHAPTER THREE

1. This problem was quickly solved by the hyperinflation of the early 1990s, when prices were liberalized as part of a drastic economic reform, and savings evaporated overnight.

2. Many Soviet enterprises employed so-called *tolkachi*, individuals who developed and maintained numerous personal ties with other enterprises' administration, and used them to procure necessary supplies. The successful fulfillment of the plan hinged on obtaining these supplies on time. Besides being undoubtedly talented "connectors" (Gladwell 2000) using personal ties to secure favors where official distribution channels failed, these individuals were skilled at two other tasks: the art of persuasion and the ability to consume large quantities of vodka with the enterprises' administration responsible for authorizing required shipments of supplies.

3. A small number of borrowers without employment, such as pensioners, could apply directly to banks (*Potrebitelskiy kredit* 1983).

4. Work was a constitutionally guaranteed right of each Soviet citizen.

5. First cooperatives engaged in a variety of undertakings, most commonly making clothes. Roman Abramovich, Russian oil tycoon, the governor of Chukotka region, the owner of the English soccer club Chelsea, and until 2007 the richest man in Russia,

started his business career from a successful plush toy-making cooperative in the late 1980s.

6. This is a clear case of the tragedy of the commons. Banks were willing to damage public trust in banking in order to attain marginal gains over their competitors (Hardin 1968).

7. See www.creditcard.ru for the history of credit cards in Russia. Accessed on June 20, 2006.

8. An average Russian had only 0.4 cards in 2005, according to the data from the Central Bank of Russia, www.cbr.ru.

9. Interview with a former employee of Kredobank. Interview no. 20 on July 22, 1998.

10. Russian credit cards have also been widely called "plastic cards" (*plastikovye kartochki*) or simply "cards" (*kartochki*).

11. Many banks started to drop security deposits in 1995–1996, mainly due to intense competition, so that only a few continued requiring them by 1998. Security deposits did not make a comeback when the card market reemerged after the 1998 crisis.

12. The use of the masculine pronoun is intentional. At least in the 1990s, the Russian card world was overwhelmingly male-dominated. Cards, it seemed, were issued by men to men. With an exception of one female journalist specializing in the card market, all of my interviews in Russia in 1998–1999 were with men. Around the same time, Russian card advertisements sometimes used images of scantily clad women selling cards alongside their bodies. For example, a popular advertisement of one of the large Moscow banks featured a strategically positioned nude woman with a card in her hand that read "All yours" (*Vsya vasha, bes ostatka*). This was a very effective ad; many prospective clients contacted the bank and inquired about obtaining a card with "naked babes" (though the card itself had a standard design). The ad ran for 1.5 months and cost $100,000. The bank estimated that it brought between $600,000 and $1,000,000 in new deposits alone (Interview no. 5 on July 7, 1998). In the next decade, the gendered world of cards started to change: some banks started to promote cards specifically designed for women users, and a few of my informants during the 2003–2004 round of interviews included women.

13. My card was once verified through a similar phone call in a local branch of a Latvian clothing store in Kharkov, Ukraine. I tried to make a purchase for slightly more than $100 and wanted to use my U.S.-issued Platinum Visa. All three factors (the size of the purchase, the fact that the card was not local, and that it was a Platinum card, which are usually more commonly stolen or forfeited due to higher credit limits) raised a red flag with the shop assistants. Several of them crowded around the only telephone found in the store to hold my card and gaze inquiringly into my face. Clearly, they were not calling my issuing bank, only their local acquiring bank. It took close to half an hour for them to get someone on the phone, dictate my name from the card and my passport, which they also asked to see, and get a positive response from the bank that the transaction could continue. My guess is that the ac-

quiring bank ran my card and my name against international stop lists of stolen, counterfeit, or fraudulently used cards. I was patient not only because I wanted my purchase, but also, and mainly, because I wanted to witness the process. Someone less curious than I might have been long gone to get cash, and would have thought twice before trying to use their card in the store again.

14. Interview with a high-ranking employee of a processing company. Interview no. 8, on June 24, 1998.

15. Interview no. 3 on September 22, 1999.

16. Interview no. 10 on July 20, 1998.   17. Interview no. 12 on June 18, 1998.

18. Interview no. 1 on July 24, 1998   19. Interview no. 19 on July 22, 1998.

20. Interview no. 2 on July 1, 1998.   21. Interview no. 1 on July 24, 1998.

22. Interview no. 12 on June 18, 1998.   23. Interview no. 12 on June 18, 1998.

24. Another popular scheme relied not on banks but on insurance companies, which would sell short-term life insurance policies to the enterprise's employees (reissued every year or even every quarter of a year), and pay annuity payments in equal increments during the policy period (Andreev 1999). In 1999, life insurance policies accounted for more than 36 percent of the total volume of premiums collected by Russian insurers (OECD 2000, 3), and in 2001 it was 50 percent. Meanwhile, the Russian Ministry of Finance estimated that more than 70 percent of this volume came from such tax-evasion schemes. Until recently, monthly annuity payments had not been taxable. Instead of a regular 35.6 percent payroll tax levied on employers (recently replaced by the 26 percent "uniform social tax") and a 13 percent income tax to be withdrawn from the employees' paychecks, such schemes cost employers 6–12 percent and employees 1.5 percent. In addition to being beneficial for enterprises, they have been extremely popular with the insurance companies, most of which used them for capital accumulation. In 2002, the Russian Parliament passed corrections to the Tax Code, which made life insurance annuities taxable for the first five years, making such schemes too expensive (Grishina 2002).

CHAPTER FOUR

1. Interview no. 4 on September 20, 1999.

2. Interview no. 10 on July 20, 1998.

3. Although those cardholders who pay their balances in full each month are often thought of as paragons of discipline and self-control, they are in fact free riders who receive interest-free loans for up to 55 days (billing cycle plus a 25–day grace period, on average) (Nocera 1994; Mandel 1990). Given the margin of profits, interest rates for those who carry balances have to be higher in order to compensate for such free riding.

4. Russia's Federal Deposit Insurance Law "O Strahovanii Vkladov Fizicheskih Lits v Bankah Rossiyskoy Federatsii" was signed in December 2003 and mandated the formation of the State Corporation "Deposit Insurance Agency."

5. The FDIC was established by the Banking Act of 1933, at the height of the Depression. Initially, it protected accounts for up to $10,000; over time, this figure has grown to the present $100,000 per account (Kindleberger 1996). The FDIC's main goals were to restore public confidence in financial institutions and to minimize the disruptions caused by bank insolvency. The agency soon was perceived as a preventive institution as well. Financial panics often turned out to be self-fulfilling prophecies, as sudden and large-scale cash demands could be a fatal blow even to solvent banks. With the existence of the FDIC, bank runs became matters of the past (FDIC 1984).

6. In 1996, Central Bank of Russia publicly selected five more banks, in addition to state-owned Sberbank, that would be supported in case of financial difficulties. These five banks were christened in the popular press "immortal," and included Avtobank, Agroprombank, Vneshtorgbank, MENATEP, and International Financial Company (Petrova, Buraya, and Akimova 1996).

7. *Card On-Line*, June 13, 1996.

8. Interview no. 2 on July 1, 1998.

9. Interview no. 5 on July 7, 1998.

10. At a training session for the card department staff from the provincial offices of a large Moscow bank, the instructor encouraged listeners to "be reasonably suspicious" when accepting applications.

11. Interview no. 24 on September 9, 1999, and interview no. 25 on September 17, 1999.

12. Interview no. 22 on September 4, 1999.

13. Interview no. 12 on June 18, 1988.

14. Interview no. 22 on September 4, 1999.

15. In Russia, telephone numbers have been traditionally fixed to addresses. Even when people move locally, they take the number associated with their new residence rather than transferring their old number to the new residence.

16. Interview with a vice president of a small bank (interview no. 13 on October 22, 1999).

17. Under salary projects, banks signed agreements with enterprises to have the salaries of all of their employees directly deposited to the bank. Both the management and the workers would then be issued cards linked to their deposit accounts, which would be regularly and automatically replenished by salary payments.

18. Interview no. 22 on September 4, 1999.

19. Interview no. 12 on June 18, 1998.

20. Anchoring is similar to methods used in microlending programs. Microlending traditionally caters to poor communities whose members cannot receive regular bank loans because they do not have any collateral and are considered "bad risks." Their membership in their community and in their group of coborrowers makes defaults infrequent. See Kamaluddin (1993); Rahman (1999); and Reinke (1998).

21. Interview no. 3a on June 11, 1998.

22. Interview no. 4a on September 20, 1999.

23. Interviews no. 12 on June 18, 1998 and no. 3 on September 22, 1999.

24. Sberbank alternatively named this risk category "managers of small organizations without [a] stable volume of operations and developed business." From Moscow Sberbank internal letter no. 1703/4903, "O vydache bankovskih kart" from November 1, 1999, signed by Deputy Head Nikolai Petrov (Prezhentsev 1999).

25. Interview no. 3 on September 22, 1999.

26. Also in interview no. 12 on June 18, 1998.

27. Interview no. 3 on September 22, 1999.

28. Interview no. 3 on September 22, 1999. The same idea was emphasized in interview no. 4a on September 20, 1999 and in interview no. 12 on June 18, 1998. (The manager of the card department said that decisions were made "in each specific case, on the basis of each application.")

29. Interview no. 8 on June 17, 1998.

CHAPTER FIVE

1. Interview no. 25 on September 9, 1999.

2. Interview no. 14 on June 23, 1998.

3. Interview no. 16 on October 20, 1999.

4. Interview no. 13 on October 22, 1999.

5. With the notable exception of Sberbank, most of the banks lack a widespread branch network and their ability to market cards via in-branch application is limited. Sberbank inherited its nationwide system of branches from the Soviet monobank system.

6. Such enterprises are called *gradoobrazuyushchie* or town-forming, making them similar to American company towns.

7. Reported on Visa International Service Association website, corporate.visa.com (accessed on March 30, 2006).

8. Interview no. 3 on September 22, 1999.

9. Interview no. 25 on September 8, 1999.

10. Interview no. 15 on June 29, 1998.

11. Interview no. 13 on October 22, 1999.

12. In a more exclusive version of salary projects, American Express made cards available only to employees approved by their enterprises ("That'll Do Nicely, Comrade," *The Economist*, August 13, 1988:67). See also "A Dragon by the Tail," *Credit Card Management* 8(4), 1995:34–45.

13. Nevertheless, salary projects have been a popular method of issuing cards to Chinese government officials.

CHAPTER SIX

1. It includes countries of Central and Eastern Europe, the Middle East, and Africa.

2. When cardholders used cards to pay for purchases, it was often out of necessity, as discussed in Chapter Five, when cash was temporarily scarce and electronic money transfers ruled—predominantly in regional towns in the mid-to-late-1990s. When cash was available, it remained the preferred mode of payment.

3. See, for instance, *PLUS-info* no. 3, 02/10/05, accessed from www.recon.ru on June 30, 2006.

4. Cash withdrawals from the banks' own ATMs eventually became free of charge by the year 2000.

5. *Platezhi. Sistemy. Kartochki.* (1997):6–7, (1997):8, (1997):9–10.

6. *Mir Kartochek* (1998):1, (1998):2, (1998):6, (1998):9.

7. A similar picture emerges from the analysis of fees for domestic card brands, such as Union Card, STB card, and Zolotaya Korona (*Card On-Line* 1998, 4/1, January 9).

8. Visa International Service Association website, accessed from corporate.visa .com on March 30, 2006.

9. This means, among other things, that salary projects do not fully account for total wages paid, and it makes applying for credit particularly difficult for individuals since one's full salary cannot be officially confirmed by the employer.

10. The only exception is small regional towns, which experienced shortages of cash in the mid-1990s. There, salary cardholders, usually employed at one large company, used cards in local retail establishments, which then settled accounts directly with that company.

11. Income data for 2005, according to the Federal Statistical Service (www.gks.ru) and Mosgorstat (www.mosstat.ru).

12. A.T. Kearney, Inc., is a global strategic management consulting firm, www .atkearney.com.

13. Interview no. 38 on June 18, 2004.

14. Interview no. 37 on December 7, 2005.

15. IPSOS Quantitative Credit Card Study, September 2006. Reported in Oliver Hughes, "Kreditnye karty v Rossii: opyt i tendentsiya," presentation at the conference "Kreditnye karty v Rossii. Novy etap razvitiya," Moscow, Russia, April 9, 2007. Accessed from www.visa.com.ru on September 11, 2007.

16. Interview no. 38 on June 18, 2004.

17. Interview no. 50 on September 2, 2004.

18. News release from May 17, 2006 on www.impexbank.ru.

19. Data from Central Bank of Russia, www.cbr.ru.

20. Reported on Visa Russia Web site, www.visa.com.ru (accessed on September 30, 2005).

21. All of the banks associated with eminent Russian oligarchs of the 1990s—Potanin (ONEXIM), Fridman (Alfabank), Vinogradov (Inkombank), Smolenskiy (Stolichny Bank Sberezheniy), Khodorkovskiy (MENATEP), and Gusinskiy (Mostbank)—were among the early card issuers.

22. One notable exception was SBS-Agro bank, which openly pursued retail as its main line of business.

CHAPTER SEVEN

1. Article 26 of the Law on Banks and Banking Activity, and Article 857 of the Civil Code define information about an individual's financial activity as part of the "banking secret." Article 26 lists the limited number of organizations that can access it and the specific situations in which it can be done (usually when ordered by a judge).

2. It was repealed in 1994 by the Riegle-Neal Interstate Banking and Branching Efficiency Act, which allowed regulated interstate mergers and acquisitions (www .fdic.gov/regulations/laws).

3. Interview no. 15 on June 29, 1998.

4. Interview no. 24 on September 9, 1999.

5. I discuss this in more detail in the Appendix.

6. In a recent case of a security breach in the Central Bank of Russia, the database of all interbank financial flows made its way onto the black market and was available for purchase on the Internet. Even more recently, the newspaper *Kommersant* reported that its journalists were able to purchase a 900-ruble (slightly over $30) CD with information on about three thousand individual borrowers of 1st OVK, a large retail bank that was purchased in 2003 by a large holding company and merged with Rosbank. The borrowers obtained loans in 2002–2003, but subsequently were put on a blacklist. The CD contained their home and cell phone numbers, passport numbers, home addresses, and reasons for their inclusion in this list. According to the sellers of the CD, in September 2006 they were going to introduce a much bigger and updated "Anticredit" database containing three million entries ("Neblagonadezhnye zaemshchiki vyshli na rynok," *Kommersant*, September 1, 2006, accessed from www.kommersant.ru on September 5, 2006).

7. There is no single recipe of what system is preferable: a pluralistic, private, market-based system featuring several credit bureaus or a monopolistic, public, state-regulated system with one public registry organized (usually) by a banking regulatory agency. There are countries such as Israel, Turkey, and France, which only have public credit registries, and there are other countries such as the United States, Great Britain, Canada, and Japan, where, on the contrary, only private credit bureaus have been established. But there are also many countries where both systems are present side by side: Germany, Mexico, Spain, Brazil, Austria, and Argentina. It is also true that the two largest credit bureaus in the world (Experian and Equifax) are private

and based in countries (the United States and Great Britain) where only private bureaus have been developed. Public credit registries and private credit bureaus differ in the goals they set for themselves. If private credit bureaus strive to improve the quality of credit information available to banks to help in their decision making, the main purpose of public credit registries is to help in general bank regulation by ensuring that the overall volume of "bad" debts does not become too overwhelming for the banking system to handle (Jappelli and Pagano 2002; Miller 2003). For this reason, public credit registries usually collect only information about borrowers' total debt amount rather than the more detailed data that identifies the amount of each loan and the creditor who extended it.

8. See Duma member Anatoliy Aksakov's Web site, www.aksakov.ru.

9. The law also excludes organizations with a 100 percent state ownership from participation in the creation of credit bureaus (this provision is waived for credit organizations).

10. This point is arguable, since preventing systemwide crises of bad debts is not the private bureaus' main goal. This is a stated goal of *public* credit registries (Miller 2003), which Russian lawmakers completely rejected as a possibility.

11. The ROMIR study has been reported by Rambler Mass Media. Accessed from www.rambler.ru/db/news/print.html?mid=6650704 on October 3, 2005.

CHAPTER EIGHT

1. Reported on the Visa International Service Association Web site, accessed from corporate.visa.com on March 30, 2006.

2. The first collection agencies were organized in Russia in 2004, and currently there are no more than ten such agencies. Among the leaders are Sequoia Credit Consolidation, Pristav, Intellect-C, Federal Agency of Payment Collections (FASP), and the collection agency "92 and Partners." They are currently working with $100–150 million of defaulted loans, while the total volume of defaults in the Russian market is close to $3 billion. Russkiy Standart is the only bank that has created its own agency, "Debt Collection Agency"; the rest of them are unaffiliated with lenders, and many were founded by lawyers experienced in preparing the paperwork to argue such cases in court. The majority of collection agencies work on commission, helping to recover debts on the banks' behalf. However, one of the leaders of the consumer credit market, Home Credit&Finance bank, has recently made an unprecedented move: it announced an open tender to buy its consumer credit debts (which according to different estimates range between 14 and 28 percent of the volume the bank lent to households). Several collection agencies have expressed interest (Korotkova 2006).

3. According to the regulator of the insurance industry in the State of Washington, "Some insurance companies believe there is a correlation between financial re-

sponsibility and insurance losses, . . . that credit information is a good measure of financial responsibility, [and] . . . that consumers who show less financial responsibility will file more claims, so they should pay more for their insurance." Accessed from www.insurance.wa.gov/factsheets on October 26, 2006.

4. Official estimates are made by the state statistical office Goskomstat. Accessed from www.gks.ru on November 5, 2006. Subjective assessments of the poverty level by the Levada Center ("Dinamika bednosti v Rossii," accessed from www.levada .ru/dynamicabed.html on November 5, 2006) name a much higher rate of 43 percent. This is the proportion of Russians who believe their income falls below what they consider to be the bare minimum acceptable level of living. Such subjective estimates of the poverty level tend to be 1.5 times the official estimated levels.

5. This number obscures the fact that around 45 percent of American households are so-called "convenience users" who pay their balances in full each month to avoid finance charges. In other words, among "revolver" households the average outstanding debt is much higher ($11,575 at the beginning of 2000) (Manning 2000, 13).

6. Other highly attractive economies for global retail banks are the rest of the so-called BRIC countries, which in addition to Russia include Brazil, India, and China. They are all experiencing exponential growth in retail financial services, while profit margins and growth in mature markets have been declining (Timewell 2006).

7. In a recent translation of *The Protestant Ethic* by Stephen Kalberg (Weber [1905] 2002, note 128), "iron cage" was replaced with "steel-hard casing."

APPENDIX

1. There might be some truth to this, as during the Soviet period, social scientists could have been approached by the KGB with the invitation to collaborate in disproportionate numbers because of the potentially influential topics of their studies. Besides, the KGB agents conducted regular public-opinion investigations that monitored moods and sentiments in the country, especially around election time (Fitzpatrick 1999, 164–65).

2. This particular employee only agreed to meet me in a public place—in one of Moscow's parks, arguing that his superiors would not approve of this interview.

Bibliography

"1000 bankov Rossii." 2007. *Kommersant* (Bank supplement) 98 (June 7). Accessed on September 12, 2007 from www.kommersant.ru.

Abolafia, Mitchell. 2001. *Making Markets: Opportunism and Restraint on Wall Street.* Cambridge, Mass.: Harvard University Press.

Adrianova, E. 2004. "Russia's Entrance into WTO—An Important Step Has Been Made." Accessed on November 20, 2004 from www.pwcglobal.com.

Andreev, A. A., A. G. Morozov, Yu. V. Selivanov, and V. L. Torkhov. 1998. *Plastikovye kartochki: rukovodstvo dlya polzovateley.* 2nd ed. Moscow: Bankovskiy Delovoy Tsentr.

Andreev, A. V. 1999. "Osnovnye 'otmyvochnye' operatsii strahovyh kompaniy v Rossii i ispolzovanie statisticheskih metodov dlya otsenki ih masshtabov." *Voprosy Statistiki* 6:59–67.

Armstrong, Mark. 2006. "Competition in Two-Sided Markets." *Rand Journal of Economics* 37(3):668–91.

Arthur, Brian W. 1994. *Increasing Returns and Path-Dependence in the Economy.* Ann Arbor: University of Michigan Press.

Aspers, Patrik. 2001. "A Market in Vogue: Fashion Photography in Sweden." *European Societies* 3:1–22.

Associated Credit Bureaus, Inc. 2001. "Who We Are." Accessed on September 9, 2001 from www.acb-credit.com.

Baker, Wayne E. 1984. "The Social Structure of a National Securities Market." *American Journal of Sociology* 89:775–811.

Batt, C. D., and Terence R. Fowkes. 1972. "The Development and Use of Credit Scoring Schemes." In *Applications of Management Science in Banking and Finance,* eds. S. Eilon and T. R. Fowkes, 191–204. Essex: Gower Press.

Beckert, Jens. 1996. "What Is Sociological About Economic Sociology? Uncertainty and the Embeddedness of Economic Action." *Theory and Society* 25(6):803–40.

Ben-Porath, Yoram. 1980. "The F-Connection: Families, Friends and Firms in Organization of Exchange." *Population and Development Review* 6(1):1–30.

Bertrand, Marianne, and Sendhil Mullainathan. 2004. "Are Emily and Greg More Employable Than Lakisha and Jamal? A Field Experiment on Labor Market Discrimination." *The American Economic Review* 94(4):991–1013.

Biggart, Nicole. 1989. *Charismatic Capitalism: Direct Selling Organizations in America.* Chicago: University of Chicago Press.

"BNP Paribas Let Russian Standard Go." 2006. *Kommersant,* September 20. Accessed on September 25, 2006 from www.kommersant.com.

Bockman, Johanna, and Gil Eyal. 2002. "Eastern Europe as a Laboratory for Economic Knowledge: The Transnational Roots of Neoliberalism." *American Journal of Sociology* 108(1):310–52.

Bogdanovskiy, Fedor. 2005. "Zaemshchik 'pod kolpakom.'" *E-xecutive.* Accessed on June 10, 2005 from www.e-xecutive.ru/bank/article_2283/.

Brint, Steven, and Jerome Karabel. 1991. "Institutional Origins and Transformations: The Case of American Community Colleges." In *New Institutionalism in Organizational Analysis,* eds. Walter Powell and Paul DiMaggio. Chicago: University of Chicago Press.

Bruszt, László. 2002. "Making Markets and Eastern Enlargement: Diverging Convergence?" *West European Politics* 25(2):121–40.

Burawoy, Michael. 1996. "The State and Economic Involution: Russia Through a China Lens." *World Development* 24(6):1105–17.

Burt, Ronald. 1992. *Structural Holes.* Cambridge, Mass.: Harvard University Press.

Bush, Jason. 2004. "More Russians Are Saying 'Charge It.'" *BusinessWeek,* October 4. Accessed on January 9, 2005 from www.businessweek.com.

Bush, Jason. 2006. "Russia: Shoppers Gone Wild." *BusinessWeek,* February 20. Accessed on April 23, 2007 from www.businessweek.com.

Buylov, Maxim, and Elena Shushunova. 2003. "15 let bez prava peredyshki." *Kommersant-Dengi* 34 (September 1–7):25–31.

Buzdalin, Alexey. 2004. "Kreditnoe byuro i bankovskaya konkurentsiya." *Bankovskoe delo v Moskve,* no. 12, December 28. Accessed on June 10, 2005 from www.buzdalin.ru.

"Bytovaya tehnika—eto ne pirozhki i ne yogurt." 2002. *Kompania,* September 2. Accessed on July 31, 2006 from www.ko.ru.

Calder, Lendol. 1999. *Financing the American Dream: A Cultural History of Consumer Credit.* Princeton, N.J.: Princeton University Press.

Cao, Yuanzheng, Yingyi Qian, and Barry R. Weingast. 1999. "From Federalism, Chinese Style, to Privatization, Chinese Style." *Economics of Transition* 7(1):101–31.

Card On-Line. Daily electronic bulletin. Moscow, Russia: Prime-TASS.

Carruthers, Bruce. 1996. *City of Capital: Politics and Markets in the English Financial Revolution.* Princeton, N.J.: Princeton University Press.

Carruthers, Bruce G., and Barry Cohen. 2001. "Predicting Failure but Failing to Predict: A Sociology of Knowledge of Credit Rating in Post-Bellum America." Paper presented at the annual meeting of the American Sociological Association, August 18–21, Anaheim, Calif.

Central Bank of Russia. 2003. *Payments Systems of Russia: Red Book*. Accessed on November 18, 2004 from www.cbr.ru/analytics/rb.pdf.

Central Bank of Russia. 2006. "Obzor bankovskogo sektora RF," April. Accessed on May 2, 2006 from www.cbr.ru.

"Chelyabinskaia oblast." 1997. *Platezhi. Sistemy. Kartochki*. 6–7:2–10.

Clarke, Simon. 2002a. *Making Ends Meet in Contemporary Russia: Secondary Employment, Subsidiary Agriculture and Social Networks*. Cheltenham: Edward Elgar.

Clarke, Simon. 2002b. "Market and Institutional Determinants of Wage Differentiation in Russia." *Industrial & Labor Relations Review* 55(4):628–48.

Cohen, Barry. 1999. "Marketing Trust: Credit Reporting and Credit Rating in the 19th Century United States." Paper presented at the 1999 ASA meeting in Chicago.

David, Paul. 1986. "Understanding the Economics of QWERTY: The Necessity of History." In *Economic History and the Modern Economist*, ed. William N. Parker, 30–49. New York: Basil Blackwell.

Dawes, Robyn M., David Faust, and Paul E. Meehl. 1989. "Clinical Versus Actuarial Judgment." *Science* 243:1668–74.

Day, Phillip. 2002. "South Korea Builds a House of Cards: Seoul Urged Consumers to Spend with Plastic; They May Both Regret It." *Wall Street Journal* (Eastern edition), May 14, p. A13.

Dementyeva, Svetlana. 2006. "Kreditnye istorii sokratiat do minimuma." *Kommersant* 98 (June 2). Accessed on June 12, 2006 from www.kommersant.ru.

Dementyeva, Svetlana, and Yulia Chaykina. 2006. "Kreditnye byuro ne mogut sdat istoriyu." *Kommersant* 79 (April 20). Accessed on April 20, 2006 from www.kommersant.ru.

"Dengi zagonyat v virtualnoe prostranstvo." 2005. *Delovoy Peterburg*, November 30. Accessed on July 31, 2006 from www.aksakov.ru.

DiMaggio, Paul J. 1988. "Interest and Agency in Institutional Theory." In *Institutional Patterns and Organizations: Culture and Environment*, ed. Lynn G. Zucker, 3–21. Cambridge, Mass.: Ballinger.

DiMaggio, Paul J., and Walter W. Powell. 1983. "The Iron Cage Revisited: Institutional Isomorphism and Collective Rationality in Organizational Fields." *American Sociological Review* 48(2):147–60.

DiMaggio, Paul J., and Walter W. Powell. 1991. "Introduction." In *New Institutionalism in Organizational Analysis*, eds. Walter Powell and Paul DiMaggio, 1–40. Chicago: University of Chicago Press.

Dinello, Natalia. 1998. "Bankers' War in Russia: Trophies and Wounds." *Post Soviet Prospects* 6(1). Accessed on June 10, 1999 from www.csis.org/ruseura/psp/pspvi1 .html.

Dobbin, Frank, and Timothy J. Dowd. 2000. "The Market That Antitrust Built: Public Policy, Private Coercion, and Railroad Acquisitions, 1825 to 1922." *American Sociological Review* 65(5):631–57.

Doti, Lynne. 2003. "Banking in the Western U.S." In *EH.Net Encyclopedia*, ed. Robert Whaples. Accessed on August 2, 2007 from http://eh.net/encyclopedia/article/doti.banking.western.us.

Economist Intelligence Unit (EIU). 2005. *Country Finance: Russia*. Accessed on November 12, 2005 from www.eiu.com.

Egorova, Viktoria. 1996. "Zarplatnye proekty Mosvodokanalbanka." *Mir Kartochek* 10:12–15.

"Eksperty sklonyayutsya k otkazu ot ogranicheniy na dolyu v kapitale kreditnyh byuro." 2004. *Interfax-AFI*, November 16. Accessed on September 11, 2007 from www.aksakov.ru/newstext/news/id/708904.html.

Euromonitor International. 2004. "Financial Cards in Russia." Accessed on September 30, 2005 from www.euromonitor.com.

Evans, David S., and Richard Schmalensee. 1999. *Paying with Plastic: The Digital Revolution in Buying and Borrowing*. Cambridge, Mass.: MIT Press.

"Experian Launches First Consumer Credit Bureau in Russia with Interfax Information Services Group." 2005. Accessed on June 9, 2005 from www.prnewswire.co.uk/cgi/news/release?id=143885.

Federal Deposit Insurance Corporation (FDIC). 1984. *The First Fifty Years: A History of FDIC 1933–1983*. Washington, D.C.: FDIC.

Fedorov, Boris. 2003. "Volshebnoe prevrashchenie." *Ekspert* 19 (May 26). Accessed on June 16, 2003 from http://archive.expert.ru/sever/03/03-19-74/srinok.htm.

Fernandez, Roberto, Emilio J. Castilla, and Paul Moore. 2000. "Social Capital at Work: Networks and Employment at a Phone Center." *American Journal of Sociology*, 105(5):1288–1356.

"Finance and Economics: Snap! Credit Cards in South Korea." 2004. *The Economist* 370 (January 10):65.

Fitzpatrick, Sheila. 1999. *Everyday Stalinism*. New York: Oxford University Press.

Fligstein, Neil. 2001. *The Architecture of Markets: An Economic Sociology of 21st Century Capitalist Societies*. Princeton, N.J.: Princeton University Press.

Fligstein, Neil, and Iona Mara-Drita. 1996. "How to Make a Market: Reflections on the Attempt to Create a Single Market in the European Union." *American Journal of Sociology* 102:1–33.

Flyvbjerg, Bent. 2001. *Making Social Science Matter: Why Social Inquiry Fails and How It Can Succeed Again*. Cambridge, UK: Cambridge University Press.

Foulke, Roy A. 1941. *The Sinews of American Commerce*. New York: Dun & Bradstreet.

Frenzen, Jonathan, Paul M. Hirsch, and Philip C. Zerrillo. 1994. "Consumption, Preferences and Changing Lifestyles." In *The Handbook of Economic Sociology*, eds. N. Smelser and R. Swedberg, 403–25. Princeton, N.J.: Princeton University Press.

Frye, Timothy. 2000. *Brokers and Bureaucrats: Building Market Institutions in Russia*. Ann Arbor: University of Michigan Press.

Gellner, Ernest. 1994. *Conditions of Liberty: Civil Society and Its Rivals*. London: Hamish Hamilton.

Gelpi, Rosa-Maria, and François Julien-Labruyere. 2000. *The History of Consumer Credit*. New York: St. Martin's Press.

Gimpelson, Vladimir, and Douglas Lippoldt. 2001. *The Russian Labour Market: Between Transition and Turmoil*. New York: Rowman and Littlefield.

Gladwell, Malcolm. 2000. *The Tipping Point*. New York: Little Brown.

Goldman, Marshall. 1983. *USSR in Crisis: The Failure of an Economic System*. New York: Norton.

Gorokhov, Konstantin. 2005. "A na zarplatu—kusochek plastika." *Komsomolskaia Pravda* (Samara Edition), September 28. Accessed on September 28, 2005 from www.samara.kp.ru.

"Gosudarstvenny Bank SSSR." Accessed on August 15, 2006 from www.cbr.ru/today/history/gosbank.asp.

Granovetter, Mark. 1973. "The Strength of Weak Ties." *American Journal of Sociology* 78:1360–80.

Granovetter, Mark. 1978. "Threshold Models of Collective Behavior." *American Journal of Sociology* 83(6):1420–43.

Granovetter, Mark. 1985. "Economic Action and Social Structure: The Problem of Embeddedness." *American Journal of Sociology* 91:481–510.

Granovetter, Mark. 1995 [1974]. *Getting the Job*. Cambridge, Mass.: Harvard University Press.

Greif, Avner. 1993. "Contract Enforceability and Economic Institutions in Early Trade: The Maghribi Traders' Coalition." *American Economic Review* 83(3):525–48.

Grishina, Tatiana. 2002. "Zarplata bez vsyakoy strahovki." *Kommersant-Dengi* 15–16 (April 24):53–55.

Guillén, Mauro. 2001. "Is Globalization Civilizing, Destructive or Feeble? A Critique of Five Key Debates in the Social-Science Literature." *Annual Review of Sociology* 27:235–60.

Guseva, Alya. 1999. "Potrebitelskiy kredit, kreditnye istorii i drugie predshestvenniki bankovskih kartochek v SShA." *Platezhi. Sistemy. Kartochki.* 8:25–28.

Guseva, Alya. 2005. "Building New Markets: A Comparison Between Russian and American Credit Card Markets." *Socio-Economic Review* 3:437–66.

Guseva, Alya, and Ákos Róna-Tas. 2001. "Uncertainty, Risk and Trust: Russian and American Credit Card Markets Compared." *American Sociological Review* 66(5): 623–46.

Guseva, Alya, and Olga Kuzina. 2004. "Kreditnye byuro i kreditny skoring na rynkah kreditnyh kartochek: teoriya i praktika." *Banki I Tehnologii* 5:54–62. Moscow: Association of Russian Banks.

Halliday, Terence C, and Bruce G. Carruthers. 2007. "The Recursivity of Law: Global Norm Making and National Lawmaking in the Globalization of Corporate Insolvency Regimes." *American Journal of Sociology* 112:1135–1202.

Harchenko, Viktor, and Andrei Ildemenov. 1999. "Raschetnaya sistema regiona." *Biznes: Organizatsiya, Strategiya, Sistemy* 5–6:34–37.

Hardin, Garrett. 1968. "The Tragedy of Commons." *Science* 162(3859):1243–48.

Heller, Michael. 1988. *Cogs in the Soviet Wheel.* London: Collins Harvill.

Hirschman, Albert O. 1970. *Exit, Voice and Loyalty: Responses to Decline in Firms, Organizations, and States.* Cambridge, Mass.: Harvard University Press.

"History collectors." 2004. *Vremya Novostei,* reprinted by *Interfax* on September 22. Accessed on September 29, 2004 from www.interfax.ru.

Iankova, Zoya. 1979. *Gorodskaya semya.* Moscow: Nauka.

Ildemenov, Andrei, and Viktor Harchenko. 1999. "Platezhnye sistemy v usloviyah bartera." *Mir Kartochek* 3:15–20.

Ingram, Paul, and Karen Clay. 2000. "The Choice-Within-Constraints New Institutionalism and Implications for Sociology." *Annual Review of Sociology* 26:525–46.

Ingram, Paul, and Hayagreeva Rao. 2004. "Store Wars: The Enactment and Repeal of Anti-Chain-Store Legislation in America." *American Journal of Sociology* 110(2): 446–87.

Jack, Andrew, and Carlotta Gall. 1998. "Russian Savers' Bank Accounts Unfrozen." *Financial Times,* December 5, p. 2.

Jappelli, Tullio, and Marco Pagano. 2002. "Information Sharing, Lending and Defaults: Cross-Country Evidence." *Journal of Banking & Finance* 26:2017–45.

Johnson, Juliet. 1997. "Russia's Emerging Financial-Industrial Groups." *Post-Soviet Affairs* 13(4):333–65.

Johnson, Juliet. 2000. *A Fistful of Rubles.* Ithaca, N.Y.: Cornell University Press.

Johnson, Juliet. 2007. "Priests of Prosperity: The Transnational Central Banking Community and Post-Communist Transformation." Unpublished manuscript.

Jordan, Henry. 1967. "Better Mousetrap?" *Forbes,* October 1, p. 67.

"Kak Avtobank rabotaet s plastikovymi kartochkami." 1996. *Bankovskie Tehnologii* 1. Accessed on October 20, 1998 from www.bizcom.ru.

Kamaluddin, S. 1993. "Banking: Lender with a Mission." *Far Eastern Economic Review* 156(11):38.

"Kartochki v Sverdlovskoy oblasti." 1997. *Platezhi. Sistemy. Kartochki.* 9–10:6–16.

Katz, Michael L., and Carl Shapiro. 1985. "Network Externalities, Competition and Compatibility." *American Economic Review* 75:424–40.

Kemme, David. 2001. "Russian Financial Transition: The Development of Institutions and Markets for Growth." William Davidson Institute Working Paper No. 455.

Kindleberger, Charles P. 1996. *Manias, Panics and Crashes: A History of Financial Crises.* New York: John Wiley.

Knight, Frank. 1957 [1921]. *Risk, Uncertainty and Profit.* New York: Kelley and Millman.

Knorr-Cetina, Karen, and Urs Brugger. 2002. "Global Macrostructures: The Virtual Societies of Financial Markets." *American Journal of Sociology* 107:905–50.

Kolyakin, Yuri. 1996. "Kartochki v Magnitogorske." *Bankovskie Tehnologii* 8. Accessed on December 16, 1998 from www.bizcom.ru.

Kopylova, Natalia, 2006. "Vsyo eshche dorogo i neprivychno." *Gazeta.ru*, April 19. Accessed on April 19, 2006 from www.gazeta.ru.

Korea Economic Institute. 2004. "A New Financial Crisis: Credit Card Excesses." *Korea Insight* 2 (February 6). Accessed on April 28, 2007 from www.keia.org.

Kornai, János. 1980. *Economics of Shortage*. Amsterdam: North-Holland.

Korotkova, Oksana. 2006. "Dolg platezhom krasen." *Nakanune*, August 28. Accessed on August 30, 2006 from www.nakanune.ru.

Kozul'kova, Kseniya. 2006. "Dayut—beri." *Kommersant* (Bank supplement) 106, June 15. Accessed on June 26, 2006 from www.kommersant.ru.

"Kreditka nedoveriya." 2006. *Argumenty i Fakty*, April 12. Accessed on July 31, 2006 from www.aksakov.ru.

"Kreditnye byuro—vchera, segodnya, zavtra." 1998. *Platezhi. Sistemy. Kartochki.* 2:26–27.

"Kreditnye byuro nachali ploho." 2006. *Izvestiia*, reprinted by *Interfax* on June 5. Accessed on June 12, 2006 from www.interfax.ru.

Krippner, Greta. 2001. "The Elusive Market: Embeddedness and the Paradigm of Economic Sociology." *Theory and Society* 30(6):775–810.

Krippner, Greta, et al. 2004. "Polanyi Symposium: A Conversation on Embeddedness." *Socio-Economic Review* 2:109–35.

Krotov, N., and B. Lapshov. 1998. *Rozhdenie kommercheskih bankov ili moment istiny rossiyskoy bankovskoy reformy. (Svidetelstva uchastnikov)*. Moscow: Bankovskoe Delo.

"Krupneyshie banki SNG." 2006. *Kommersant* (Bank supplement) 106, June 15. Accessed on June 26, 2006 from www.kommersant.ru.

Kulagin, Vasiliy. 1997. "Marketingovaya shema 'zarplatny proekt.'" *Mir Kartochek* 7:6–11.

Kulikova, Maya. 2003. "Otdalis shoppingu." *Ogoniok* 41 (October 11). Accessed on April 25, 2007 from www.ogoniok.com/4993.

Kuzina, Olga. 2006. "Credit Card Market in Russia." Unpublished manuscript.

Kuzmenko, Irina. 2005. "Sberbank sozdaet svoe kreditnoe byuro." *Biznes* 105(124), June 10. Accessed on June 16, 2005 from www.b-online.ru.

Kuznetsov, K., and I. Spiranov. 1999. "Voprosy uchrezhdeniya kreditnogo byuro v Rossii." *Mir Kartochek* 9:1–4, 30.

Lamoreaux, Naomi. 1991. "Information Problems and Banks' Specialization in Short-Term Commercial Lending: New England in the Nineteenth Century." In *Inside the Business Enterprise: Historical Perspectives on the Use of Information*, ed. Peter Temin, 161–204. Chicago: University of Chicago Press.

Langlois, Richard N. 1986. "The New Institutional Economics: An Introductory Essay." In *Economics as a Process: Essays in the New Institutional Economics*, ed. Richard N. Langlois, 1–26. Cambridge: Cambridge University Press.

Lazarsfeld, Paul F., and Robert Merton. 1954. "Friendship as a Social Process: A Substantive and Methodological Analysis." In *Freedom and Control in Modern Society*, eds. M. Berger, T. Abel, and C. H. Page, 18–66. New York: Van Nostrand.

Ledeneva, Alena V. 1998. *Russia's Economy of Favours: Blat, Networking and Informal Exchange*. Cambridge: Cambridge University Press.

Lee, Raymond M. 1981. "Interreligious Courtship and Marriage in Northern Ireland." Unpublished Ph.D. thesis, University of Edinburgh.

Lee, Raymond M. 1993. *Doing Research on Sensitive Topics*. Newbury Park, Calif.: Sage Publications.

Lewis, Edward M. 1992. *An Introduction to Credit Scoring*. San Rafael, Calif.: Fair, Isaac and Company.

Leyshon, Andrew, and Nigel Thrift. 1999. "Lists Come Alive: Electronic Systems of Knowledge and the Rise of Credit-Scoring in Retail Banking." *Economy and Society* 28:434–66.

Lie, John. 1997. "Sociology of Markets." *Annual Review of Sociology* 23:341–60.

Logvinova, Natalia. 2005. "Metamorfozy 'sluzhebnogo' plastika." *Finans* 33 (September 12–18). Accessed on September 27, 2005 from www.finansmag.ru.

"Lou Naumovski: 'Uspeh bankovskoy roznitsy opredelyaetsya masshtabom biznesa.'" 2005. *Mir Kartochek* 3. Accessed on September 29, 2005 from www.cardworld.ru.

Lovett, Robert W. 1975. "Nineteenth-Century Credit Information." In *Shop Talk: Papers on Historical Business and Commercial Records of New England*, ed. J. Lawton, 47–52. Boston: Boston Public Library.

Macaulay, Stuart. 1963. "Non-Contractual Relations in Business: A Preliminary Study." *American Sociological Review* 28:55–67.

MacKenzie, Donald, and Yuval Millo. 2003. "Negotiating a Market, Performing Theory: The Historical Sociology of a Financial Derivatives Exchange." *American Journal of Sociology* 109:107–45.

Madison, James H. 1974. "The Evolution of Commercial Credit-Reporting Agencies in Nineteenth-Century America." *Business History Review* 48:164–86.

Mainville, Michael. 2007. "Rising Middle Class Ready to Shop." *Washington Times*, February 5. Accessed on April 25, 2007 from www.washingtontimes.com.

Mandel, Lewis. 1990. *The Credit Card Industry: A History*. Boston: Twayne Publishers.

Manning, Robert. 2000. *Credit Card Nation*. New York: Basic Books.

Maxwell, Joseph A. 1998. "Designing a Qualitative Study." In *Handbook of Applied Social Research Methods*, eds. Leonard Bickman and Debra J. Rog, 69–100. Thousand Oaks, Calif.: Sage Publications.

McDermott, Gerald. 2002. *Embedded Politics: Industrial Networks and Institutional Change in Postcommunism*. Ann Arbor: University of Michigan Press.

McLean, Paul D., and John F. Padgett. 1997. "Was Florence a Perfectly Competitive Market? Transactional Evidence from the Renaissance." *Theory and Society* 26:209–44.

McMillan, John, and Christopher Woodruff. 1998. "Interfirm Relationships and Informal Credit in Vietnam." *The Quarterly Journal of Economics* 114(4):1285–1320.

Meyer, John, and Brian Rowan. 1991. "Institutional Organizations: Formal Structure as Myth and Ceremony." In *New Institutionalism in Organizational Analysis*, eds. Walter Powell and Paul DiMaggio, 41–62. Chicago: University of Chicago Press.

Meyer, John W., John Boli, George M. Thomas, and Francisco O. Ramirez. 1997. "World Society and the Nation-State." *American Journal of Sociology* 103(1):144–81.

Milgrom, Paul, Yingyi Qian, and John Roberts. 1991. "Complementarities, Momentum and the Evolution of Modern Manufacturing." *American Economic Review*, 81(2):84–88.

Miller, Arthur. 1971. *The Assault on Privacy.* Ann Arbor: University of Michigan Press.

Miller, Margaret J. 2003. *Credit Reporting Systems and the International Economy.* Cambridge, Mass.: MIT Press.

Min, Kim Jung. 2003. "Plastic Panic." *Far Eastern Economic Review*, December 18, p. 45.

Mizruchi, Mark, and Linda Stearns. 2001. "Getting Deals Done: The Use of Social Networks in Bank Decision-Making." *American Sociological Review* 66(5):647–71.

Moiseev, Igor. 2004. "Kreditnaia byuro-kratizatsia." *Finansovye Izvestiia*, May 27. Accessed on June 17, 2007 from www.finiz.ru/economic/article849085.

Nee, Victor. 2005. "The New Institutionalism in Economics and Sociology." In *The Handbook of Economic Sociology*, 2nd ed., eds. N. Smelser and R. Swedberg, 49–74. Princeton, N.J.: Princeton University Press.

Nelson, Richard R. 1994. "Evolutionary Theorizing About Economic Change." In *The Handbook of Economic Sociology*, eds. Neil J. Smelser and Richard Swedberg, 108–36. Princeton, N.J.: Princeton University Press.

Neuhauser, C. Kimberly. 1993. "Two Channels of Consumer Credit in the USSR." *Berkeley-Duke Occasional Papers on the Second Economy in the USSR*, eds. G. Grossman and V. Treml.

Nezavisimy institut sotsialnoy politiki. n.d. "Sotsialny atlas rossiyskih regionov." Accessed on September 14, 2007 from http://atlas.socpol.ru/overviews/settlement/index.shtml.

Nocera, Joseph. 1994. *A Piece of the Action: How the Middle Class Joined the Money Class.* New York: Simon and Schuster.

North, Douglass. 1977. "Markets and Other Allocation Systems in History: The Challenge of Karl Polanyi," *Journal of European Economic History* 6:703–16.

North, Douglass. 1989. "Institutional Change and Economic History." *Journal of Institutional and Theoretical History* 145:238–45.

"Noveyshaya kreditnaya istoriya." 2006. *Bankovskoe Delo*, reprinted by *Interfax* on May 31. Accessed on August 30, 2006 from www.interfax.ru.

"Obyazatelnaya karta." 2006. *Vedomosti*, March 17. Accessed on July 31, 2006 from www.aksakov.ru.

Olegario, Rowena. 1999. "That Mysterious People: Jewish Merchants, Transparency, and Community in Mid-Nineteenth Century America." *Business History Review* 73:161–90.

Olney, Martha. 1991. *Buy Now, Pay Later: Advertising, Credit, and Consumer Durables in the 1920s.* Chapel Hill: University of North Carolina Press.

Orekhova, Irina. 2003. "Konferentsiya po plastikovym kartochkam 'Potrebitelskie finansovye uslugi v Rossii.'" *Mir Kartochek.* Accessed on October 31, 2004 from www.bizcom.ru.

Organization for Economic Co-operation and Development (OECD). 2000. "Russian Insurance Market: Structure of the Insurance Market and Expectations in Its

Development." Accessed on May 31, 2002 from www.oecd.org/pdf/M00008000/M00008728.pdf.

Ó Riain, Seán. 2000. "States and Market in the Era of Globalization." *Annual Review of Sociology* 26:187–213.

Padgett, John, and Paul Mclean. 2002. "Elite Transformation and the Rise of Economic Credit in Renaissance Florence." Unpublished manuscript.

Pagano, Marco, and Tullio Jappelli. 1993. "Information Sharing in Credit Markets." *The Journal of Finance* 48(5):1693–1718.

Panfilova, Yulia, and Elena Kiseleva. 1998. "Riskuyut vse." *Kommersant* 163 (September 4). Accessed on September 12, 2007 from www.kommersant.ru.

Papernaya, Inessa. 2004. "Strana vozvrashchentsev." *Profil*, November 29. Accessed on January 17, 2005 from www.aksakov.ru.

Pavlov, V. 1975. "Razvitie kollektivizma v bytu rabochey molodezhi." In *Issledovanie i planirovanie duhovnoy kul'tury trudyashchihsya Urala*, eds. L. Kogan and A. Sharova, 104–24. Sverdlovsk, Russia: Uralskiy Nauchny Tsentr AN SSSR.

Petersen, Mitchell A., and Rahuram G. Rajan. 1994. "The Benefits of Lending Relationships: Evidence from Small Business Data." *The Journal of Finance* 49(1): 3–37.

Petrova, Svetlana, Zoya Buraya, and Natalia Akimova. 1996. "Pyatero v lodke, ne schitaya Sberbank." *Kommersant-Dengi* 29, August 21. Accessed on September 10, 2007 from www.kommersant.ru

"Plastikovye kartochki v Cherepovtse." 1998. *Platezhi. Sistemy. Kartochki.* 4:12–20.

"Plastikovye kartochki v Permskoy oblasti." 1998. *Platezhi. Sistemy. Kartochki.* 5:2–16.

"Pochti tret' rossiyan poluchayut zarplaty v konvertah." 2006. *Lenta.ru*, October 10. Accessed on November 5, 2006 from http://wciom.ru/arkhiv/.

Podolny, Joel. 1994. "Market Uncertainty and the Social Character of Economic Exchange." *Administrative Science Quarterly* 39(3):458–83.

Podolny, Joel. 2005. *Status Signals: A Sociological Study of Market Competition*. Princeton, N.J.: Princeton University Press.

Polanyi, Karl. 1957 [1944]. *The Great Transformation*. Boston: Beacon Press.

Popov, V. P. 1995. "Pasportnaya sistema v SSSR (1932–1976)." *Sotsiologicheskie Issledovaniya* 8–9.

Potrebitelskiy kredit. 1983. Moscow: Znanie.

Powell, Walter W. 1985. *Getting into Print*. Chicago: University of Chicago.

Powell, Walter W., Kenneth W. Koput, and Laurel Smith-Doerr. 1996. "Interorganizational Collaboration and the Locus of Innovation: Networks of Learning in Biotechnology." *Administrative Science Quarterly* 41:116–45.

Prezhentsev, Pavel. 1999. "Sberbank boretsya s prestupnostyu sredi pensionerov i domohozyayek." *Kommersant* 224 (December 3). Accessed on September 10, 2007 from www.kommersant.ru.

Prokop'ev, Yuri. 2006. "Banki upovayut na 'dedushkinu ogovorku.'" *Rossiyskaia Biznes Gazeta*, January 31. Accessed on July 31, 2006 from www.aksakov.ru.

Putnam, Robert. 1993. *Making Democracy Work: Civic Traditions in Modern Italy*. Princeton, N.J.: Princeton University Press.

Pyle, William. 2002. "Overbanked and Credit-Starved: A Paradox of the Transition." *Journal of Comparative Economics* 30(1):25–50.

Pyle, William. n.d. "Reputation Flows." Unpublished manuscript.

Rahman, Aminur. 1999. "Micro-Credit Initiatives for Equitable and Sustainable Development: Who Pays?" *World Development* 27:67–82.

Reinke, Jens. 1998. "How to Lend like Mad and Make a Profit: A Micro-Credit Paradigm Versus the Start-Up Fund in South Africa." *The Journal of Development Studies* 34:44–61.

"RF Economic Development Ministry Picks Out Credit History's Supervisor." 2005. *Kommersant*, May 25. Accessed on June 10, 2005 from www.kommersant.com.

Robinson, William I. 2001. "Social Theory and Globalization: The Rise of a Transnational State." *Theory and Society* 30(2):157–200.

Rochet, Jean-Charles, and Jean Tirole. 2005. "Two-Sided Markets: A Progress Report." Institut d'Économie Industrielle (IDEI), University Toulouse 1, Working Paper No. 275.

ROMIR. 2005. "Tsifry i fakty," July 14. Accessed on September 11, 2007 from romir.ru/news/res_results/145.html.

Róna-Tas, Ákos. 1998. "Social Capital and Path-Dependency: Sociology of Postcommunist Economic Transformation." *East European Politics and Society* 12(1): 107–31.

RosBusinessConsulting. 2004. "Samye zarplatnye banki." Accessed on November 23, 2004 from http://rating.rbc.ru.

RosBusinessConsulting. 2006. "Obzor rynka bankovskih plastikovyh kart Rossiyskoy Federatsii." Accessed on June 20, 2006 from http://research.rbc.ru.

Rosenthal, James A., and Juan M. Ocampo. 1988. *Securitization of Credit: Inside the New Technology of Finance*. New York: John Wiley.

"Roustam Tariko." 2004. *BusinessWeek*, June 7. Accessed on September 30, 2005 from www.businessweek.com.

"Russians Get Taste for Credit as Consumerism Takes Hold." Accessed on January 15, 2003 from *Johnson's Russia Home*, www.cdi.org/russia/johnson.

"Russia's Capital: Beacon or Bogey?" 1997. *The Economist* (September 6):50.

Russkiy Standart. 2003. *Annual Report*. Moscow: Russkiy Standart.

"Russkiy Standart sozdaet svoe sobstvennoe kreditnoe byuro." 2005. *Vestnik Banka Rossii* 30 (June 8). Accessed on June 16, 2005 from http://banker.ru/news/newsline.

Rysman, Marc. 2003. "Competition Between Networks: A Study of the Market for Yellow Pages." *Review of Economic Studies* 70:1–30.

Rysman, Marc. 2006. "An Empirical Analysis of Payment Card Usage." *Journal of Industrial Economics* 55(1):1–36.

Salnikov, Denis. 1997a. Kartochki-97. *Mir Kartochek* 10. Accessed on December 16, 1998 from www.bizcom.ru.

Salnikov, Denis. 1997b. "'Plastikovye dengi' v Neryungi." *Mir Kartochek* 1:5–12.

Saloner, Garth, Andrea Shepard, and Joel Podolny. 2001. *Strategic Management*, 305–28. New York: John Wiley.

Samotorova, Anastasia. 2005. "Banki na potrebu." *Profil* 35 (September 26). Accessed on August 30, 2006 from www.profile.ru.

Samovarshchikova, Olga. 1998. "Kartochki v Irkutskoy oblasti." *Mir Kartochek* 7:40–45.

Sberbank. 2005. *Annual Report*. Moscow: Sberbank.

"Sberbank ne verit klientam v magazinah, nadeyas uvidet ih v svoih otdeleniyah." 2006. *Gazeta* 103 (June 19). Accessed on October 3, 2006 from wciom.ru/arkhiv/tematicheskii-arkhiv.

"Sberbank sozdaet kreditnoe byuro." 2005. *Lenta.ru*, June 9. Accessed on June 16, 2005 from http://lenta.ru/news/2005/06/09/credit/.

"Sberbank vedut na rynok." 2005. *Vedomosti*, reprinted by *Interfax*. Accessed on June 22, 2005 from www.interfax.ru.

Schotter, Andrew. 1986. "The Evolution of Rules." In *Economics as a Process: Essays in the New Institutional Economics*, ed. Richard N. Langlois, 117–34. Cambridge: Cambridge University Press.

Scott, Richard W., Martin Ruef, Peter J. Mendel, and Carol A. Caronna. 2000. *Institutional Change and Healthcare Organizations*. Chicago: University of Chicago Press.

Sedaitis, Judith. 1998. "The Alliances of Spin-offs versus Start-ups: Social Ties in the Genesis of Post-Soviet Alliances." *Organization Science* 9(3):368–81.

Seligman, Adam. 1992. *The Idea of Civil Society*. New York: Free Press.

Shadalin, Oleg. 1997. "Banki kak zerkalo burzhuaznoy revolyutsii." *Delovye Lyudi* 82:19.

Shepherdson, Nancy. 1991. "Credit Card America." *American Heritage* 42:125–32.

Shlapentokh, Vladimir. 1989. *Public and Private Life of the Soviet People: Changing Values in Post-Stalin Russia*. New York: Oxford University Press.

Shleifer, Andrei, and Robert Vishny. 1998. *The Grabbing Hand: Government Pathologies and Their Cures*. Cambridge, Mass.: Harvard University Press.

Simon, Herbert. 1986. "Rationality in Psychology and Economics." *Journal of Business* 59(4):S209–S224.

Smirnov, Aleksandr. 1998. "Chto zhdet rossiyskie banki v 1998 godu?" *DiasoftINFO*, May, pp. 10–15

Smith, Hedrick. 1976. *The Russians*. New York: Quadrangle.

Smith, Charles W. 1989. *Auctions: The Social Construction of Value*. Berkeley: University of California Press.

Spicer, Andrew, and William Pyle. 2003. "Institutions and the Vicious Circle of Distrust in the Russian Household Deposit Market, 1992–1999." William Davidson Institute, University of Michigan Business School, Working Paper No. 588.

Stark, David. 1996. "Recombinant Property in East European Capitalism." *American Journal of Sociology* 101:993–1928.

Starkov, M. 2005. "Kollektorskie agentstva ne nashli obshchego yazyka s bankami." November 14, no. 42. Accessed on November 16, 2005 from www.dkvartal.ru.

Stigler, George. 1967. "Imperfections in the Capital Market." *Journal of Political Economy* 75:287–92.

Stiglitz, Joseph E. 2000. "The Contributions of the Economics of Information to Twentieth Century Economics." *Quarterly Journal of Economics* 115:1441–78.

Stiglitz, Joseph E. 2001. "Whither Reform? Ten Years of Transition." In *The Rebel Within*, ed. Ha-Joon Chang, 127–71. London: Wimbledon Publishing Company. Originally presented at the World Bank Annual Bank Conference on Development Economics, Washington D.C., April 1999.

Swedberg, Richard. 1994. "Markets as Social Structures." In *The Handbook of Economic Sociology*, eds. N. Smelser and R. Swedberg, 255–82. Princeton, N.J.: Princeton University Press.

Swedberg, Richard. 2003. *Principles of Economic Sociology*. Princeton, N.J.: Princeton University Press.

Swedberg, Richard. 2005. "Markets in Society." In *The Handbook of Economic Sociology*, 2nd ed., eds. N. Smelser and R. Swedberg, 233–53. Princeton, N.J.: Princeton University Press.

Swidler, Ann. 1986. "Culture in Action: Symbols and Strategies." *American Sociological Review* 51(2):273–86.

Sztompka, Piotr. 1996. "Looking Back: The Year 1989 as a Cultural and Civilizational Break." *Communist and Post Communist Studies* 29(2):115–29.

Sztompka, Piotr. 1999. *Trust: A Sociological Theory*. Cambridge, UK: Cambridge University Press.

Tennenbaum, Jonathan. 2002. "Russia's Economy 1999–2001: Strong Growth, But Exhausting Its Foundation." *Executive Intelligence Review* 24(4), February 1. Accessed on April 25, 2007 from www.larouchepub.com/other/2002/2904russ_econ.html.

Thorne, Susan. 2002. "Russia Warming to Development." *International Council of Shopping Centers*, December. Accessed on August 20, 2006 from www.icsc.org.

Timewell, Stephen. 2006. "Bring Me Your Consumers, Your Unbanked Masses." *The Banker*, June 1.

Uzzi, Brian. 1996. "The Sources and Consequences of Embeddedness for the Economic Performance of Organizations: The Network Effect." *American Sociological Review* 61:674–98.

Uzzi, Brian. 1997. "Social Structure and Competition in Interfirm Networks: The Paradox of Embeddedness." *Administrative Science Quarterly* 42(1):35–67.

Uzzi, Brian. 1999. "Embeddedness in the Making of Financial Capital: How Social Relations and Networks Benefit Firms Seeking Financing." *American Sociological Review* 64:481–505.

Velthuis, Olav. 2005. *Talking Prices*. Princeton, N.J.: Princeton University Press.

"Visa COPAC: Reshenie dlya Rossii?" 1997. *Bankovskie Tehnologii* 4. Accessed on December 16, 1998 from www.bizcom.ru.

Visa International. 2004. *Annual Report.* Accessed on November 6, 2005 from http://corporate.visa.com.

Volkov, Vadim. 1999. "Violent Entrepreneurship in Post-Communist Russia." *Europe-Asia Studies* 51(5):741–54.

Wallerstein, Immanuel. 1998. *Utopistics: Or, Historical Choices of the Twenty-First Century.* New York: The New Press.

Weber, Max. 2002 [1905]. *Protestant Ethic and the Spirit of Capitalism*, trans. Stephen Kalberg. Oxford: Blackwell Publishers.

Weitz, Rose. 2006. *Sociology of Health, Illness and Health Care.* Belmont, Calif.: Wadsworth/Thomson Learning.

White, Harrison. 1981. "Where Do Markets Come from?" *American Journal of Sociology* 87(3):517–47.

White, Harrison. 2002. *Markets from Networks: Socioeconomic Models of Production.* Princeton, N.J.: Princeton University Press.

Williamson, Oliver. 1975. *Markets and Hierarchies.* New York: Free Press.

Wolters, Timothy. 2000. "'Carry Your Credit in Your Pocket': The Early History of the Credit Card at Bank of America and Manhattan Chase." *Enterprise and Society* 1:315–54.

Woodruff, David. 1999. *Money Unmade: Barter and the Fate of Russian Capitalism.* Ithaca, N.Y.: Cornell University Press.

Yakubovich, Valery. 2005. "Weak Ties, Information and Influence: How Workers Find Jobs in a Local Russian Labor Market." *American Sociological Review* 70(3): 408–21.

Yakubovich, Valery, and Irina Kozina. 2007. "Recruitment at Russian Enterprises." In *Human Resource Management in Russia: The Current State of Leadership, Recruitment, Payment, and Training Practices Within Russian Enterprises*, eds. Michel Domsch and Tatjana Lidokhover, 153–69. Aldershot, UK: Ashgate Publishing Group.

Yevtyushkin, Alexandr. 1996. "Plastikovye kartochki v Rossii: problema pobuditelnyh motivov." *Bankovskie Tehnologii* 1. Accessed on August 19, 1998 from www.bizcom.ru.

"Za kazhduyu pokupku po plastikovoy karte 'Rossiyskiy Kredit' nachal platit dengi." 1998. *Moskovskiy Komsomolets* 108 (June 10):1.

Zarshchikov, Aleksandr. 2006. "Chuvstvo dolga." *Profil* 8 (March 6). Accessed on August 30, 2006 from www.profile.ru.

Zaslavskaya, Olga. 2005. "Novye vozmozhnosti 'zarplatnyh proektov.'" *Bankir*, June 8. Accessed on July 20, 2005 from www.bankir.ru.

Zelizer, Viviana. 1978. "Human Values and the Market: The Case of Life Insurance and Death in 19th Century America." *American Journal of Sociology* 84:591–610.

Zelizer, Viviana. 1988. "Beyond the Polemics on the Market: Establishing a Theoretical and Empirical Agenda." *Sociological Forum* 3(4):614–34.

Zelizer, Viviana. 1994. *The Social Meaning of Money.* New York: Basic Books.

Zelizer, Viviana. 2005. "Culture and Consumption." In *The Handbook of Economic Sociology*, 2nd ed., eds. N. Smelser and R. Swedberg, 331–54. Princeton, N.J.: Princeton University Press.

Zhirinovskiy, Vladimir, and Vladimir Jurovitskiy. 1998. *Novye dengi dlya Rossii i mira.* Moscow: Graal.

Zucker, Lynne. 1986. "Production of Trust: Institutional Sources of Economic Structure." *Research in Organizational Behaviour* 8:53–111.

Zuckerman, Ezra. 1999. "The Categorical Imperative: Securities Analysts and the Illegitimacy Discount." *American Journal of Sociology* 104:1398–1438.

Zukin, Sharon, and Paul DiMaggio. 1990. "Introduction." In *Structures of Capital: The Social Organization of the Economy*, eds. Sharon Zukin and Paul DiMaggio, 1–36. Cambridge, UK: Cambridge University Press.

Index

Page numbers followed by *f* or *t* indicate figures or tables, respectively.